SELL TOWN

D0966259

WASHINGTON
A Centennial History

WASHINGTON

A Centennial History

Robert E. Ficken
Charles P. LeWarne

University of Washington Press
Seattle and London

Washington: A Centennial History
is published with the assistance of
the 1989 Washington Centennial Commission.

Library of Congress Cataloging-in-Publication Data

Ficken, Robert E.
Washington: a centennial history.
  Commissioned by the Washington State Centennial Commission.
  Bibliography: p.
  Includes index.
  1. Washington (State)—History.
I. LeWarne, Charles Pierce, 1930– . II. Washington Centennial
Commission. III. Title.
F891.F49   1988   979.7   88-20459
ISBN 0-295-96693-9

Jacket lithograph: "Bird's-Eye View of the City of Olympia, East Olympia
and Tumwater, Puget Sound, Washington Territory, 1879," by E. S. Glover.
Courtesy of Carolyn Staley.

Endsheet illustrations: (front) Seattle, W.T., 1884; *(back)* Spokane Falls,
W.T., 1880s. From *The West Shore* magazine, courtesy of Carolyn Staley.

For Robert E. Burke and Vernon Carstensen,
mentors and friends

Contents

Illustrations

Aftermath of the Seattle fire
Seattle streetcar strike, 1903

Preface

This centennial history of Washington was commissioned in 1986. At that time, we were given a series of mandates. We were to avoid writing a textbook and to avail ourselves of up-to-date research and interpretation in the field of state history. The book was to be scholarly, yet appeal to the general reader. Working from an agreed-upon outline, we divided responsibility for drafting specific chapters. These chapter drafts were then exchanged and revised. The result is a collaborative account focusing on the major developments of the past century.

Much of the book is based on research in primary source materials. The section on the atomic bomb, for instance, relies heavily on the recently declassified diary of the wartime commander at Hanford and on the records of the Manhattan Project. In consideration of our intended audience, footnotes have been omitted. Also, the bibliographical section is more a guide to additional reading than a listing of all items consulted in preparation of this book.

With considerable pleasure, we dedicate this book to Robert E. Burke and Vernon Carstensen. These two scholars share and richly deserve the distinction of being deans of Pacific Northwest history. Through their own work and the work of their many students, they have made a great contribution to our understanding of Washington state history.

R.E.F.
C.P.L.

Introduction

The Statehood Year

1889.

The year has no magic or intrinsic importance. Only by political happenstance did 1889 become the year of statehood for Washington. Statehood might have come in any of the half-dozen earlier years when the territorial legislature petitioned Congress for admission to the Union. It might well have been achieved in 1878, when territorial voters approved a state constitution drafted at a Walla Walla convention—only to see it derailed by partisan politics when it reached Congress. Had proceedings moved faster, or a trifle slower, in the fateful months, Washington State might have been born in 1888 or 1890. But 1889 it was.

There were sixty-two million people in the United States that year. A tier of well-settled states lined the west bank of the Mississippi, with three jutting into the prairies. To the west, sparsely settled desert and mountains separated the eastern states from distant California, Oregon, and Nevada. Three railroads, among them the six-year-old Northern Pacific line, crossed the continent. In March, Democrat Grover Cleveland turned the presidency over to Republican Benjamin Harrison; this succession of rivals, little remembered today, augured well for the admission of states likely to support the Grand Old Party. Not since Colorado's admission in the centennial year of 1876 had a new state entered the Union. Through October of 1889 there were thirty-eight states, then suddenly forty-two, and in nine months two more.

Among the sudden half dozen was Washington. A territory for the preceding thirty-six years, its borders had been subject to controversy and two alterations during the span. Its population in 1889 was

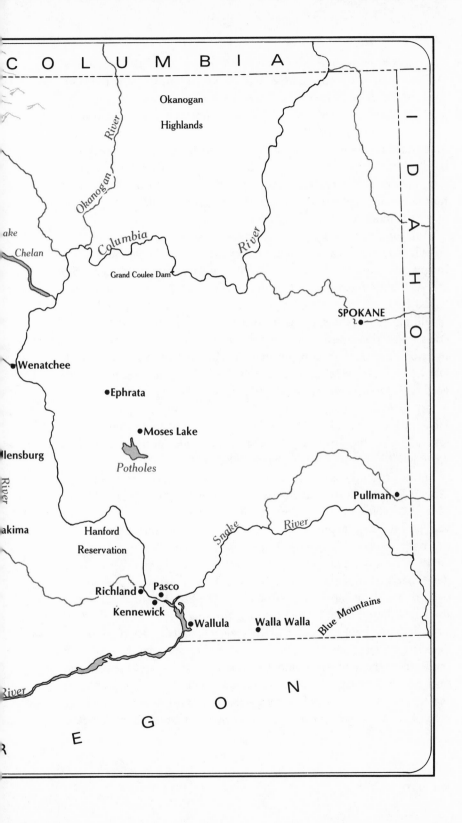

C O L U M B I A

Okanogan

Highlands

Okanogan River

I D A H O

Columbia

River

ake

Chelan

Grand Coulee Dam

SPOKANE

●Wenatchee

●Ephrata

●Moses Lake

Potholes

llensburg

River

akima

Hanford

Reservation

Snake

River

Pullman●

Richland●

●Pasco

Kennewick

●Wallula

Walla Walla

Blue Mountains

River

E   G   O   N

R

R   E   G   O   N

239,544—four times the minimum recommended in the Northwest Ordinance of 1787 and double that used in recent years as the standard for statehood. Located in a far corner of the United States, never made famous by incidents of drama or notoriety, Washington remained remote and unknown. Naturalist John Muir observed at the time that "to many, especially in the Atlantic States, Washington is hardly known at all. It is regarded as being yet a far wild west—a dim, nebulous expanse of woods—by those who do not know that railroads and steamers have brought the country out of the wilderness and abolished the old distances."

Most of the new state's population lived along Puget Sound, a complex water highway crisscrossed by small steamboats that carried freight and passengers between shoreline villages and up sluggish rivers. Although a generation had passed since the first settlements, the Sound buzzed with youthful vigor. "The newcomers," observed Muir, "building their cabins where beavers once built theirs, keep a few cows and industriously seek to enlarge their small meadow patches by chopping, girdling and burning the edge of the encircling forest, gnawing like beavers, and scratching for a living among the blackened stumps and logs, regarding the trees as their greatest enemies— a sort of larger pernicious weed immensely difficult to get rid of." Here and there cities were aborning, "young, and loose-jointed . . . fast taking on the forms and manner of old cities, putting on airs, as some would say, like boys in haste to be men."

Three little towns—Whatcom, Sehome, and Fairhaven—curved around Bellingham Bay, their merger into Bellingham still over a decade away. Near the mouth of the Skagit River, LaConner struggled to retain its early prominence as steamers chugged on upriver and a railroad connected booming Anacortes with the interior hinterland. At Port Gardner Bay, Everett was but a gleam in the eye of land developers. Across the Sound, bustling Port Townsend was at the peak of its Victorian glory. West along the Strait of Juan de Fuca, the Puget Sound Cooperative Colony, thriving with two hundred visionaries and hangers-on, tried to create an ideal society near the fledgling village of Port Angeles. Large lumber ports were located on the western shore of the Sound and along Hood Canal. One of them, Port Gamble, boasted a sawmill that was the industrial pacesetter in the region in this era before Weyerhaeuser. Port Gamble's orderly pattern of white wooden houses and other structures gave it the air of a typical New England company town transplanted into a western forest.

Seattle was emerging as the metropolis of the Sound, having enjoyed a remarkable decade of growth and change. At the beginning of the 1880s, it had been, in the words of one historian, "a small town hacked out of a huge and shaggy wilderness. . . . small enough for people to walk or ride to work easily and while doing so to run in to most of its citizens." Then, between 1880 and 1889 its population soared from 3,553 to almost forty-three thousand. Enormous physical and social improvements were made, and Seattle acquired the look and feel of a confident, medium-sized city.

Upsound, rival Tacoma lagged behind but it was still a challenger. Tacoma, the terminus of the Northern Pacific, had already survived enough growth spurts and declines to develop a certain resiliency. Rudyard Kipling, visiting in 1888, described the city as "staggering under a boom of the boomiest." To complement its railroads and lumber, Tacoma in the statehood year acquired its famous smelter, and Andrew and Thea Foss assembled a few rowboats that would eventually blossom into the Sound's best known tug company. Farther south, in contrast to the activity on Commencement Bay, Steilacoom languished, and the lumber and shipping village of Olympia fought to ensure its continuation as Washington's capital. Farming and logging centered around Chehalis and Centralia, the latter founded by a former slave named George Washington who was now patriarch of the town.

Along Grays Harbor development was just getting underway. The first of its sawmills and the tapping of vast inland forest reserves dated only to the early 1880s. In 1889 residents anticipated construction of a railroad connection with Puget Sound. Hoquiam's population jumped from four hundred to fifteen hundred that year and the town formally incorporated. Auspicious plans were launched for Grays Harbor City on the northwestern shore by speculators hopeful of creating the great port of the region. In typical boom-and-bust fashion, Grays Harbor City was a ghost town within two years.

Kelso, Kalama, and other towns on the lower Columbia watched commercial traffic between the sea and Portland pass them by. Opposite that metropolis, Vancouver, once the Hudson's Bay Company headquarters for the entire Pacific Northwest, bustled with sawmills and other industries. Nearby LaCamas boasted its paper manufacturing plant. Farther east, on both sides of the Columbia's great cut through the Cascades, occasional villages were located at portage and transshipment points. Wallula, where the Walla Walla River entered the Columbia, remained a crucial transport point even after the railroads came.

In Eastern Washington, most of the good land appeared to have been taken by settlers by 1889. But "good land" in those days meant green and fertile river valley tracts, and irrigation projects of the time were small, private, and uncertain propositions. Planning was already underway for the Yakima Valley's Sunnyside Canal, which in a few years would commence widespread reclamation of arid lands. The town of North Yakima was flourishing; five years earlier the Northern Pacific had hauled in a hundred or more buildings by flatcar from the original Yakima City to create this new terminus.

Tucked away in the southeast corner of the new state, Walla Walla—until recently courted by both the older Oregon and the proposed state of Washington—still filled its accustomed role as the center of a rich agricultural region. Its days as Eastern Washington's most important community, however, were passing.

To the north, Spokane (then still commonly called Spokane Falls) had nineteen thousand people in 1889. Scarcely a decade old, the city was a railroad center that thrived on flour milling and on wheat, pine, lead, and silver brought in from its hinterland. Already it was assuming the air of a comfortable, stable city of homes, and the local elite built mansions in choice neighborhoods. That year, Louis Davenport established the downtown restaurant that would grow into the most elegant hostelry east of Cascades.

Elsewhere Eastern Washington held scattered villages, some on new railroad lines, that were entrepôts for their surrounding areas. A few were located on Indian reservations. Except for forests in the northeast highlands, most of Eastern Washington was arid country with the untamed Columbia River circling through. Settlers grazed livestock, but as yet knew little about how to use such land.

Most of the people of this new state were recent arrivals, many from the Midwest, restless and in quest of cheap land and new opportunity. Amidst the established white population came increasing numbers of northern and eastern Europeans, many settling along Puget Sound to farm, log, and fish. By 1889, most Indians had been placed on reservations, and several hundred Chinese had been driven from Seattle, Tacoma, and smaller places (though a few continued to work in remote areas on short-line railroad construction). Blacks resided throughout the larger cities, where they enjoyed a quiet middle-class livelihood. Only in the coal-mining town of Roslyn were blacks prominent; a few years earlier several hundred had been brought in as strike-breakers and many remained.

Eighteen eighty-nine would be remembered not only as the year statehood arrived but as the year that great fires destroyed parts of several towns, causing possibly ten million dollars' worth of damage. Seattle's famous conflagration began in the midafternoon of June 6, when a glue pot boiled over in a Front Street paint shop. Understandably but unwisely, the proprietor poured water on the nascent blaze, spreading it to wood chips and other litter. Within minutes flames leapt to neighboring saloons and other buildings. Before long the fire was completely out of control, thanks to the ample fuel available in a community of sawmills, wharves, and other wooden structures. Ironically, the fire marshal was out of town attending a fire prevention conference, and efforts to pump water from Elliott Bay proved futile because of a low tide.

As the reddish glow above Seattle became visible about the Sound, neighboring towns from Portland to Victoria responded. Even Tacoma, where schoolchildren were taught to sing, "Seattle, Seattle, Death Rattle, Death Rattle," proved an invaluable friend when death actually threatened. Scarcely an hour after the fire began, a special train arrived from Tacoma carrying fire-fighting equipment, with relief supplies soon following. The fire continued throughout the night, devouring two dozen business blocks and all the bayside wharves and mills. But the residential areas on the hillside were untouched and loss of life was limited to the waterfront's enormous rat population. The following morning six hundred citizens met to assess the losses and to prepare for immediate rebuilding. They voted down a suggestion to keep five hundred dollars recently raised to aid victims of the recent Johnstown flood. They would reorganize the city, alter blocks, widen streets, and rebuild with stone and brick—not wood. Amid tents and temporary structures, the rebuilding got underway almost immediately. By fall, surprised visitors found a new and improved city. The fire, however costly, enabled Seattleites to lay the foundations of an expansive urban center.

In late summer, Spokane suffered similar devastation. Haze drifting from forest fires in the Coeur d'Alene region at first obscured a minor blaze spewing from a Railroad Avenue lodging house. Here too, a key official—this time the water superintendent—was out of town, and hydrants failed to provide water. Uncontrolled, the fire spread through businesses and rooming houses as people fled across the river to supposed safety. But burning mills along the river's south bank sent sparks high into the sky, igniting buildings on the north side. A wind change eventually brought matters under control, but not until thirty-five blocks had been destroyed. As in Seattle, disaster inspired the rise of a new and sturdy downtown on the ashes of the old. Nor were these cities the only places visited by fire in 1889, flames also devastated much of downtown Vancouver, while parts of Ellensburg, Goldendale, and Roslyn were destroyed.

But the critical event of the year was statehood. In 1887 Washington's petition for admission to the Union had run afoul of a fundamental obstacle: Democrats controlling Congress were unwilling to increase Republican representation there. The Republican triumph in the 1888 elections, however, changed all that. Proposals immediately came to admit five new states: New Mexico, Montana, North Dakota, South Dakota, and Washington. Thinly populated New Mexico was soon eliminated from the list, but on Washington's Birthday enabling legislation was approved allowing the others to proceed.

In Washington, a constitutional convention convened in Olympia on July 4 and continued until late August. Seventy-five delegates, over half Republican, assembled from every county. Some had previous legislative experience in other states. Almost a third were lawyers, and only thirteen were farmers. Delegates borrowed much from constitutions of Oregon, California, Illinois, and other states viewed as appropriate models. The sensitive issues of woman suffrage and prohibition were set before the voters, who promptly rejected both. A popular referendum endorsed the constitution by a margin of nearly four to one and selected Olympia as state capital over North Yakima, Ellensburg, and other contenders. A state seal was adopted. According to legend, a committee devised an elaborate design depicting various industrial activities of the new state, but the chosen jeweler rejected this, took a postage stamp bearing a picture of George Washington, stuck it over the committee's proposal and said, "Here's your seal!"

Such duties concluded, territorial residents anxiously awaited word from the nation's capital. On November 11, the message arrived—collect—that President Harrison had signed the bill admitting Washington as the forty-second state, Montana and the Dakotas having been admitted in recent days. As word spread, it was greeted with cannon fire, oratory, and public celebrations.

A week later, scores of visitors arrived at gaily decorated Olympia by train and steamer. Symbolically, morning rain gave way to sunshine as festivities began. Bands, national guard units, and dignitaries including early settlers Michael T. Simmons and Ezra Meeker paraded to the modest white-frame capitol building. Here official proclamations were read and officials of the new state were sworn in. Banners honoring Isaac Stevens, the first territorial governor, and Elisha P. Ferry, the first state governor, flew above the assembled throng. A third banner carried the Indian words *Chinook quanism ancotty alta chee chaho alki*, roughly translated, "Living hereto in the past we now begin to live in the future."

The passing of power between the two governors was in itself symbolic. The last territorial governor, Miles Moore, was a merchant and civic leader from Walla Walla, which in earlier days had been the most urban settlement of the region. Now there was Ferry, political leader and town booster from aggressive young Seattle.

Territory to state, Moore to Ferry, Walla Walla to Seattle: change was occurring, a new era was under way.

WASHINGTON

A Centennial History

~ 1 ~

The Land Is Opened

The land never rests. Wind, water, earth movements, volcanoes, and glaciers constantly alter its shape. Change, imperceptible to the human eye, is always taking place. Only now and then do we notice. A sudden earth tremor disrupts daily routines. Flood waters engulf a valley. Winds carry off topsoil. Forest fires blacken the summer sky and leave scars that foster erosion. High-country backpackers hear the thunder of avalanches that alter the face of nearby mountains. And the peace of a pleasant Sunday morning in May is shattered when Mount St. Helens hurls a black plume ten miles into the sky, thirteen hundred feet of the mountain cone is blown away, a mud flow surges toward the Columbia River destroying everything in its wake, and fine ash blankets much of Eastern Washington.

Humans have also changed the earth. Early Indians who set fires to clear woodlands foster ecological changes. Monoliths of steel and concrete convert the free-flowing Columbia River into a chain of placid lakes. Canals cross and bring new life to barren deserts. Hills are moved and mountains sliced through to facilitate the transport of goods and people. Rivers and harbors are dredged; meandering streams are narrowed, deepened, and straightened; swamps and tidal basins are drained and filled. The earth is buried beneath layers of asphalt and cement; highrise structures of steel, concrete, and glass, their foundations embedded deep in the ground, rise higher than surrounding hills.

The events that shaped the basic lay of the land began eons ago. Almost a billion years ago, a small continent slowly drifted eastward toward older landforms, the collision creating the succession of

3

mountain ridges and narrow valleys in what is now Northeastern Washington. As the small Juan de Fuca plate has been shifted and squeezed against adjacent plates of the earth's crust, earthquakes and volcanic action have created mountains, troughs, and valleys. Volcanic eruption shaped the Cascade Mountains and threw out layers of basalt to build the plateaus of the Columbia Basin, later to be covered with fine particles of loess from periodic dust storms. Continual folding and shifting produced the Olympics Mountains and the Willapa Hills.

Ancient glaciers had dammed rivers high in the Rockies. With warming trends twelve thousand years ago came deep floods, carving out the scablands and ancient coulees of Eastern Washington.

Nature will never cease to shape the land, but now humans change it as well, even as they adapt to what nature provides. North America's first human inhabitants were of Asian origin, most likely from Siberia or Mongolia. In search of game and forage, over untold generations they moved eastward over an eight-hundred-mile-wide North Pacific land bridge that connected Asia and North America. Their trek followed a natural route exposed by melting glaciers, and the dry, flat steppes they encountered were not much different from the land they left behind. Most anthropologists believe that these people journeyed inland toward the heart of North America and then fanned out in all directions, adapting to the varying topography, climate, and resources they found in different regions. Some came eventually to the Pacific Northwest. Recent archaeological excavations indicate that at least twelve thousand years ago humans stalked and killed giant mastodons on the northern plains of the Olympic Peninsula, and remains of villages nearly as ancient have been uncovered at sites in Eastern Washington. Tools, weapons, amulets, and other artifacts indicate an established but mobile culture based on hunting and gathering and salmon fishing. In body structure and skin, hair, and eye color, they probably resembled present-day Native Americans.

Millennia later, Indians, possibly descendants of those earliest immigrants, benefited from the natural wealth of the Pacific Northwest. Cultures on opposite sides of the natural barrier of the Cascades differed. East of these mountains, Indians as far as the Rockies were culturally similar. West of the Cascades people inhabited the long coastal plain and inland valleys between Northern California and Southeast Alaska. Except for the Makah on the tip of the Olympic Peninsula and the Chinook on the lower Columbia River, most

Indians west of the Cascades had language patterns of Salish derivation. Salish also predominated in the northern part of Eastern Washington, while Sahaptin groups lived to the south.

Most lived well, amid abundant big and small game, fish and other seafoods, berries, nuts, roots, and small plants. Large trees, particularly red cedar, covered the land west of the Cascades and were easily felled and split. Natural bounty assisted a thriving culture to emerge without dependence upon agriculture or domesticated animals. Inland Indians lacked some of these advantages but they also fared well.

Many coastal villages were large and permanent with cedar longhouses clustered together on a beach. These were rectangular houses of cedar planks, similar to Indian homes of the eastern American woodlands and structures built by early white settlers. Inside, platforms and shelves for sleeping and daily activities lined the walls around a central fire pit. Mats, baskets, and other furnishings graced the houses. In addition, small seasonal campsites were set up near favored fishing spots or where berries or game were plentiful.

East of the Cascades, the traditional dwelling was a circular shelter dug three or four feet into the earth, its roof of brush and woven mats attached to a pole framework. The house was warmed or cooled by adding or removing these coverings. One ancient village containing more than a hundred such houses was located near the mouth of the Snake River. Inland people were mobile, moving to seasonal hunting, fishing, and gathering places; their houses of poles and mats could be easily carried, set up, and removed. These Indians also took advantage of natural shelters such as caves and rock overhangs. Only after acquiring horses in the early 1700s did they begin to use teepees like the Indians of the Great Plains.

On both sides of the mountains, life centered around the villages, with influence extended and strengthened over vast regions by marriage and kinship. Social and political organization, though stratified, was informal. Persons with great skills and spiritual gifts emerged as leaders. Authority might be inherited along with wealth and prestige, but leaders out of favor were easily deposed. In coastal communities, class structure was based on family lineage. A large class of "good families" was traditionally accorded prestige, while others held lower status, although above that of the numerous slaves. Inland, experienced hunters might be chosen to lead in the chase. Everywhere, great temporary power was granted during war or other emergency, to be given up when the crisis subsided. Shamans, medicine men or women who were in contact with spirits and able to cure illness and offer advice, also enjoyed prestige.

Everywhere, the quality of life was directly related to the abundance of food and other necessities. Salmon, plentiful and easily caught, was central to Indian diet and culture on both sides of the mountains. Salmon swimming upriver to spawning grounds were so abundant that they could be caught easily. At some spots nets were dropped to pull in large catches; elsewhere Indians used harpoon-like spears fitted with pointed heads that sprang open upon penetrating the fish, to be drawn in by an attached cord. Some Indians extended fence-like wiers across watercourses to channel fish into traps. At the mighty Celilo Falls of the Columbia, Indians fished from high wooden platforms extending out above the current. Women prepared the fish for eating, boning, scraping, and cutting them, and placing them on long frames to smoke or dry. The supernatural powers attributed to the salmon were reflected in elaborate rituals after the catch and during the feast.

Shellfish and other seafood were also important in the west. Off the coast, whalers pursued their prey using sturdy boats, bone-tipped hardwood lances, and balloon-type floats made from hair-seal hides. Hunters brought down bear, deer, and other large game with bows and arrows, hunting clubs, pikes, and traps, while women set out with baskets and digging sticks to gather berries, roots, wild fruits, or nuts.

Clothing differed according to the need to shed rain or to protect bodies from extremes of hot and cold. On the coast, robes of animal skins and pelts typically signified wealth. Salish women wove brightly colored blankets of mountain goat wool, vegetable fibers, and the hair of tiny dogs raised for the purpose. Decorations and jewelry were often woven or sewn into the clothing itself.

Puget Sound, rivers, lakes, and the ocean itself provided natural routes for fishing, hunting, trading, and visiting. Swift canoes of red cedar made possible rapid and easy passage of these waterways. Travel east of the Cascades was at first by foot. Then, a century before whites arrived, horses, originally brought by Spanish conquistadores to the south, began to appear. First used by the Nez Perce and by the Cayuse, they later spread to other groups. Now Indians could travel greater distances at a faster pace and contacts, peaceful and otherwise, were enhanced in all directions. Northwest Indian groups were never isolated from each other. They made contact with one another in common gathering areas such as The Dalles, where they met for trade and ceremonies. Among coastal Indians, periodic potlatches allowed ostentatious displays of personal and tribal wealth, brought people together for festivities that lasted over several days, and provided a mechanism for redistributing as well as affirming a leader's wealth and power.

Northwest Indians had a strong sense of family, based on the extended family, with several generations living together in a single house or village. Old age was honored, and elders were accorded profound respect and were expected to pass on to the young their knowledge, skills, and wisdom. Deceased family members were mourned with ceremony and weeping. Made comfortable, the deceased was prepared for burial as if for a journey.

Indians revered animals, and in legends endowed them with human characteristics and particular attributes or powers. Spirits in the natural world could assist with everyday activities. Their voices were heard in creaking trees, the hum of the wind, and the ripple of water, and each individual human might seek one particular spirit helper.

Life was good for most Washington Indians, but their favorable circumstances could not last forever. Long before actual encounters with whites, Pacific Northwest Indians received hints of impending change. Along with horses, strange trade items began to appear: iron hatchets, knives, and guns. Stories circulated about light-skinned men with beards and bizarre costumes who were trading among distant tribes. Unfamiliar diseases decimated entire villages, leaving survivors stunned and confused and threatening their ability to provide enough food by traditional means. Then, one summer day, a coastal band spotted a strange vessel off the Olympic shore, huge with masts and sails. They paddled out to meet it and exchanged furs for trinkets and pieces of metal with the light-skinned men on board. The encounter was peaceful, but seven sailors who came ashore the following evening were slaughtered by Indians swarming from the bushes. Horrified witnesses aboard the ship put to sea as soon as the tide allowed, with cannon firing. The vessel was soon gone, but white men would return, and they would not be vanquished so easily again.

⌒ジↄ

The mariners killed by the band of Quinaults on that July afternoon in 1775 were from the *Sonora,* a schooner commanded by Juan

Francisco de la Bodega y Quadra. A league south rested the *Santiago* of Bruno de Heceta, leader of this small expedition out of San Blas, Spain's naval station in Baja California. In the three centuries since Christopher Columbus had precipitated the first great explorations in the New World, Spanish adventurers had conquered rich civilizations and explored much of the Americas, allowing Spain to reign as the foremost trading power and cultural center of Europe. Now rival nations threatened the periphery of His Catholic Majesty's empire. Aggressive English sailors and Russian traders were joined by merchants and experienced seamen from a new nation emerging from the discontented British colonies of North America.

During recent decades Spanish crews had explored north along the California coast, establishing trading posts, garrisons, and missions. In 1774 Juan José Pérez Hernandez sailed to the northern shore of Vancouver Island, but this cautious man remained far offshore and recorded only general descriptions of the land he passed. Heceta led a second expedition the following year. On July 14, 1775, he landed at Point Grenville where he erected a cross and formally claimed the area for Spain. Elation was shattered a few hours later when Bodega y Quadra came alongside to relate his disastrous encounter with the Indians. His own crew weakened by scurvy, Heceta turned south toward San Blas. En route he noted the mouth of a river, which he named the *Rio de San Roque,* but he failed to enter it. Later it would be called the Columbia.

Spain had good reason to fear Russian encroachment. Russia under the Romanovs, though vast, undeveloped, and largely isolated from international affairs, nevertheless contemplated exploration and expansion in the North Pacific. With czarist encouragement, the Russian-American Company was by the early 1800s directing a large, prosperous fur business out of New Archangel, now Sitka. As Russians looked further south, their intentions became a factor for Spain to reckon with.

Rivalry with the British was of greater significance. Rising to challenge Spanish power in the Old World, they had plundered galleons crossing from the New and established their string of American colonies. Two centuries after Sir Francis Drake saw California, English ships returned to the western North American coast. In 1776, Captain James Cook, famed for earlier Pacific expeditions, was seeking navigation routes in the North Pacific. Commanding the *Discovery* and the *Resolute,* Cook discovered the Hawaiian Islands, then proceeded eastward, raising the northwest coast in the spring of 1778. At Nootka on Vancouver Island, he claimed the area for England before heading out to sea and a violent death in Hawaii. His crew returned home rich with geographic and scientific knowledge, and the significant observation that sea otter pelts from the North American coast could bring fabulous profits in China.

Several men who sailed with Cook would make contributions in their own right. A young Yankee adventurer named John Ledyard became the first American on the northwest coast. Enthralled by what he saw, Ledyard sought to imbue his countrymen, including Thomas Jefferson, with his enthusiasm for the far American West. Charles Barkley entered the Strait of Juan de Fuca in the summer of 1787, naming it for the possibly mythical Greek sailor said to have described an opening there two centuries earlier. A year after Barkley, John Meares sailed along the Olympic Peninsula, naming many features. At Nootka he secured land from the Indians, built a house, launched the first European-style vessel constructed in the Pacific Northwest, and started an international political crisis. Spain was asserting possession of Nootka and erecting fortifications, and an impetuous commandant, Don Esteban José Martínez, seized ships belonging to Meares and hustled the crews to a Mexican prison. He was overridden by his superiors, but England still protested, and relations between the two nations deteriorated amidst mutual preparations for war.

Because both governments desired to avoid hostilities, an agreement was reached whereby Spain and England would respect each other's rights in the North Pacific. To settle the details, the Spanish government selected Bodega y Quadra as its representative, and England chose George Vancouver, formerly of Cook's expedition. Their meeting at Nootka in the fall of 1792 was conducted cordially amid a hum of activity and festivity. Nootka had become the most active center on the coast, and twenty-seven ships of five nations lay in the harbor. Neither negotiator could relinquish his nation's claims, although each confirmed that the other's ships could stop at Nootka. Nevertheless, Spain's pretended monopoly in the region had ended. Spain would independently abandon its north coast claims while England increased its presence and interests.

Sea otter furs and other pelts brought increasing profit. Indians, alert to new trading opportunities, traded pelts for metal objects, buttons, snuff, and beads. The fine furs of the small otters that played on rocks from California to Alaska brought high prices in China, and England's cross-Pacific trade thrived.

En route to Nootka, George Vancouver had entered the Strait of Juan de Fuca. Anchoring at an inlet he named Discovery Bay after his command ship, Vancouver surveyed the immediate waters, forested foothills, and mountains beyond. He named Mount Baker for a crew member and the snow-covered hulk on the southeast horizon became Mount Rainier, after a rear admiral in the Royal Navy. Turning south, Vancouver divided his command among himself and his lieutenants, Peter Puget and Joseph Whidbey. Rowing small boats and sailing when wind allowed, the crews investigated all inlets and waterways that appeared navigable. The result was a detailed description of the area accompanied by charts and sketches. Many outstanding geographical features were named, among them Puget Sound, Whidbey Island, Hood Canal, Bellingham Bay, Vashon Island, Port Orchard, Admiralty Inlet, Birch Bay, and Port Gardner. At this last spot, on June 4, 1792, Vancouver went ashore at the site of Everett and claimed the region for England.

But the English commander also heard disquieting information. An American captain named Robert Gray, sailing out of Boston, had discovered and entered a giant river to the south and named it Columbia. Feigning disinterest, Vancouver nevertheless assigned William Broughton to investigate. Broughton sailed over a hundred miles upriver, passing sandbars, breakers, and Gray's anchorage. Penetrating deeper than had Gray, Broughton thus improved England's later claims to the Northwest.

Meanwhile, even more momentous events had been occurring on the eastern coast of North America as British colonials declared independence, confirmed it by war, and established a new government. Over the years, New Englanders had honed skills of seamanship and trading, but the revolution had closed traditional British markets and the immediate hinterlands lacked sufficient marketable resources. Seafaring traders looked outward in search of new opportunities. To exploit the North Pacific trade, a party of Boston and New York merchants outfitted two ships. While John Kendrick sailed in the *Columbia Rediviva,* Robert Gray commanded the *Lady Washington.* Often sailing separately, the two successfully traded at Nootka and in China. Gray's second trip altered Northwest history.

Having returned from his first voyage with a degree of fame as the first American to circumnavigate the globe, Gray, now commanding the *Columbia Rediviva,* touched the Washington coast in May 1792. After finding and investigating Grays Harbor, he returned south to a spot where he hoped to find the mouth of the great river noted by Heceta. There, a wide band of discolored water rushed seaward to meet ocean breakers. Early on the morning of May 11, Gray maneuvered through the breakers and around dangerous sandbars. The entry in his log was profound with understatement: "When we were over the bar we found this to be a large river of fresh water, up which we started." Curious but friendly inhabitants of a Chinook village greeted him, supplying fresh water and following the boat. Gray anchored about four miles upriver, naming the river Columbia after his ship. For more than a week, his crew investigated the immediate hinterland, but they sailed no farther upriver before returning seaward.

American interest in the Northwest coast increased following Gray's discovery. Yet the focus of investigation brought Americans overland, and half a century passed before a major maritime exploration—under command of Charles Wilkes in 1841—was carried out. Part of a global scientific expedition, the Wilkes contingent of scientists added to the geographical and physical knowledge of the region.

Despite the monumental crossing of the north country by the Canadian Alexander Mackenzie and other fur trading ventures, the heart of the continent between the Missisippi River and the Pacific Ocean remained an unknown when Thomas Jefferson became President in 1801. Even before the Louisiana Purchase in 1803, Jefferson was planning an overland expedition to the Pacific. As leader Jefferson selected his personal secretary, Meriwether Lewis, a scholarly military officer interested in engineering and natural history. William Clark, a frontier fighter, was officially subordinate but acted as co-leader. The interests and personalities of the two men complemented each other.

Departing from St. Louis, the expedition went up the Missouri River to winter among the Mandan Indians in the Dakotas, setting out the next April farther up the Missouri and its tributaries, then tramping on foot across snow-covered Rocky Mountain passes. On October 16, they became the first whites to view the Columbia River east of the Cascades. Proceeding downstream in dugout canoes they encountered Indians fishing in the great rapids. On November 7, the party reached the north side of the river's mouth and made camp. "Great joy in camp," Clark wrote. "We are in view of the Ocian, this great Pacific Octean which we have been so long anxious to See."

The excitement of reaching the end of the outward journey was tempered by wind, pounding rain, chill, and an unpalatable diet of dried fish and roots. Within days the men moved to better ground south of the Columbia where they built the campsite of Fort Clatsop near a sheltered stream. After a dreary but busy winter, they set out for home in early spring. Dividing their forces so that Lewis could seek a land route farther north, they reunited in North Dakota. The rejoined parties arrived at St. Louis on September 23, 1806, having been gone for twenty-eight months.

The trek's significance can hardly be overestimated. Lewis and Clark clarified much of the geography of interior North America, and they brought or sent back countless plant and animal specimens. Sacajawea, the young Indian woman carrying her baby on her back as she accompanied the expedition, and Lewis's black servant York, became Northwest legends. Moreover, Lewis and Clark gave their young nation a strong claim to the entire Northwest and helped establish an overland route linking the oceans.

Five years elapsed before the next overland expedition, a private venture launched in 1811 by wealthy New York merchant John Jacob Astor. Astor had grandiose plans to establish a fur-trading monopoly throughout the continent. His Pacific Fur Company was to establish headquarters at the mouth of the Columbia. Two expeditions were sent west, one overland and one by sea; both experienced hardship and tragedy. Duncan McDougall founded Fort Astoria on level ground above the Columbia and efforts to inaugurate fur trading got under way. During the War of 1812, however, a British ship arrived to accept the surrender of Astoria. After the war, the fort and its outlying posts passed to Britain's North West Company, a giant and colorful company whose men trapped, hunted, and exchanged goods with Indians for beaver and other pelts. From a chain of posts including Fort Nez Perce and Spokane House, peltries were shipped to market. These "Nor'Westers" came to know the area intimately and to chart and map it; they dominated the region for a time, but their dominance was not to last.

After the powerful and older Hudson's Bay Company moved from northern Canada into North West Company territory, competition between them became ruthless. These companies engaged in brutal and sometimes violent rivalry until 1821 when the British government forced their merger, retaining the Hudson's Bay Company name. Briefly, the HBC continued to direct its Pacific Northwest operations from Astoria, but it soon established a new headquarters a hundred miles up the Columbia River. In March 1825 George Simpson, resident governor for North America, personally dedicated this post, which was named Fort Vancouver as a reminder of English explorations and claims. The fort quickly became the economic, social, and political center of the entire Northwest and its chief factor or administrator, Dr. John McLoughlin, dominated the region for two decades. Supported from afar by Simpson and aided by his own imposing stature and strength of purpose, McLoughlin ran company affairs with an iron hand while he encouraged the fort's self-sufficiency. Representing stability and government in the area, he insisted upon fair treatment for Britons, Americans, and Indians alike. Wheat and apples, those eventual staples of Washington agriculture, were first planted at Fort Vancouver. Livestock was raised for both meat and hides. Shipping and fishing flourished and a sawmill was erected. Goods for the entire area passed through Vancouver.

Possibly five hundred people lived in or near the fort, a cosmopolitan blend of English, Americans, French Canadians, Indians, and Hawaiians. Inside a stockade were workshops, storerooms, a bakery, a flour mill, Protestant and Catholic churches, and the homes of the McLoughlins and his chief assistant, James Douglas. Vancouver was also the social headquarters of the region, a customary stopping place for visitors and travelers, a source of food, provisions, information, and gossip.

But Fort Vancouver was above all the heart of a fur-trading empire. Smaller posts, some new and others inherited from the North West Company, replicated Fort Vancouver: Fort Nisqually on southern Puget Sound, Okanogan at the mouth of the Okanogan River, and Spokane and Walla Walla farther east. In the Cowlitz Valley, HBC subsidiary Puget Sound Agricultural Company opened a large farm. In 1836 the company brought the first steam-powered boat, appropriately named the *Beaver,* into the Pacific Northwest.

By the late 1830s increasing numbers of Americans were arriving in the Northwest. The HBC had treated American fur traders as competitors, but settlers posed a greater threat. British settlers were not arriving, but Americans were, and their uses of the land directly conflicted with those of the company. Fur trading required that the area remain free, wild, and unpopulated; settlers cultivated fields, erected fences, organized villages, and attracted more people. Apparently McLoughlin shrewdly encouraged Americans to settle south of the Columbia River, away from major company interests. In 1843, the HBC moved its headquarters north to Vancouver Island, causing speculation that it intended to surrender its interests on the Columbia. More than a few company employees, McLoughlin among them, left fur trading to settle in the Willamette Valley. Distrusted now by both British and Americans and beset by debt, McLoughlin lived out his remaining years far from the power and glory of his past.

For twenty formative years, Fort Vancouver had represented an unofficial government for all groups in the region. It commenced or controlled major economic activities and was the leading social outpost in a region lacking European amenities. The company was the chief catalyst in the transitional years between exploration and settlement.

Despite British dominance, a few Americans attempted to trade in the Pacific Northwest. "Mountain men," individualistic fur traders of the Rocky Mountain Fur Company, only touched the fringes of the Far Northwest, but their intimate knowledge of the mountains, streams, valleys, and climate made them ideal guides for the wagon trains of early overlanders. Army Captain Benjamin L. E. de Bonneville brought the first wagons across the continental divide and was the subject of a book by Washington Irving. Two Boston acquaintances, Hall J. Kelley and Nathaniel Wyeth, proposed grandiose colonial settlements—which perished under company opposition and for lack of interest. But Kelley's enthusiastic writings increased eastern awareness of the area, and Wyeth attracted some settlers west.

Among those Kelley attracted were Connecticut Methodists Jason and Daniel Lee, the first American missionaries to actively work in the region. Like the fur traders, they would help transform the Northwest from a wild, unknown area to one of settlement. Arriving in 1834, the uncle and nephew took residence in the lush Willamette valley where retired HBC employees and some Americans lived without benefit of religious guidance. Satellite posts were started at The Dalles and at Nisqually, such activities peaking by 1840. Sent to convert Indians, the Lees increasingly concerned themselves with the white settlers. Writing home, they sought financial support and reinforcements while at the same time glorifying the area and its potential. The Lees saved few souls but they helped attract American immigrants and prepare the region for American control.

Marcus and Narcissa Whitman arrived in 1836 in a party sent west by the Protestant-supported American Board of Commissioners for Foreign Missions. Whitman selected a mission site in the Walla Walla Valley at a place local Cayuse Indians called Waiilatpu, "the place of rye grass." Sheltered by trees and surrounded by rounded hills of grass, a small settlement was built near a winding creek. Henry and Eliza Spalding, their contentious associates, settled farther east in Nez Perce country on Lapwai Creek. Two years later Mary and Elkanah Walker and Cushing and Myra Eells established Tshimakain among the Spokane Indians. Differences of opinion and personality afflicted the scattered and individualistic missionaries. Whitman believed that their first purpose was religious conversion, while others felt that the Indians should first be taught farming and other settlement skills.

Nevertheless, settled routines took shape at the three missions. Farming and assorted chores shared time with meditations and religious instruction. Waiilatpu, on a trail to Vancouver, had frequent visitors and the Whitmans took in the children of mountain men and immigrants. The mission became lively and busy. Nevertheless, the Whitmans had difficulties with the Cayuse who refused to work as if slaves, and Narcissa found their life style disturbing.

Disharmony among the missionaries, the lack of Indian converts, and high expenses led the American Board to consider closing Lapwai and Waiilatpu. The energetic Marcus Whitman journeyed east and successfully appealed the closures, at the same time becoming something of a celebrity.

Returning west in 1843, Whitman, now the seasoned traveler, helped guide one of the first large trains across the Oregon Trail and demonstrated that a four-wheeled wagon could cross the Rockies. Clearly, large numbers of people with heavy loads of supplies could make the trip west.

Narcissa Whitman grew increasingly depressed in her isolation. Her only child had drowned in the stream, and relations with the Cayuse, never good, deteriorated. Laxatives and poisons, intended to ward off wild animals from the garden, sickened Indians who ate the vegetables. Although white patients treated by Dr. Whitman usually got well, many Indians died. The death of half the Cayuse tribe from measles in 1847 aroused suspicion and anger. Furthermore, white settlers continued to filter into the area, clearly threatening Indian security.

On the morning of November 29, 1847, the seventy-four people at Waiilatpu went about normal activities. The Whitmans rested and children played. Several Indians quietly milled around the buildings after burying a young Cayuse. After noon, Tilaukait, the father of the dead man, and Tomahas arrived to confront the doctor. From another room Narcissa and several children heard the three men talking loudly and then a shot.

Soon, angry Indians were storming the house. Narcissa was shot when she went to a window searching for help. By the time the incident ended, the Whitmans and twelve other mission residents were dead, and buildings, fields, and orchards were destroyed. When HBC men from Fort Walla Walla reached the scene they found smoldering ruins and scattered bodies. Forty-seven people, abducted by the Indians, were later ransomed by the company. A few escaped. Soon, the Lapwai and Tshimakain stations were closed, although Elkanah Walker returned to live among the Nez Perce in later years.

The killings alarmed American settlers throughout the region and gave some an excuse to rid the area of Indians. A force of five hundred vigilante volunteers entered the Cayuse country, but little actual fighting ensued. In April 1850, five Cayuse, including the supposed murderers, surrendered. Tried in Oregon City, they were convicted and hanged. The so-called Cayuse War ended, but the continued movement of whites across Indian lands invited future difficulties.

Among their many prejudices, the Whitmans harbored deep mistrust of the Roman Catholic "Black Robes" they feared were infesting the Northwest. Encouraged by Dr. John McLoughlin, himself a convert, Father Francois Blanchet established headquarters in the Willamette Valley while Father Modeste DeMers and the Jesuit John Peter DeSmet ranged much of the Far West. Catholic missionaries had certain advantages over their Protestant rivals. The priests were well schooled; unburdened by families, they could circulate widely among Indians and whites. Not intent on settlement, they scrupulously attended to religious duties. Catholics were less demanding than Protestants in the matter of conversion and not so easily shocked by "uncivilized" practices. Often shunned by Protestant settlers, Catholic priests were free to concentrate on their Indian charges.

Together, Catholic and Protestant American missionaries played a significant role in developing the Pacific Northwest. Efforts to convert Indians generally failed, but the missionaries' accomplishments lay in other directions. They brought American religion to the frontier and established early settlements. Most important, missionary letters to home congregations and church newspapers painted a glowing picture of an Eden beyond the Rocky Mountains. Marcus and Narcissa Whitman became legendary martyrs and pioneers symbolizing the area.

For half a century, Europeans and Americans had explored and exploited the Pacific Northwest, setting the stage for the great influx of settlers from the United States during the 1840s and 1850s.

~ 2 ~

The Land Is Settled

It was called the Oregon Country, that slanting rectangle that reached from the Pacific Ocean to the crest of the Rockies and between the forty-second parallel and the fifty-four forty line. Spain after 1819 and Russia after 1824 confined themselves respectively to the south and north. A peculiar if pragmatic treaty in 1818 allowed British and American "joint occupation" of Oregon. Renewable each decade, the treaty was amended to allow abrogation by either nation on a year's notice. As a practical matter, governmental authority during most of the "joint occupation" period was exercised by the Hudson's Bay Company, with John McLoughlin as chief factor. Harmony was generally maintained as fur traders, missionaries, and assorted adventurers went about their diverse activities. Wisely if unknowingly, the diplomats of 1818 decided to delay decision on sovereignty until events themselves determined the final disposition of the region.

Fur traders and missionaries competed for beaver and for souls. Journals of exploration, books by Washington Irving, promotional broadsides from Hall J. Kelley and Nathaniel Wyeth, missionary letters and lectures, and William Cullen Bryant's evocative line from *Thanatopsis*, "where rolls the Oregon," combined to fix the Pacific Northwest in the national mind. The image emerged of a rich and open territory that was rightfully and logically American. A New York editor would coin the phrase "Manifest Destiny" to express the view that occupation of the West was both inevitable and just. Who could better use the land and its resources, change prairies into farms and isolated bays into bustling harbors, than the people of this young, aggressive nation?

And so sixty-five thousand Americans, a fifth of all who travelled the overland trails west, journeyed to the Northwest between 1830 and 1860. Until 1849, when California gold became a stronger magnet than farmland, the overwhelming majority of migrants chose Oregon. It was a great historical migration, its participants driven by myriad motivations. Economic or personal hardship at home, the availability of cheap land and excellent growing conditions, and a desire for adventure were among individual reasons. Ezra Meeker expected to make his fortune farming; Morton McCarver to found a city; David Maynard to escape a shrewish wife; George Washington to find a place where his black skin was no detriment; Samuel Wilbur "Wild Bill" Condit to find gold; and Cushing and Myra Eells to do God's work. Antonio B. Rabbeson hoped "to kill buffalo, deer, elk, etc., and have a good time."

Typical emigrants were Midwestern Protestants firmly devoted to such rural American ideals as piety, patriotism, family, hard work, and clear distinctions between the sexes. Most started out in the spring for a journey of anywhere from three-and-a-half to seven months, depending upon such vagaries as weather, disease, and Indian hostility. They assembled at one of the busy outfitting towns on the Missouri River, places dedicated to starting such groups on their way. There migrants picked up supplies, heard abundant advice, found traveling companions, hired guides, and learned how to yoke oxen or drive a prairie schooner. Although costly, overland travel was less expensive than sea voyages via Panama or Cape Horn.

Parties organized into trains, some several hundred wagons long. These caravans plodded up the North Platte River along a "highway" forty feet wide that would eventually harden under years of wagonwheel pressure. Dry and flat, the prairies offered little fresh water and insufficient wood for fuel and repairs. A slow, barely noticeable climb led to the Sweetwater River, then steepened near Rocky Mountain foothills where pine trees thickened and water became abundant. The legendary gateway to the Far West was South Pass, a valley so wide and grassy that many failed to recognize it as a pass at all. Just beyond, Utah-bound Mormons and California-bound argonauts turned southwest. Legend relates that the California road was marked by a gleaming pile of gold-laced quartz and the northern fork by a sign reading "To Oregon." Clearly, a generation boasted, literate persons chose Oregon. Descending from the Rockies, the trail wound though desert valleys and beneath the rock cliffs that held the

Snake River. Above the mouth of that stream, pioneers set off across the piney Blue Mountains toward the Columbia. Rapids on the Columbia were the last physical obstacles encountered before arrival in the fabled valley of the Willamette; after 1846, many preferred the road Samuel Barlow built along an old cattle trail circling south of Mount Hood.

From jumping off to destination, the trail experience meant hardship and danger. Deaths resulted from sickness, accidents, or drowning, but rarely—despite popular period fiction to the contrary—from Indian attacks. Some Indians and lawless whites stole goods, harassed trains, robbed fresh graves, extracted tolls at passage points, and frightened the faint of heart, but they were rarely dangerous. Indeed, Indians often assisted travelers, offering advice or carrying messages between trains. Monotony, illness, and extremes of heat and cold were more bothersome than Indian encounters.

There were good moments. Nightly stops provided opportunities to visit, sing, dance, and compare notes. Travelers deposited mail along the way and posted messages of general import; this was how many immigrants learned of President Zachary Taylor's sudden death in 1850. Trading posts offered welcome respite and supplied goods. Wagon trains became communities on the move, the members forming close and enduring friendships and an occasional courtship. Leaders emerged and travelers with specialized skills were valued. Most took turns standing watch or caring for animals.

Arrival in the Northwest allowed little time for relaxation. Early pioneers congregated in the Willamette Valley, but by the early 1850s increasing numbers moved north of the Columbia. They sought sites where rivers joined, where soil was fertile, or where a harbor was deep. Finding a desirable spot, the newcomer filed claim at the nearest government land office and prepared to improve his land. Few wanted to live in isolation. Many intended to build towns on the frontier. The Northwest, distant from established centers, needed urban services to support an increasing population: stores, warehouses, offices, banks, schools, churches, and other amenities. Most settlers expected to become active in these new communities.

The land north of the Columbia was settled slowly at first. Simon Plomondon, the French Canadian who had established the Hudson's

Bay Company farm on the Cowlitz Prairie, built his own home there in the late 1820s, becoming apparently the first permanent white settler above the Columbia. Other settlers scattered near that outpost and near Fort Nisqually. A few homes spread along the north bank of the Columbia, but settlement in Eastern Washington was slight after the deaths of the Whitmans. Isolated land holdings were less common than settlement by organized groups that established villages. Many newcomers cleared land and planted crops, but they also turned their efforts toward providing such urban features as sawmills and gristmills, docks, community stores, and governmental institutions.

The first organized party to reach Puget Sound was led by Kentucky-born Michael T. Simmons and George W. Bush. With friends and neighbors, these men came west from Missouri in 1844. Learning that Bush, who was black, would be prohibited from owning land south of the Columbia, they looked to the north. Simmons first scouted out the Cowlitz prairie, but preferred the falls of the Des Chutes River on the southern Sound. In late September, he led a party of thirty-two overland from the Columbia and claimed land alongside the falls. Bush took higher prairie land, with the Bert Kindred and James McAllister families on nearby tracts. They cooperated to build a split-log house, and survived that first harsh winter with help from HBC officials at Fort Nisqually and from local Indians who showed the newcomers how to live off the land.

These scattered land holdings became the nucleus of a village that slowly attracted other immigrants. At the falls, Simmons built a gristmill and then a sawmill. In 1847 eight settlers formed the Puget Sound Milling Company which initiated the lumbering business of the region. Edmund Sylvester and Levi Lathrop Smith claimed land along Budd Inlet at the mouth of the Des Chutes. When Smith drowned, Sylvester became the sole owner of what would become Olympia. Sylvester prospered, but Michael Simmons suffered a series of setbacks. Selling his mill interest, he became embroiled in a lengthy lawsuit and was then swindled out of a modest fortune by an employee.

As Olympia grew, it was selected as site of the first customs house on the Sound, promising stability. One general store was joined by others. There were the inevitable saloons and successive newspapers, a livery stable, churches, a public school, and a Masonic temple. Buildings were hardly auspicious: the schoolhouse collapsed under heavy snow, and Smith's log cabin was the only hotel. Weather could be unpleasant, and streets were muddy. But two hundred and fifty settlers made Olympia the largest village on Puget Sound and by 1853 it was the clear choice for territorial capital.

Meanwhile George Bush was prospering south of town, raising grain, vegetables, fruit, and livestock and hosting travelers. Yet discriminatory laws impeded his ownership of this land. Memorializing Congress to allow his title under the Donation Land Act, the first territorial legislature vouched that his habits were "exemplary and industrious; and that by a constant and laborious cultivation of his said claim, and by an accommodating and charitable disposal of his produce to emigrants, he has contributed much towards the settlement of this Territory, the suffering and needy never having applied to him in vain for succor and assistance." It was praise, grand and generous, and there lay the rub: the same legislature defeated a bill that would have granted Bush citizenship and the vote.

Other villages began to appear on harbors and at river mouths around Puget Sound in the early 1850s. Just beyond Nisqually and near the Army's Fort Steilacoom, Lafayette Balch in 1850 built a house and then a store. In 1853, Balch's Steilacoom became the first incorporated town in the territory. Five years later there were seventy homes, six stores, three hotels, a sprinkling of shops, and a wharf, with three sawmills and a flour mill nearby. The hundred inhabitants included discharged soldiers and former HBC employees. Cultural amenities abounded: a library association, a public school, and the first Protestant and Catholic churches north of the Columbia. Steilacoom's fortunate location, beside an Army post and between Olympia and settlements to the north, helped it to thrive.

Meanwhile, Nicholas Delin, a husky Swede from California, stopped in Olympia just long enough to find backers for a sawmill on Commencement Bay. After clearing land, he commenced manufacturing, and by 1852 his mill was operating and advertising. A year later a hundred and seventy-one persons crossed Naches Pass over the new wagon road from Walla Walla and settled in or near this town, recently named Tacoma. The newcomers engaged in such activities as barrel making, seining, and fish packing, along with logging and farming.

Thirty miles north, early in the fall of 1851, two young friends from Illinois, John Low and David Denny, took land at a triangular point jutting into Puget Sound just south of Elliott Bay. On a rainy November day, they were joined by Denny's older brother Arthur and twenty others, who debarked from the brig *Exact*. The pioneers constructed several cabins and began selling timber to California-bound vessels. With superlative optimism, the Dennys named their settlement New York, adding "Alki," Chinook Jargon for "by-and-by."

But bothersome winds and tides made landings at Alki difficult, and accesible timber was soon used up. Before spring, Arthur Denny and two other men moved to a deep-water site on the eastern side of Elliott Bay, staking out claims that became Seattle. There was little to suggest that this bayside village, named after a helpful Suquamish leader, would eventually become the regional metropolis.

As his community grew, Denny became involved in almost every aspect of city building and civic affairs. Early on, Henry Yesler arrived and built a steam-powered sawmill, the settlement's first industrial enterprise. From surrounding hills logs skidded down greased runners to his mill, originating the term "skid road," later designating the rundown area of any city. Yesler's log cookhouse served as Seattle's first public meeting house and his business interests reached into other parts of the region. Meanwhile, David S. Maynard arrived to open the first hospital in the Northwest, start a fish-packing plant, and plat a portion of the bayside area. Often competing vigorously with each other, Arthur Denny, Yesler, and Maynard were the ambitious triumvirate of founders who dominated Seattle during its formative years.

Tideflats south and east surrounded a small point where Yesler's wharf extended into the bay. A growing business district stretched parallel to the shore. Logged-off spots were soon filled with yards and houses below forests that rimmed the eastern skyline.

Still farther north, Port Townsend was founded where the Strait of Juan de Fuca meets Puget Sound. High land, expansive views, and a deep harbor made this location attractive. All ships entering or leaving the Sound and its growing number of mills passed by. Therefore, in 1853 the customs house was relocated from Olympia to this strategically placed village and prosperity seemed assured. A mix of loggers, sailors, Indians, and gold seekers bound for the Fraser River strike in 1858 enlivened early Port Townsend. Like port towns the world over, it teemed with liquor, gambling, thievery, smuggling, prostitution, and violence.

Attracted to Oregon by green valleys and temperate climate, few settlers considered the arid lands of the Cascades. They were further inhibited by the Indian wars of the 1850s. Those who came sought valleys and river bottoms such as the Walla Walla Valley, which drew a few whites in the late 1850s. Farmers concerned with livestock and crops needed a town, and Walla Walla emerged near the old HBC fort. A gristmill was built and customary evidence of white civilization appeared. Walla Walla remained a major stopping point for travelers, especially after 1860 when Lt. John Mullan completed a military road between the mouth of the Snake River and Fort Benton on the Missouri. By 1860, over thirteen hundred whites were living in a valley which two years earlier had had practically no settlers. Idaho gold rushes and later railroad links with the Columbia River and Portland joined with agriculture to ensure the dominance of Walla Walla, long the largest city in Washington Territory.

Settlement was not limited to these nascent urban areas, and town building was the focus of the Washington frontier. Although many early villages failed, the process was repeated again and again across the territory. The legend of the solitary settler little fits the history of Washington; people who came west sought to reestablish conditions much like those they had left behind. An energetic or far-seeing settler claimed a site, platted a town, and attracted others to take up residence. A basic industry was established, amenities were added, and patterns of leadership emerged. Institutions that symbolized or assured permanence were sought. Most towns experienced one or several setbacks, becoming more stable in the process.

Effective settlement of the Pacific Northwest could not take place in a political vacuum. Lacking an adequate legal system, Willamette Valley settlers took matters into their own hands in the 1840s as the authority of the Hudson's Bay Company ebbed. When Ewing Young, a fur trader turned settler and grown wealthy in the cattle trade, died without heirs or a will, the disposition of his property became a matter of community concern. Neither laws nor courts were available to handle the problem, so resourceful neighbors met to devise a workable solution. They appointed an executor who followed New York statutes to dispose of Young's estate. This and other concerns highlighted the need for a working governmental apparatus.

Depredations by packs of wolves were one problem. Distraught farmers gathered at Champoeg on the Willamette to agree on united action. Their efforts to raise money for a bounty on wolves led to subsequent meetings and the formation of a provisional government for Oregon on July 5, 1843. Temporary governance had to suffice, for under the joint occupation agreement neither Great Britain nor the United States could extend formal administration over the Oregon Country. The 1844 Presidential election brought matters to a head. James K. Polk's victorious campaign resulted in the call of "Fifty-four forty or Fight!" demanding American control over all of Oregon from the forty-second parallel to Russian Alaska.

Slogans to the contrary, most observers anticipated a division of the region, but the actual line remained in contention. Although England preferred a Columbia River boundary, negotiations resulted in the extension of the forty-ninth parallel west from the Rockies to the main channel between Vancouver Island and the mainland. England thus retained that island, but the United States acquired Puget Sound and undisputed control of the Columbia's navigable portion. Failure to clearly define the main channel led to tension among American and British nationals residing in the San Juan Islands; the "Pig War" incident of 1859, when an HBC pig was killed after invading an American potato patch, sparked thirteen years of boundary dispute. The combative nations maintained an uneasy truce until at last arbitration by Germany settled the border dispute in the Americans' favor. Haro Strait became the dividing channel making the San Juan archipelago American.

Oregon Territory had been created in 1848 and a territorial government established with its seat at Oregon City. The governorship was offered to a former congressman from Illinois named Abraham Lincoln, but he declined, and the post went instead to a Democratic politician and Mexican War general, Joseph Lane. The region north of the Columbia was divided into two counties, Lewis and, in a misspelling later corrected, Clarke. Growing numbers of settlers gradually moved north beyond the river to take up residence.

In 1850 over a thousand settlers lived north of the Columbia, three times as many as in the previous year. Opportunity beckoned, but obstacles hindered rapid growth. An obvious problem was that Oregon Territory, some 285,000 square miles in extent, was unmanageable. While needs of the Willamete Valley received attention, northern concerns seemed to be ignored by distant and uncaring officials. Travel south for legislative sessions and other governmental business was arduous, especially after the capital was moved to Salem in 1851.

Little wonder that northerners sought redress. With Mike Simmons in the lead, disgruntled delegates met in November 1852 at Monticello near the mouth of the Cowlitz River, and formally petitioned Congress to create a new territory named Columbia. The petition was quickly approved, although the name was changed in a near-sighted attempt to avoid confusion with the District of Columbia. Thus Washington Territory came into being in March 1853, its southern boundary following the Columbia to the forty-sixth parallel and then east to the crest of the Rockies.

Under provisions similar to the Oregon Donation Land Law, a single person settling in Washington could acquire 320 acres of public land, or a married couple 640 acres, by living on it for four years. Thus settlers arriving soon after mid-century found a territory under clear U.S. control, with generous land laws to facilitate the acquisition of property.

President Franklin Pierce appointed Isaac Ingalls Stevens, a West Point graduate and politically well-connected engineer, as the first governor of the new territory. Stevens was also instructed while traveling west to survey a northern transcontinental railroad route and to conclude treaties with Northwestern Indians. Legend recounts that the disheveled Stevens, reaching Olympia a day earlier than anticipated, was unrecognized and therefore ignored by townspeople preparing for the formal reception of their governor. Shortly, Stevens would be well known and controversial.

Once the basics of government were in place, Stevens turned to the matter of extinguishing Indian title to the land encompassed within the territory. Guided by the examples of Oregon and the Missouri Valley, Stevens began a treaty-making tour of Western Washington. Accompanied by an entourage of interpreters and hangers-on, he set up camp at selected places where Indian bands were ordered to assemble. The resulting treaties—at Medicine Creek, Point Elliott, Point No Point, the Quinault River, and Neah Bay—were essentially the same in content and effect. In return for small reservations and specified government services, the Indians would cede their lands. Treaty in hand, Stevens explained the terms to his listeners, appointing "chiefs" to represent various tribal groups. The terms were translated into Chinook Jargon and then into the various Indian languages. The jargon, consisting of some three hundred and fifty Indian, French, and English words, had long been useful for trading purposes but was scarcely sufficient for complex diplomacy. If the means of communicating was unclear, however, the major point was obvious: Indians would forfeit their traditional lands and move to reservations selected by the U.S. government. Indian negotiators expressed their desire to retain customary fishing grounds and methods and this privilege, unimportant at the time to whites preoccupied with farm and timberlands, was granted. However reluctantly, the assembled chiefs (some of them Stevens's appointees) affixed their marks to prepared treaties. A few refused. Leschi, long a friend to white settlers, repudiated his mark on the Medicine Creek treaty and fled, to live as a fugitive suspected of inciting attacks against white settlers. Eventually he surrendered for trial and was hanged.

His goals in Western Washington achieved, Stevens proceeded east of the Cascades for similar treaty-making councils, first at Walla Walla and then in the farthest reaches of the territory. In less than a year Stevens persuaded or coerced over seventeen thousand Indians to give up sixty-four million acres of land and move onto reservations. Nevertheless, large areas of Eastern and southwestern Washington were never covered by treaties.

Meanwhile, Steven's earlier work was unravelling. The Puget Sound treaties had not been ratified by the United States Senate, but many settlers anxious to take land did so without awaiting the necessary ratification. Indians could not understand why settlers were allowed to trespass on tracts still formally theirs. After the discovery of gold in the Colville region of northeastern Washington, violent encounters occurred when prospectors crossed the promised Yakima reservation en route to the mining country. An agent sent to investigate was killed, and a full-scale war broke out in Eastern Washington in 1855.

Thus, Stevens's treaty-making brought not peace but wars. Periodic fighting erupted at various spots in Oregon and Washington. A two-pronged assault from The Dalles and from Western Washington was planned against the Yakimas. The Dalles contingent was routed with the embarrassing loss of five men and a prized howitzer. Forewarned, the Puget Sound force retreated to Seattle, finding that village terrorized by the recent killing of settlers on the White River.

Governor Stevens rushed home from eastern areas to deal with the crisis. Declaring martial law, he ordered the arrest of six French-Canadian settlers who chose to remain neutral. When Chief Justice Edward Lander of the territorial supreme court attempted to hold a civilian hearing for the defendants, the governor ordered his arrest; Lander countered by declaring Stevens in contempt of court. Lander eventually won on legal points, but Stevens ingratiated himself with settlers bent on fighting the Indians. Stevens also quarreled with General John Wool, commander of Regular Army forces on the Pacific Coast. From his San Francisco vantage point, Wool concluded that the hasty white settlers, aided by an impetuous governor and other officials, were more to blame than the truculent Indians for the conflict. The general and the governor barraged one another with insults and counter orders as the military emergency worsened.

Although Seattle was briefly attacked in early 1856, most of the fighting occurred east of the Cascades. Several expeditions were sent to control the region. In 1858 Colonel E. J. Steptoe suffered defeat in the upper Palouse country. Colonel George Wright then carried the main thrust, leading a punitive expedition of five hundred men. Near the Spokane River falls these well disciplined troops, armed with long range rifles, easily defeated the Indians; moving east, they cut a swath of destruction through Indian lands. More troubles lay ahead, but Wright's campaigns marked the end of real warfare in the territory. Eastern Washington was declared safe for settlement. Meanwhile, Steven's long-delayed treaties won U.S. Senate approval. By the end of the 1850s, the earliest phase of American settlement had ended.

~ 3 ~

The Timber
Commonwealth

Eleven stern Midwesterners sat at a polished table in the Tacoma Hotel on a midwinter day in 1900. Below their comfortable vantage point, bustling activity on Commencement Bay testified that prosperity had returned after the long economic despair of the 1890s. Steamships loaded grain brought from east of the Cascades to the Pacific terminus of the Northern Pacific Railway. Sawmills on the sweeping mudflats at the mouth of the Puyallup River turned out lumber for export on schooners or eastbound railroads. Dredging machines excavated tidal muck from the first of the bayfront's deepdraft waterways. Above, in the placid isolation of their conference room, the visitors from the Great Lakes finalized a stupendous economic undertaking.

Although all of the businessmen gathered about the table were wealthy and powerful, attention centered on the spare and white-bearded Frederick Weyerhaeuser. Born in Germany in 1834, he had immigrated to America as a teenager ambitious to become a brewmaster. Instead, Weyerhaeuser ventured into lumbering, first as a salesman and then as sawmill proprietor, on the Mississippi River. After the Civil War, he assembled a syndicate of companies reaching across a half-dozen Great Lakes states and emerged as the most famous timberman in America, "richer than John D. Rockefeller," according to one muckraking journalist.

Yet Weyerhaeuser was an unassuming man who was often mistaken by tourists for the gardener as he puttered about the grounds of his California winter estate. Self-effacement was crucial to his knack of welding together disparate interests and conflicting egos in the pursuit of mutual profit. The coalition process perfected on the Great Lakes was transferred to the Pacific Northwest. With Weyerhaeuser himself supplying a third of the capital, one of the greatest real-estate transactions in American history was formalized: the acquisition of nine hundred thousand acres of Northern Pacific timberland for $5.4 million. To manage this property, syndicate members created the Weyerhaeuser Timber Company. At the stroke of several pens, Washington's forest economy was instantly transformed. The Tacoma proceedings, moreover, symbolized the state's advance from the era of pioneer lumbering to the status of the nation's leading producer of lumber.

What cod was to New England and gold to California, timber was to the land west of the Cascades: the fundamental resource upon which settlement and fortune building rested. Marine air currents deposited heavy rainfall upon inviting soil to produce an awesome forest extending from beachfront to mountainside. Mighty Douglas fir—80 percent of the nation's supply of this species was found in Western Washington and Oregon—joined with hemlock, spruce, and cedar to make up the forest cover, the exact composition of a given stand dependent upon factors ranging from degree of shade to Indian burning practices. There were enough trees, said early lumbermen, to build a city forty miles long and twelve miles wide or to line a street from the Pacific to the Atlantic coast with wooden buildings. The land around Puget Sound and along the ocean shore was clearly, in the words of one observer, "the lumber-man's paradise."

In early 1848, James Marshall's discovery of gold in the California Sierra determined the future course of Washington history. News of the discovery precipitated the most famous stampede after wealth ever experienced in the United States. San Francisco, made over from nondescript Yerba Buena, became the prototype of all subsequent boomtowns, while Sacramento and other interior communities were hurriedly thrown together to house invading prospectors. Lumber was essential to build wharves, warehouses, hotels, saloons and brothels, but local supplies were miniscule. For Puget Sound residents, the opportunity was as great as it was unexpected: their land was covered with trees, anchorages were numerous and secure, and sailing time to San Francisco was a matter of days.

Men of experience and wealth took note of Puget Sound. Andrew J. Pope, William C. Talbot, Asa Mead Simpson, and William Renton,

Yankee seafaring merchants all, arrived in San Francisco in 1849 to establish lumberyards and sell building materials imported from New England. Although lumber brought enormous profits, a more convenient source of supply could ensure even greater returns. The problem was that all harbors north of the California metropolis were blocked by treacherous bars, making exploitation of their forested hinterlands risky. The storied mouth of the Columbia, for instance, was so hazardous that passengers and crews alike often fortified themselves with prayer or drink before crossing the bar. And Shoalwater Bay—modern Willapa Bay—and Grays Harbor were at low tide virtual mudflats.

In happy contrast, Puget Sound offered every possible attraction. So far on the map but so near by trim sailing vessel, it was the ideal site for creation of a great industry. But implementation required careful planning. The men of San Francisco envisioned large, efficient steam-powered plants to rival the leading lumber manufactories of the world. There were dozens of superficially attractive millsites, but the Californians sought locations near high-quality timber, with few homesteaders or government officials to hinder exploitation. Shipping facilities had to be arranged to allow prompt export of lumber. Thus, several years passed between the discovery of California gold and the realization of that event's great meaning for Washington: the making of Puget Sound into an economic dependency of San Francisco.

Several important California-owned sawmills were built on the Sound in 1853. William Sayward erected the first mill at Port Ludlow, Captain William Renton began the operation that would become the Port Blakely Mill Company, and George Meigs founded the Port Madison Mill Company. These firms paled into insignificance when compared to a final Puget Sound entrant. On a visit to Maine in December 1852, Andrew J. Pope and William C. Talbot contracted with New England associates to organize the Puget Mill Company "for the purpose of manufacturing lumber . . . at Puget Sound." The following summer, Talbot selected a millsite at Port Gamble on the northeastern shore of Hood Canal, a place also known by the Indian name of Teekalet. Josiah Keller, one of the eastern partners, arrived in September via Cape Horn with boilers and other equipment for the plant he had agreed to superintend.

Shortly thereafter, Port Gamble saws began turning out lumber. In the first full year of operation, four million feet were produced and

Puget Mill established itself as the leading concern in the region. "I think we do about as much business as all the rest of the Sound," an exultant Andrew Pope soon boasted. A second mill was added at Gamble and the older Sayward plant at Port Ludlow was acquired and expanded. Until the arrival of Weyerhaeuser in 1900, the firm remained Washington's most important enterprise.

The Puget Mill Company and its competitors were organized in similar fashion. A parent company operated out of San Francisco, where senior partners handled sales and scheduled shipping. The milling subsidiary on the Sound was managed by a colleague who either had junior status in the overall operation or who preferred manufacturing to distant administration. Disputes among partners were constant, except at Puget Mill. In 1862, Pope and Talbot bought out their original associates. Because both men preferred the civilized comforts of San Francisco to the drizzly rudeness of Puget Sound, they admitted Cyrus Walker, a long-time employee, to partnership as mill manager. Walker, a severe Yankee who sneered at such fanciful notions as debt and labor unions, was for four decades thereafter the leading lumberman on the Sound. The close bonds between Pope, Talbot, and Walker, and then between their heirs, gave the concern an additional competitive advantage.

Visitors who approached the mill ports by steamboat—virtually the only means of travel on the Sound—were struck by evidence of the industry's New England heritage. Store, manager's house, cottages, and company hotel were arranged above the wharfside sawmill. The more civilized towns also contained a school, a church, and a saloon, the latter offering an essential diversion for workers after many days in the forest. Customarily, buildings were of white-painted clapboard and surrounded by picket fences, suggesting a deliberate effort to recreate Maine three thousand miles from home.

At the wharf, vessels tied up stern-to for loading by crews of Indian stevedores. Lumber was placed on board green and wet, literally straight from the saws; because freight charges were assessed according to board feet there was no need to dry the lumber to reduce weight. In any event, lack of storage space made drying impossible and pointed to the necessity of always having ships at hand. Holds were filled through special port openings and much lumber was stowed on deck. This made vessels unwieldy, and cargo was frequently jettisoned during storms at sea, to the benefit of beachcombers from the Strait of Juan de Fuca to San Francisco.

But irony is a constant traveler on the pathway of history, and the industry founded to supply California almost immediately found that market unpredictable. Busts in the southern state were more numerous and often more dramatic than booms. Demand for lumber was easily and frequently exceeded by supply. Millmen made assorted and occasionally ingenious efforts to control prices in San Francisco. The energy devoted to making such agreements, however, was soon exceeded by efforts to violate them.

Early on, coastwise business had to be supplemented by foreign trade. Resurrecting the old Hudson's Bay Company connection, Washington mills established a significant commercial relationship with Hawaii. The growth of Honolulu and the rapid expansion of sugar plantations made lumber the leading import of the kingdom, thus helping bind the islands to the mainland. Other overseas markets at various times included the west coast of South America, Australia, and China.

By the end of the 1850s, enduring trade patterns were established. Most Washington lumber was sold in California and the territory's prosperity depended largely upon the uncertain rise and fall of that state's economy. Connected by the lumber trade with other farflung Pacific ports, Puget Sound was a vital part of the Pacific Rim economy, its well-being dependent more upon San Francisco, Honolulu, Callao, Sydney and Melbourne than upon eastern American cities.

Roughly eight of every ten dollars invested in manufacturing in Washington Territory between 1860 and 1880 went to lumbering. Unfortunately, stagnation plagued the industry throughout the period. Deflated markets in California and delays in building a transcontinental railroad prevented the opening of an alternative domestic trade with eastern states. Consequently, overall mill production increased only slightly. By 1880, Washington's lumber output ranked only thirty-first among the nation's states and territories. In the quarter century after 1857, only one significant new firm, the Tacoma Mill Company, was founded. A massive transformation, however, would recast the industrial scene of Western Washington.

Opening its direct line across the Cascades to Tacoma in 1883, the Northern Pacific Railway revolutionized Washington history. In apparently endless succession, trains deposited settlers and developers on the inviting shoreline of a new dominion. Seattle, recently dismissed by perceptive visitors as "a veritable mudhole," and Tacoma, previously unworthy of inclusion in federal census figures, became bustling urban centers. The territory's population increased by nearly 400 percent during the 1880s and statehood was attained. The lumber industry both reflected and contributed to the new prosperity: output increased eightfold during the decade and at its birth the state bounded to fifth place among producers of forest products.

The transcontinental railroad was completed just as major changes occurred in the national timber industry. For decades, that industry had centered on the Great Lakes, with Michigan, Wisconsin, and Minnesota producing a third of America's lumber. By the 1880s, however, sustained over-cutting had depleted those forests, forcing the region's timbermen to look elsewhere. Traveling west in convenience and style on the Northern Pacific, investors discovered Washington's attractiveness. There, the average acre of timber contained five times as much wood as the Great Lakes region. Happily, the prevailing price of timber was less than a third of the figure required for acquistions at home.

That timber had to be purchased was telling evidence of changing times in Western Washington. In the first years of the industry, San Francisco—owned milling companies made no acquisitions. There were obvious reasons: legal purchases were under most circumstances impossible and were in any event unnecessary. Federal land policy stressed agricultural settlement and no law expressly provided for sale of public timberland until 1878. Lumbermen filed claims on their mill ports under the Oregon Donation Act, which was intended to encourage farming, or other preemption legislation. Josiah Keller, for one, happily referred to his Port Gamble sawmill complex as "our farm."

Such laws left timber, that wealth-producing resource, virtually free for the taking. A federal investigation concluded that by the late 1870s, $40 million worth of timber had been "stolen" from the public domain on Puget Sound. Efforts to curb thievery were sporadic and easily corrupted. In 1861, for instance, the energetic new U.S. attorney, John McGilvra, secured the indictment of several prominent mill operators for timber theft. McGilvra soon concluded that such prosecutions could harm both the territorial economy and his own career. The letter of the law was honored by sentencing the indicted timbermen to a few hours of convivial partying in the Port Townsend jailhouse. The larger issue was resolved by instituting an honor code under which mills paid nominal fees to the government based upon their own estimates of timber removed from federal land.

The first successful effort against thievery was made not by a public authority, but by the Northern Pacific Railway. Under the beneficient terms of its federal land grant, the railroad eventually acquired over seven million acres in Washington Territory. Northern Pacific management, astutely recognizing that railroading at its finest was a means to profit in other areas, worried that resale value of this acreage was threatened by timber theft. In 1871, they instructed their Puget Sound attorney, Hazard Stevens, the son of territorial governor Isaac Stevens, to put an immediate end to the practice. Displaying an energy reminiscent of his father's, Stevens secured an appointment as deputy U.S. marshal and rapidly traveled the inland waters confiscating suspect rafts of logs. When these rafts were sold at government auction, Stevens appeared in the guise of private citizen to bid up prices before dropping out to allow sale to outraged timbermen. Fear of retaliatory violence prompted the Northern Pacific to adopt a more orderly approach, under which the railroad charged fees for timber on land within its grant. Although Stevens was dismissed in 1873 for allegedly skimming earnings under this scheme, his campaign did end the free and easy use of Washington's forest.

Not long thereafter, a means of legally acquiring tracts of public timber at last became available. Reformers reasoned that carefully worded legalization would end thievery, and they therefore endorsed the Timber and Stone Act of 1878, which authorized sale to residents of Washington, Oregon, California, and Nevada of up to 160 acres of timber or mineral land at $2.50 per acre. Few observers noted that spokesmen for industry from those states were the principal congressional sponsors of the legislation. Reform advocates appeared to be even more naive than speculators were greedy.

Meant to eliminate corruption, the Timber and Stone Act instead allowed the mill companies to acquire sizeable holdings. The 160-acre limitation was easily circumvented by using dummy entrymen. Once these original entrants received patents—companies paid them from $50 to $125 for their brief service—title was transferred to the mill firms, often through third parties. Despite some efforts at concealment, the process was conducted so openly that it was anything but secretive; newspapers even reported regular departures of organized groups of entrymen for the Olympia land office.

Two hundred thousand acres of Washington timberland passed into private hands by this process in 1882 and 1883 alone. Fraud was so widespread that on two occasions the government temporarily halted entries pending investigation. But, in their own words, mill owners "fixed" or "entertained" federal agents assigned to the investigations. By 1890, however, the importance of the legislation was waning. Creation of the nation's first forest reserves—predecessors of the National Forest system—protected vast tracts from entry and shifted the emphasis to privately owned land. Because the value of private holdings was rising due to investment from the Great Lakes, old-line milling companies could not afford to acquire such timber.

True to their Yankee heritage, San Francisco–based lumbermen avoided publicity, making it difficult to determine the exact acreage owned by lumber firms. The Puget Mill Company owned 186,000 acres by the early 1890s, slightly under half of that acquired through the Timber and Stone Act. The Port Blakely and Tacoma mill companies, both heavy users of the legislation, held around 30,000 acres apiece, the Port Madison mill claimed 55,000 acres, and the Washington Mill Company 15,000.

These long-lived firms from the founding era of Washington's lumber industry were subjected, from the late 1880s onward, to ever-mounting rivalry from the Great Lakes. Tacoma, where the Northern Pacific planned to sell industrial sites and nearby timber, became the center of the reorganized industry. In June 1888, Chauncey Griggs, a wealthy Minnesota grocer, and several associates acquired 80,000 acres from the railroad and organized the St. Paul and Tacoma Lumber Company. Their mill on the Commencement Bay tideflats was the most modern on the Sound and the first to deliver its logs entirely by rail.

Seattle also felt the impact of railroading, after James J. Hill's Great Northern Railway built into the city in early 1893. The community's sawmills, while numerous, were small. Only the Stimson Mill Company, organized by a Michigan family, ranked among the state's important firms. Instead, the focus was upon shingle manufacturing, concentrated in Ballard, north of the Seattle city limits. Cedar shingles were shipped east by rail as far as the Mississippi River and beyond. In the early 1890s, a third of the nation's shingles came from Washington, and Ballard ranked as the largest producer in the world.

Lumbering was also a key factor in the creation of new urban areas. Most dramatically, in 1890 Henry Hewitt, Jr., a partner in the St. Paul & Tacoma Lumber Company, organized a syndicate to found Everett at the mouth of the Snohomish River. The investors were buffeted in quick succession by James J. Hill's refusal to make the community his Puget Sound terminus and and by the Panic of 1893. By decade's end, however, Everett was firmly established as a center of lumber and shingle manufacturing. In these same years, the timber ventures of J. J. Donovan, J. H. Bloedel, and other Midwesterners produced economic and population growth to the north on Bellingham Bay.

Meanwhile, the timber commonwealth also expanded to embrace Grays Harbor, a backwater previously ignored by settlers and speculators alike. The original impetus came from an old direction. In 1882, Captain Asa Mead Simpson, a San Francisco merchant of 1849 who had invested in sawmills along the California and Oregon coastline, dispatched George Emerson to the Harbor. The attraction was twofold: cheap timber and government plans for the excavation of a navigation channel across the bar and through the interior tideflats. Emerson, a nervous sort who chafed for years under the dictation of the elderly and eccentric Simpson, established the North Western Lumber Company at Hoquiam and became the progenitor of modern Grays Harbor. Competitors from the Great Lakes soon built sawmills as well and by 1890 Hoquiam, Aberdeen, and Cosmopolis were all important participants in the trade. Cargoes could be safely exported to California, and the arrival of the Northern Pacific in the mid-1890s opened up eastern rail markets. Grays Harbor, proudly boosted as the "Duluth of the Pacific," was a firm industrial rival of Puget Sound.

Thus, two distinct lumber industries operated in the early period of statehood. The older centered upon the isolated mill ports of Gamble, Ludlow, Madison, and Blakely and relied upon waterborne trade with California and Pacific ports; the newer, centered at Tacoma and Grays Harbor, also shipped east by railroad. When ocean-going trade was bad, as it often was, rail business provided an alternative route to profit. Thus, the new lumbermen enjoyed a competitive advantage of enormous importance. The economic future lay with them, not with their competitors from the era of San Francisco domination.

Change was also evident in other aspects of lumbering. For decades, straining teams of oxen dragged logs out of the forest over greased skid roads. Ox-hauling, however, was inefficient at distances of more than a mile from tidewater, a factor of mounting concern as depleted timber forced loggers inland. In 1881, the invention of the steam-powered donkey engine by John Dolbeer of California resolved an impending crisis. Cables driven by the engine moved logs farther, faster, and more cheaply. Stock and feed no longer had to be purchased and employers did not need to contend with the demands of teamsters. Washington became a center of the new technology; by 1900 the state had three times as many steam donkeys as Oregon and California combined.

Development of logging railroads also reflected the arrival of the machine in the forest. Neither ox nor donkey engine could haul logs over excessive distances to landings where rafts were assembled for towing to the mills. In 1881, a short line near Olympia opened the rail age in the woods. Traditionally, mill firms had contracted out their logging to independent operators, but the heavy capital required for railroading forced millmen to handle logging directly. The Puget and Port Blakely mills commenced extensive railroad projects in the Olympic foothills in 1885. Several years later, Blakely interests formed the Simpson Logging Company, the largest logging concern in the state. Manufacturers involved in railroad ventures secured logs at reduced cost and thus attained a significant competitive advantage over rivals.

Traditional relationships between management and labor also changed. The lumber industry was an obvious and fertile ground for union organizers who wanted to bind workers together in pursuit of common interest. True, food in mills and camps was usually good—employers learned early that entire crews would desert if the grub was inferior—and wages were high in comparison with the national standards. In 1890, Washington sawmill workers earned an average of $56.44 a month, compared with $35.83 on the Great Lakes; nine of every ten logging workers earned more than $40 a month. Still, workers in the woods labored for weeks at a time without civilized comforts, while life in mill towns was drab. Around highspeed saws and power-driven cables, accidents were frequent and gruesome. All too frequently, producers shut down to reduce supply and increase prices, giving no thought to how laid-off workers would survive; at the time, only eccentric visionaries advocated unemployment insurance or old-age pensions. This was a young man's industry, and those who persisted in it rapidly became old and haggard and maimed.

Unionization in the Northwest forest began with the Knights of Labor. Founded nationally in 1869 with the near-utopian goal of uniting all gainfully employed persons, the Knights claimed two thousand members in Western Washington by the early 1880s. The organization's regional campaign focused on expelling Chinese workers, whose willingness to accept low wages supposedly deprived whites of employment. This was a concern primarily in urban areas along the eastern shore of the Sound, but it also affected lumbering ports where Chinese performed menial tasks. Although the racial agitation came to a head in urban centers in 1885 and 1886 and isolated mill towns were spared, lumbermen took note of the portents. "Their next attack," a worried Cyrus Walker wrote of the Knights, "will be on the corporations and capital."

Walker's fears were realized in mid-1886 when the Knights of Labor launched a campaign to reduce the lumber industry workday from twelve to ten hours. Strikers forced closure of the Tacoma Mill Company and only timely intervention by the territorial militia prevented a similar occurrence at Port Blakely. Operations in general were so disrupted, however, that management acceded to the new standard. Cyrus Walker voluntarily introduced a ten-hour workday at Gamble and Ludlow in order to avoid any appearance of giving in to employee demands.

The ten-hour day was the main and surely not insignificant legacy of the Knights of Labor, which soon collapsed. The violence of the anti-Chinese movement alienated respectable opinion, which preferred more subtle forms of bigotry, while private detectives employed by mill owners sowed confusion between union leaders and the rank and file. Still, the initial success of the organization demonstrated that fundamental change had come. To hardbitten lumbermen, prideful products of a self-reliant age, men were men and union members were something less. "There is a strong inclination among all the employees," lamented Cyrus Walker, hardest of the hardbitten, "to become high toned as to how they shall live, the time they shall work, the amount of work they do & the pay they receive, which makes things run harder than in times past."

All of these momentous changes—the arrival of Great Lakes lumbermen, technological advance, and worker militance—began in the early 1880s and culminated in the first years of the twentieth century. The pace of change, though, was temporarily slowed by the national depression following the Panic of 1893, the most severe economic crisis yet in American history. On the Pacific coast, the collapse began with financial hysteria in San Francisco and rapidly spread north to Puget Sound. The few banks that survived the initial blow refused thereafter, according to reliable account, to loan one thousand dollars on fifty times that amount of collateral. Shingles, it was reported, were accepted by merchants in lieu of cash and gladly received in church collection boxes.

Several developments testified to the scope of the disaster experienced by lumbermen. The newly opened rail trade with the East collapsed; shipments from Washington declined by over a third even though railroads cut shipping rates. Three of every four shingle plants doing business in 1893 were closed two years later. The California and foreign markets became dumping grounds for lumber that could not be sold elsewhere and prices dropped to record lows. Investment from the Great Lakes ended as timbermen hoarded their dollars for the uncertain day when prosperity would return.

If that were not enough, workers, who had in past crises shouldered layoffs and wage reductions, declined to accept peacefully such conventional antidotes to economic depression. A shingle weavers' strike convulsed Ballard in 1893 and the next year workers on Grays Harbor organized to protest pay cuts. Nationally, the employers' fear of impending revolution was increased in 1894 by the Pullman strike, which halted rail shipments of lumber, and by the march of Jacob Coxey's motley army of the unemployed upon the nation's capital. A Northwest version of that effort roused fears in Puyallup and several other communities. Attending that year's Fourth of July celebration in Hoquiam, a distraught George Emerson suggested that "memorial services are more in order."

Mill owners finally threw off their funereal gloom when prosperity suddenly returned in 1897. William McKinley's presidential triumph the previous fall over William Jennings Bryan, whose advocacy of inflationary silver coinage was regarded by conservatives as dangerous to the American way of life, restored business confidence. Rail shipment of lumber to the East picked up dramatically in the first year of McKinley's governance. The discovery of gold in the Yukon, meanwhile, opened an important new market for Washington lumbermen. The war with Spain in 1898 and the acquisition of Hawaii and the Philippines stimulated Pacific trade. Finally, in the surest sign that times were good and bound to get better, Great Lakes investors dramatically resumed their westward migration.

Frederick Weyerhaeuser first considered moving to the Pacific Northwest in the mid-1880s. The German-born lumber magnate, however, was not a reckless plunger. In 1887, he and his associates allowed an option on Northern Pacific timber and mill sites to lapse. Nothing further was done prior to the Panic of 1893, an event that sapped the confidence of even the wealthiest. Weyerhaeuser made millions by paying attention to his pennies. He sat up nights on trains rather than pay for sleeping compartments and when a forest fire devastated one of his Great Lakes mills he seriously contemplated closing up his St. Paul mansion and moving to a rooming house to cut costs. There could be no investment in Washington until the depression had run its course.

McKinley, gold and America's new imperial stature appeared to signal the end of the bad years. In 1898, Weyerhaeuser began to actively investigate opportunities west of the Cascades. Newspapers and trade journals, chronically misspelling his name, avidly followed the comings and goings of the famous lumberman. Mill operators as important as Cyrus Walker and George Emerson, rigid men unable to cope with modern times, hoped to sell their properties. But Frederick Weyerhaeuser was interested in timber rather than in sawmills and no existing firm owned enough land to satisfy his ambitions.

Decades of mismanagement leavened with peculation left the Northern Pacific forever on the brink of bankruptcy. The railroad was often forced to sell assets for vital infusions of cash. Weyerhaeuser's desire for timber and the Northern Pacific's need for capital combined in late 1899 to produce serious negotiations. On behalf of his syndicate, Weyerhaeuser offered to purchase a million acres at five dollars an acre. The railroad demanded six dollars. A compromise soon allowed the Northern Pacific its price, but with acreage reduced to a not insubstantial 900,000. Three million dollars was transferred on January 3, 1900 as a down payment and the Weyerhaeuser Timber Company commenced business life as far and away the leading force in the Pacific Northwest woods.

Frederick Weyerhaeuser was not the sole owner of the firm carrying his name, but the largest stockholder with slightly under a third of the stock; the remainder was spread among longtime associates. Moreover, although Weyerhaeuser was a major figure in the history of Washington, he never resided in the state and rarely visited. Actual management of the company was handled by George S. Long, a veteran sales executive of the syndicate's Midwestern operations. Tall and skinny with receding chin and prominent Adam's apple, Long did not look like a lumber baron. Yet for three decades his employers gave him virtually free rein to run the firm. His ability and personal integrity, backed by Weyerhaeuser's fiscal might, made him the great historical figure of Pacific Northwest lumbering.

As the name Weyerhaeuser Timber Company suggested, the firm was in the land business rather than the lumber trade. Because the railroad's land grant consisted of odd-numbered sections, George Long's initial task was to fill in the checkerboard of the Northern Pacific purchase. By mid-1903, Weyerhaeuser holdings had increased to 1.3 million acres in Western Washington, making possible efficient administration of the entire tract. In contrast to its energetic land purchases, the company made only one tentative step toward manufacturing lumber when it acquired a small Everett sawmill. Not until after World War I did Weyerhaeuser become a major lumbering enterprise. Timberland was an investment for distant, rather than immediate, return. "This is not for us, nor for our children," Frederick Weyerhaeuser had asserted in 1900, "but for our grandchildren."

Weyerhaeuser's founding culminated the decade-and-a-half-long transformation of Washington lumbering from a San Francisco orientation to a focus on the Great Lakes. Two of the principal California-owned concerns, the Port Blakely Mill Company and the North Western Lumber Company, were sold to Midwest investors by 1903. These transactions, along with bankruptcies, meant that only the Puget Mill Company survived from the territorial era. And Puget Mill, increasingly vexed by its lack of rail connections, was a pale imitation of its once-vigorous self. Symbolically, Cyrus Walker, that embodiment of olden times, was forced into retirement in 1906 by physical decrepitude and senility.

A sophisticated response to issues confronting lumbermen characterized the new Great Lakes industry. Traditionally, relations with government had relied on what George Emerson called "metallic argument." With progressive reforms, however, lumbermen, who were handy targets for criticism, paid increasing attention to public opinion. After primary elections replaced the corrupted convention method of selecting candidates, politicians had to be elected instead of purchased.

In the past, few timbermen had heard of conservation and few of those who had could conceive that the vast Western Washington forest would ever be exhausted. As long as timber could be stolen, through one pretext or another, there was no need to conserve for tomorrow what was not needed today. If timber was free, or at least cheap, why spend money upon its preservation? Labor issues were more pressing, in any case. By 1900, employers had coped for two decades with worker militance in camps and mills. Assorted local unions formed

Inauguration of Elisha P. Ferry, first governor of the one-week-old State of Washington, Olympia, November 18, 1889 (Washington State Capital Museum)

Major General Isaac I. Stevens, first territorial governor of Washington (Special Collections Division, University of Washington Libraries, neg. no. 3436)

Facing page: top, *John C. McLoughlin, chief factor of the Hudson's Bay Company and its most prominent representative in the Pacific Northwest (Oregon Historical Society, neg. no. Or Hi 49848)*; bottom, *Meriwether Lewis and William Clark (Special Collections Division, University of Washington Libraries)*

Indians on the Colville Reservation (photo by L. D. Lindsley, Special Collections Division, University of Washington Libraries)

An Indian family at their home on the Puyallup Reservation (Washington State Historical Society)

Pioneer outfitters in Seattle, a booming business in the gold-rush era (Special Collections Division, University of Washington Libraries)

Lumbermen of the Pacific Northwest (photo by Cress, Special Collections Division, University of Washington Libraries, neg. no. 390)

WASHINGTON

Chicago, Milwaukee & St. Paul Railway.

Early railroad brochure promoting tourism in Washington (Special Collections Division, University of Washington Libraries, neg. no. 436)

during the depression of the 1890s were easily squelched. But the labor problem—or menace, as management preferred to call it—remained and a response more effective than disdain and force was clearly needed.

An indication that shrewd lumbermen could come to grips with modern times was first evident in the area of conservation. Nineteenth-century logging was notoriously wasteful, especially after the advent of the steam donkey, which was useful only on cleared terrain. Only high-quality timber bringing a premium price was removed and the remainder was strewn across the forest floor to decay. Industrial leaders knew that this was inefficient, and even hidebound Cyrus Walker worried about "the way logs are being slaughtered." But trees were relatively inexpensive and there was no demand for inferior grades or species, so economic incentive for better woods habits was lacking.

Destruction by fire also wasted the region's great natural resource. Debris left from logging was ready kindling in periods of high temperature and wind, while farmers added to the problem by carelessly burning fields. Early settlers even set woods ablaze as a spectacular celebration of holidays. By 1905, more timber west of the Cascades had actually been destroyed by fire than had been removed by logging. Each summer, navigation on Puget Sound was impaired by drifting clouds of smoke. The fortifications at the entrance to the Sound would be useless if enemy ships could slip past unnoticed, concealed in smoke.

The problem was evident, but its solution awaited a time when timber was scarce and expensive. That time arrived by the end of the 1890s. Creation of national forest reserves—7.4 million acres were encompassed within such tracts in Washington by 1905—greatly reduced availability of timber from the public domain. Extensive purchases by Weyerhaeuser and other Great Lakes investors further reduced supply and drove up values. Millions of dollars were invested in timberland and there was now incentive to protect the forest. Every tree that was destroyed represented loss of return on investment.

If the need was clear, the remedy foundered on two obstacles: fire and taxation. The ever-present possibility that conflagration would destroy one's timber, and thus one's investment, encouraged rapid cutting regardless of market conditions. Holding timber for long-term profit meant exposure to more than just loss by fire. Every year that a tract was withheld from logging meant an additional year's payment of property taxes. Lumbermen, skilled at cultivating the sympathies of county assessors, still bore an enormous burden. Combined in frightful partnership, nature and public policy stifled conservation.

Resolution of this destructive dilemma was regarded by Gifford Pinchot, chief of the U.S. Forest Service in the first years of the twentieth century, as his principal task. With President Theodore Roosevelt, his good friend and political mentor, Pinchot argued that overcutting had produced an actual timber famine. There was nothing difficult about determining the correct strategy to stave off this calamity. The "underlying principle of conservation," Roosevelt and Pinchot believed, was simply "the application of common sense to common problems for the common good." Effective and practical policies must merge private and public interest.

Forestry as originally advocated by Pinchot amounted to two basic things. Federal, state, and local governments, in cooperation with private landholders, must reduce destruction by forest fires. And the tax burden must somehow be lessened to enable timber owners to retain their properties until the dictates of efficient management called for logging. These precepts dovetailed nicely with the needs of industry and Washington lumbermen became enthusiastic supporters of the Forest Service chief. "I am a Pinchot man in every respect pertaining to forestry matters," wrote Weyerhaeuser's George Long.

In September 1902, a major natural disaster provided the opportunity to introduce practical forestry measures. The fateful triad of dry weather, soaring temperatures, and high winds blew several smoldering fires into a week-long conflagration in southwestern Washington. The main blaze, the Yacolt Burn, spread destruction over twenty-five thousand acres between Mount St. Helens and the Columbia River. Three dozen people were killed as the storm of flame swept through the Lewis River Valley. Newspapers graphically described the charred remains of entire families huddled together and watercourses choked by heaps of dead animals. Public interest generated a chance for lumbermen to win acceptance of Pinchot's concepts.

The press reported damages of $13 million, but this figure was misleading. Much of the Yacolt Burn area was owned by Weyerhaeuser and other large holders capable of withstanding the loss. And most of the timber in that region had been killed, not destroyed. Fallen timber could still be salvaged within a period of seven or eight years; after that, damage from insects would be extensive. Weyerhaeuser even realized a slight profit logging the Yacolt Burn, although less than if the forest had not been damaged. Little notice was taken of this significant fact as lumbermen took advantage of the fire and loss of life in order to pursue their own ends.

An industry committee chaired by George Long proposed to the 1903 legislature a statewide fire warden organization, forest patrols, and a burning permit system. Two years later, a state forest commission was established. Supplementing this, lumbermen in 1908 created the Washington Forest Fire Association. In 1909, the Western Forestry and Conservation Association was established to publicize the cause and to campaign for property tax relief on a regional basis. Timber owners also supported establishment of the University of Washington forestry school, launched in 1907.

These advances showed that lumbermen could be reformers when reform was in their economic interest. Harmonious relations within the forestry movement, however, soon came to an end. In 1910 Gifford Pinchot provoked a public quarrel with Interior Secretary Richard Ballinger, a former Seattle mayor, and was fired by President William Howard Taft. Following the old adage that politicians out of office are more radical than when in office, Pinchot abandoned his previous cautious views to favor mandatory planned forestry, whether or not economical. Lumbermen recoiled with horror at the prospect of federal regulation, and the Pinchot men of yesteryear became steadfast Pinchot haters.

In the first years of the century, the response to labor also demonstrated that reform and business were not necessarily antithetical. The conditions that had given rise to unionization in the 1880s persisted into the early twentieth century, and there arose a threat to employers more serious than that posed by the Knights of Labor. In 1905, alienated unionists and socialist intellectuals created the Industrial Workers of the World, with the loudly proclaimed aim not merely of winning better pay and shorter hours, but of overthrowing the capitalist system and erecting a new social fabric "within the shell of the old." For two decades, the appeal of this message in the Northwest forests horrified employers.

The IWW first appeared in the region in March 1907, when Wobblies closed Portland sawmills for three weeks in a strike to demand a nine-hour workday. Concerned Washington mill owners, fearing what they regarded as an infectious disease, employed undercover detectives to infiltrate the IWW. The Grays Harbor Commercial Company became widely known as the "Western Penitentiary" for its use of armed sentries and guard dogs to intimidate employees. Several companies employed Asians, in the hope of dividing crews along racial lines. The Bloedel-Donovan mill at Bellingham, one of the largest in the state, engaged immigrants from India, a tactic that backfired when outraged whites drove the foreigners from the city. These were old-fashioned measures, but the newfangled approach of actually remedying abuses proved more valuable in countering discontent.

Employer and employee found they shared views on the issue of accidents. Death and crippling injury were ever-present fears of workers. But management also felt victimized; in its view, accidents resulted from employee carelessness and indifference to safety measures, yet the company suffered because morale suffered and production inevitably fell off after a grizzly death or maiming. Washington's courts, moreover, seemed overly sympathetic to the plight of the injured and the survivors of the deceased. "Hardly a day passes," insisted an industry publication, "that a mill man is not mulcted [out of] a sum in many cases ridiculously high, and on evidence that would not be accepted in the ordinary civil or criminal action." Management's suggested approach would reduce employer costs, while at the same time providing money directly to the affected parties, not their attorneys.

Because the second part of this proposition was agreeable to mainstream labor leaders—as distinct from the IWW—basic reform was possible. In 1911, a committee of businessmen and American Federation of Labor representatives drafted a plan under which employers would fund a state compensation program. That year's legislature approved one of the first workmen's compensation systems in the nation, a triumph for progressivism in Washington. The benefit was also obvious in what the Puget Mill's Edwin G. Ames termed "a great saving to the manufacturers" through elmination of damage suits. The Wobblies were not destroyed by this reform—no palliative would accomplish that—but an effective counterpoint to the radical threat was in place.

Forestry and labor reforms were telling manifestations of the transformation of Washington's lumber industry. By 1905, the state was the nation's number one lumber producer, a position it retained until the late 1930s. Industrial enterprise west of the Cascades, however, remained fundamentally unstable because more lumber was manufactured than could be profitably sold, except for rare periods when there was high demand in all markets. This basic truth was again demonstrated in 1907 when a short but destructive depression struck the United States. Eastern shipments were especially affected as the railroads chose this inopportune moment to increase freight rates, sharply reducing the territory in which the Pacific Northwest could compete with other regions. Although most sectors of the economy soon rebounded, lumbering remained depressed until World War I.

One new weapon, at least, was at hand to fight this depression. Washington lumbermen were among the pioneers of the trade association movement. In 1901, Puget Sound and Grays Harbor mill owners established the Pacific Coast Lumber Manufacturers Association, which later evolved into the regional West Coast Lumbermen's Association. This venture had some important early successes. Inspection of lumber shipments reduced the common practice of cheating customers on quality and the association lobbied congress for federal regulation of railroad rates. But the principal goal, control of prices, was never achieved. Price fixing violated the law, but was so openly attempted that committees assigned the task held their meetings in the Tacoma federal building. The problem was that for every mill willing to abide by official price lists, several others eagerly engaged in underselling.

This habitual failure of cooperation suggested that some things were eternal. San Francisco control had given way to Great Lakes domination. The rail business had grown to match and in some years exceed the ocean-going trade. Heedless destruction of timber had largely been abandoned in favor of the new forestry doctrine. Iron-fisted resistance to labor had been replaced by relatively sophisticated responses, ranging from improved camp conditions to the state compensation law. Through it all, lumbering remained a highly individualistic enterprise, in which competitors had divergent interests and only in the rarest of circumstances came together in honest pursuit of common objectives.

The history of Washington west of the Cascades, from the beginning of white settlement down to World War I, cannot be understood without full comprehension of the importance of forest usage. The vast stands of fir, cedar, hemlock, and spruce made that history one of industrialism rather than agriculture. Beginning in the early 1850s, an economy based upon logging and lumbering developed on Puget Sound and then on Grays Harbor. Enormous wealth was derived, first by merchants from San Francisco and then by men from the Great Lakes. Much of the industrial workforce, meanwhile, depended upon the camps and the mills. If the forest and the existence of deep-water anchorages dictated the nature of these developments, there was still something haphazard about the course of Washington history. Gold was discovered in the Sierras, and distant Puget Sound turned out to be the closest navigable timbered region to California. The transcontinental railroad reached Tacoma just when the forest of the Great Lakes was being depleted, making possible a shift of the nation's's lumbering center to Washington state.

~ 4 ~

The Wheat Commonwealth

In March 1885 a party of Army engineers arrived at Priest Rapids, there to survey the legendary hazard of the upper Columbia River. The terrifying stream surged over seven rapids in the course of eleven miles. As confining volcanic bluffs fell away, the river spread out, becoming wider and more shallow; partially hidden rocks and reef barriers tested the nerve of adventurous steamboat crews. The sane and sober considered navigation frankly impracticable. Even the engineers had to approach Priest Rapids on horseback and haul in supplies and boats by wagon.

Because funds were chronically short in that era of strict economy, the Army had planned to hire for low wages some of the Indians who lived along the river. These were so-called renegades who had resisted removal to government reservations, preferring to fish and tend their stock in freedom. But a tour of villages near the rapids soon revealed that no men would agree to work. "Some of them asked $3 per day and board," reported the Army's surveyor, "and some of them would not work for any price." Even more disheartening, some were decidedly opposed to the planned navigation work itself. The white engineers perceived this as superstition: "They do not much enjoy the prospect of having the river improved, as they are afraid it will spoil the fishing."

But civilization would be served. A less "superstitious" point of view prevailed on the nearby Yakima Indian reserve, which had been long under religious and secular missionary influence. Residents were willing "to work for about $1.50 per day, some provisions and tobacco." They only waited to find out how many men were wanted.

This obscure episode in Columbia River history reflected the tripartite nature of life east of the Cascades on the eve of statehood. Large numbers of Indians, unreconciled to reservations, still strove to live by their old ways in their traditional homes. Others were making the difficult adjustment to reservation life. And finally, the need of commerce to remake the Columbia River for navigation attested to the new era of settlement and organized economic activity.

From distant high mountain origins in Canada, the Columbia River flows for 1,200 miles through a series of aptly named "Big Bends," to reach the sea. Its vast drainage basin exceeds a quarter million square miles, more than New England and the Mid-Atlantic states combined. Numerous tributaries—the Kootenai, the Clark Fork—Pend Oreille, the Spokane, the Okanogan, and the Yakima among them— are major rivers in their own right. The most important of the subsidiary streams, the Snake, actually drains a larger territory than does the Columbia above their juncture. Early travelers often referred to the two as the northern and southern branches of the same river.

Clearly, the Columbia was one of the world's great rivers. For much of its course east of the Cascades, it was walled in by broken rock battlements suggesting the ruined fortifications of a vanished civilization. Descriptions readily flowed from the pens of awed visitors. The Columbia's "current," wrote a tourist of 1890, "is as impetuous as that of the Mississippi; its mountain walls and palisades are far loftier than those of the Hudson; cataracts, like those of the Yosemite Valley, dash over its basaltic cliffs." The Mississippi was more important, but its muddy sluggishness offered no challenge to the powerful clarity of the Columbia.

If the appearance of the Columbia inspired awe, other qualities brought despair to the hearts of those who would develop Eastern Washington. Over countless centuries, the river cut deeply into its volcanic bedrock. "It must be remembered," observed Captain Thomas Symons, "that the Columbia flows through a great canyon or depression from 2,000 to 3,000 feet and more below the general level of the country drained by it." The Columbia rolled on to the Pacific, carrying water away from tens of thousands of square miles.

Erosion's ceaseless, minute work transformed Eastern Washington's original volcanic cover into soil potentially rich for agriculture, if only moisture were present. To speculators and objective commentators alike, the horizon-spanning spread of bunch grass indicated an underlying fertility. Such grass, it was said, was "the synonym for things good, strong, rich, and great." Where it grew, so too could wheat. Where grain was grown, a new frontier society could be built by men and women eager to reap the sure rewards of hard work.

Informed observers also knew that the great plain of the Columbia—from the Cascade Range east to the Bitterroots and from the Blue Mountains north to the Canadian Selkirks—encompassed distinct regions of varying attraction. On the southeast, the rolling Palouse was well watered by numerous wandering creeks. The rugged and forested Spokane sector to the north had little to offer agriculturalists, but its timber and the mineral wealth of the Coeur d'Alene attracted industrial investors. The Big Bend country, where the eerie Grand Coulee hung suspended in magnificent isolation above the Columbia, stretched westward from the plains of Spokane; although the soil was nearly as rich as that of the Palouse, water was lacking. In the 1870s, the only non-Indian inhabitants were a few cattlemen whose names—Portugee Joe, Wild Goose Bill—bespoke a primitive existence beyond the pale. Promoters nevertheless hoped to discover artesian wells and irrigate the region.

Opportunities for settlers existed in the Palouse, with some hope even in the Big Bend, but neither could be reached easily. Rivers, as Thomas Symons noted, were the "natural highways for travel and trade" in the Pacific Northwest, but the Columbia was a disappointment. Although largescale maps might portray the river as a great artery of commerce, residents of Washington and Oregon confronted a constricting reality. Above The Dalles, the upper Columbia was divided by rapids into navigable sections. One informed account reported sixty-two rapids between the Snake and the Canadian border, of which a dozen were "Great Rapids," barring passage. Kettle Falls, Hell Gate, Rock Island Rapids, Priest Rapids, and other fearsome names suggested death and destruction for the unwary.

Good land in the Columbia Basin was useless if it could not be reached or if its agricultural produce could not be shipped out. Issac Stevens wrote enthusiastically about the prospects of Eastern Washington in the 1850s and recommended locks and canals to open the river. Most observers, though, dismissed Stevens's dreams as reflections of his excessive political ambition. Surveying the upper Columbia in 1853, Captain George McClellan, flinching before snowy mountain passes as he would before the guns of Richmond, concluded that "no white man can ever make anything of this country." Other Army officers recommended that everything east of the Cascades be reserved for the Indians, who were suited to a wasteland environment. The military, like fur traders of the past, stood on the periphery at The Dalles, Walla Walla, and Colville, leaving the interior unoccupied.

Steamboating, the initial means of penetrating the country, began on the upper Columbia in 1859 with the launching at The Dalles of the *Colonel Wright*. In the following year all of the boats on the river, down to Portland and Astoria, were brought into a giant monopoly, the Oregon Steam Navigation Company. Regular passenger service was opened between Portland and Wallula, where a wagon road connected to Walla Walla. Passengers had to change vessels at the Cascades and The Dalles, where portages linked the steamer landings.

The steamboats were elegant but the places they served were desolate. Barren Wallula, with several dozen unpainted buildings, ranked for a time as the most woebegone community in Washington Territory. "Sand . . . insinuates itself everywhere," observed California author Frances Fuller Victor in 1872. "You find it scattered over the plate on which you are to dine; piled up in little hillocks in the corner of your wash-stand; dredged over the pillows on which you thoughtlessly sink your weary head." Another visitor, noting the swift current at Wallula, speculated that the Columbia was "anxious to get away" from the "dessert waste."

The discovery of gold in Idaho enabled the O.S.N., as the company was informally known, to take maximum advantage of its monopoly. Where sensible settlers would never go, prospectors by the thousands rushed in a frenzy to dig wealth from the ground. In 1860, the year of its founding, the O.S.N. commenced its most profitable trade; between late spring and early fall, men and goods were shipped up the Columbia and the Snake to Lewiston, headquarters of the mining boom. New discoveries during the decade resulted in steamers on the upper Snake, on the Clark Fork above Pend Oreille Lake, and on the Columbia itself north from Colville to Canadian mine districts. Crude wagon tracks linked navigable portions of the rivers.

Lewiston's boom forced the Nez Perce Indians off much of their reservation and inspired the organization in 1863 of Idaho Territory from out of easternmost Washington. The first large influx of settlers into the valley of the Walla Walla was another result. Flour from local mills was shipped to interior mining regions and grain was hauled by wagon to Wallula for export to Portland. Unfortunately, much of the harvest came in after water level in the Columbia had fallen, ending navigation for the season. "Every available house in Wallula," reported the O.S.N.'s John C. Ainsworth in late 1871, "is now filled with wheat" that would have to be held until spring.

Pressed by the O.S.N., the Army Corps of Engineers began removing obstacles of navigation on the middle and upper rivers. A comprehensive improvement scheme was approved in 1877, at a planned cost in excess of five million dollars. Canals were planned to bypass the Cascades and The Dalles. A year-round 5½-foot channel was authorized between The Dalles and the mouth of the Snake, with a 4½-foot channel upstream to Lewiston. Various complications delayed completion of the canals, perpetuating for many years the historic bottleneck to river travel. The principal rocks and bars above The Dalles, however, were removed by the late 1880s.

Long before then, railroads superseded river navigation as the means of opening the country, relegating steamboats to places without rail connections. By the end of the 1870s, a locally financed line linking Walla Walla with Wallula passed to the control of the O.S.N., which was reorganized as the Oregon Railway and Navigation Company. The enlarged operation constructed a railroad from The Dalles to Wallula and connected Walla Walla with the Snake River. Meanwhile, the Northern Pacific, in one of its periodic flurries of construction, launched its long-discussed segment between Pend Oreille Lake and the mouth of the Snake. There, the terminus of Ainsworth rivalled Wallula for unattractiveness. Ainsworth, according to a visitor, was "one of the most uncomfortable, abominable places in America," and its residents justifiably called the place Hades.

Two decades after Army officers recommended that Eastern Washington be left to the Indians, the railroad and the steamboat made white settlement possible. This forced the government to confront a grave dilemma. Without protection and other assistance, few whites would settle where Indians still occupied the land. Under the treaties of the 1850s, Indians were supposed to be confined to reservations, safe from contact with unwholesome whites, and there trained in the methods of agricultural civilization. But in the absence of a significant settler presence, little had been done to actually enforce residence upon the reserves. Now, all that was changing. The bloody course of American history taught in graphic terms what would happen when unrestrained whites and Indians came into contact.

At the beginning of the settlement era, two vast Indian reservations occupied a large part of Eastern Washington. The Yakima reserve created by Isaac Stevens encompassed over a million acres in the valley of the Yakima River. The Colville Reservation, established by executive order in 1872, was bounded by Canada to the north, by the Columbia River on the south and east, and by the Okanogan on the west. (A third reserve, the Spokane, was established in 1881.) They were isolated and thus well suited to prevent mutually destructive intercourse between Indians and whites. Wagon roads linked the Yakima with The Dalles and Colville with Walla Walla; contact with the outside world was cut off in wintertime.

Half of those assigned to the Yakima reserve preferred to live instead at their traditional village sites along the Columbia. At Colville, three thousand Indians stayed east of the Columbia and refused to occupy a reserve conceded by one government official to be in "a most undesirable locality." Although those living off reservation were often portrayed as drunken and licentious layabouts, most were as civilized as the typical white settler. Many had cattle and horses and farmed on land they had cleared by their own efforts. Others worked as laborers or as servants in the steamboat towns of The Dalles, Umatilla, and Wallula. Indians paid taxes and voted in Washington Territory's local elections. Some even engaged lawyers to protect fishing rights and other treaty provisions.

Indians usually failed to secure legal title to their lands. Under the Indian Homestead Act of 1875, it was possible for Indians to file claims, provided that they renounce their tribal affiliation. Most, however, were unwilling to make that renunciation. Furthermore, travel to distant land offices and payment of fees and commissions were difficult and confusing. As a result, settlers were able to move onto tracts that had been occupied for years by Indians who saw no recourse except to meekly depart or violently resist.

Because Indian agriculturalists had picked out and cleared choice land, their holdings were prime targets for settler trespass. "The whites want what good lands [the Indians] have and seem determined to get them," General Irwin McDowell, Army commander on the Pacific coast, summed up in 1878. The defiant were driven off by mounted terrorists known as "cow-boys." Agents of the Indian Department occasionally assisted the vigilantes by burning villages to force removal to reservations. Even those Indian agents who expressed sympathy for the dispossessed still believed that that they deserved their fate, having defied the government or failed to take advantage of the homestead legislation.

Acculturated, off-reservation Indians were outnumbered by white settlers, demoralized, and posed no serious threat to peace. Government attention, therefore, focused on those Indians who rejected both the reservations and assimilation into white society. One such group was called the "Dreamers," influenced by Smohalla, a prophet living at Priest Rapids. Characterized by government officials as an exceedingly shrewd leader, Smohalla preached that if Indians stood by their traditions, the settlers would soon be overthrown and the land restored to its true owners. His immediate following was variously estimated at between three hundred and a thousand persons, but his influence was believed to be the sinister force behind all Indian discontent throughout the Pacific Northwest.

As settlement spread across the interior in the mid-1870s, the continous assault on the lands and stock of off-reservation Indians made war seem probable. Smohalla appeared to be the figurehead for all opposition to government policy, and settlers perceived a terrifying Indian conspiracy brewing east of the Cascades. They pinned their hopes on a formal organization of Indian affairs that would confine roving bands to the reserves and open the territory safely for the advance of settlement.

The first demonstration of government resolve came in 1877 with the attempt to force Nez Perce Indians living along the Snake and in the Wallowa Valley of northeastern Oregon—the latter led by Chief Joseph—to move to the Lapwai agency in Idaho. The resultant Nez Perce War, featuring the dramatic flight of the Indians through Idaho and Montana toward sanctuary in Canada, sparked fears of a region-wide conflict. Great effort was expended to placate or intimidate other off-reservation Indians in Eastern Washington. General Oliver O. Howard, in command in the Pacific Northwest, even met Smohalla in uncomfortable council in a Wallula warehouse. The failure of other Indians to assist the Nez Perce suggested not so much the effectiveness of this campaign as the shallowness of the alleged "Dreamer" conspiracy.

A central figure in the continuing struggle to move unwilling Indians to reservations was Chief Moses. The government hoped to remove Moses and his followers from their homes along the Columbia, south of modern-day Wenatchee, to the Yakima reserve. The reservation Indians opposed this effort. In late 1878, a ludicrous near-war occurred in the Yakima country as whites tried to manipulate Moses so as to open both his land and the reservation to settlement. The murder of a settler was quickly blamed on the chief. Despite the protestation of venerable agent James Wilbur that there was "not the least indication of hostility," hysteria gripped the valley.

Although Moses's followers numbered less than five hundred men, women, and children, reports had him rampaging across the countryside with a thousand or more warriors. A sheriff's posse sent to arrest him was supposedly surrounded and faced with annihilation. One hundred good and strong volunteers rode out from Yakima City to risk death in the ongoing fray. This intrepid little army apprehended the deadly Indian and nine of his companions as they slept blissfully unaware of the mayhem attributed to them. Moses was hauled back to Yakima in irons and incarcerated amid public rejoicing.

Agent Wilbur, with assistance from the military, managed to extricate Moses from jail before the citizenry turned from its revelry to organize a lynch mob. He was taken into protective custody on the reservation pending resolution of the dispute. After three months in this confinement, Moses was again seized by local authorities. Passions had cooled, however, and he was released for lack of evidence; three other Indians were eventually hanged for the murders. Moses journeyed to Washington, D.C., where the negotiations produced a new reserve, the Columbia, between the Okanogan River and the Cascades.

As matters turned out, Chief Moses never resided on the new reservation, preferring instead the Colville. According to military observers, only about 4 percent of the Columbia reserve was suitable for agriculture and even that required irrigation. But grass-covered benches above the Okanogon were well adapted to grazing and Moses rented land to white stockmen. From the beginning, miners insisted that their claims in the region took precedence over those of the Indians, assertions that were stiffened when a gold rush broke out in the early 1880s. In February 1883, the mining region was removed from the reserve by presidential order and in July the remainder of the reservation was purchased from Moses.

In yet another exercise in maladministration, the government decided to make Nespelem, in the southern Colville Reservation, the permanent home of Moses and his people. No consideration was given to the views of Skolaskin, leader of the Indians living in this section of the reserve. Skolaskin, a noted "Dreamer," saw Moses as an unwelcome interloper who meant to take over the entire reservation. "If they can annoy Moses in any petty way they will do it," the Colville agent wrote of Skolaskin's band.

Finally, Moses and Joseph, the two personifications of resistance to the government's removal policy, wound up as neighbors. The Nez Perce, for years exiled to the Indian Territory (in present-day Oklahoma) were allowed to return to the Pacific Northwest in 1885. They could not return to their old homes, however, because settlers threatened to kill Joseph on sight. Nor could they go to the Nez Perce reservation in Idaho, due to opposition from tribal leaders who had sided with federal authority in 1877. The Colville reserve was the only practicable alternative. From the typically uninformed perspective of Washington, D.C., one part of the Northwest was just as good and suitable for Indians as another.

With a hundred and fifty of his people, Joseph arrived at the Colville agency in March 1885. Moses was on hand to greet him and urge him to settle at Nespelem, where he would be a useful ally in the rivalry with Skolaskin. From the start, the government seemed bent on persecuting Joseph. The Nez Perce were forced to make the difficult sixty-mile ride from Nespelem to the agency, located on the east bank of the Columbia, to pick up supplies. Because the government's Indian Department refused to provide wagons, timber for houses could not be hauled from the mountains. Draft animals and farm implements were denied, making it impossible to clear land and plant crops. Even more galling was mistreatment inflicted by the indigenous Colville Indians. Skolaskin was as aggravated by the arrival of Joseph as he had been by that of Moses. Horses belonging to the Nez Perce were stolen and repeated threats were made upon Joseph's life. The situation became so bad that the authorities eventually imprisoned Skolaskin.

The Army, well acquainted with the military skill of the Nez Perce, feared that these troubles would result in war east of the Cascades. There was, however, little chance of an outbreak by the mid-1880s. Settlers were by now so numerous that resistance was futile. Powerful leaders such as Joseph and Moses turned their energies to accepting and adjusting to the restrictions of reservation life at Nespelem. Smohalla still lived at Priest Rapids, but his hopes for the "Dreamer" religious movement had faded, and the "Dreamer" conspiracy had been exposed as a fiction. Indians and settlers were finding a new equilibrium. They hunted the same mountains, occasionally meeting there. They traded and worked together, though not always in complete ease. As they learned to share the land, the worst of the bloodshed seemed to be over.

❧

Western and Eastern Washington, separated by the snowy Cascades, have always been regarded as two distinct provinces. To the west, rainfall is plentiful and to the east, scarce. The year-round climate on the west side is mild; while on the east summer brings searing heat and winter uncomfortable chill. The land on the ocean side was covered at the time of settlement by forest and on the other, except on the north, by grass. Industry predominates west of the Cascades and agriculture to the east. Clearly, those officials who created Washington's boundaries had little regard for its geographic logic.

Yet the factors motivating settlement and the qualities required of the settlers were identical on both sides of the Cascades. Western Washington's economy, dependent upon seaborne trade, lacked efficient overland transport, thus slowing population growth away from the waterline. Development of Eastern Washington was also closely related to transportation patterns. Until railroads came, few could reach the hinterland or export its products. The obstructed Columbia-Snake water route, impassable during low water, was simply not up to the task. Moreover, farmers had to be both pioneers and businessmen. Capital was needed to finance the journey west and to purchase land and equipment upon arrival. Most of those who settled in agricultural regions were financially dependant on distant markets.

While Walla Walla's first farmers grew oats to supply packtrains setting off for the Idaho mines, wheat, that constant companion of western settlement, quickly became the valley's dominant crop. By the mid-1860s, the best land was occupied by settlers eager to capitalize on the successive mining bonanzas to the east. Flour was shipped to Lewiston and from there distributed throughout the mountain interior. Grain in increasing amounts also went downriver, and in 1867 the first cargo of Columbia Basin wheat was exported from Portland to Liverpool. Wheat ranchers demanded that the Snake and the Columbia be opened to year-round navigation so that the valley might realize its full potential.

Settlers first moved across the Snake into the Palouse in 1869. This harbinger of expansion reflected the filling up of the Walla Walla country rather than faith in the land beyond the river. Indeed, a distinct lack of transportation retarded the making of claims in the Palouse. "The fear of not being able to send their crops to market at once," reported an Army engineer, "has deterred many settlers from locating there." To remove this fear, the Army planned rock removals and canals at The Dalles and the Cascades: "If farmers could only be certain of getting their grain to market in the fall, the vicinity of the Snake River would soon be fully settled, and extensive wheat fields, yielding from 30 to 40 bushels to the acre, would cover the whole country."

Steam-driven travel by land quickly replaced water travel. The dramatic arrival of the railroad in Eastern Washington involved complex speculations, ownership changes, and territory-splitting arrangements. The initial penetration came from two directions. Aggressively directed by Henry Villard, the Oregon Railway and Navigation Company by 1882 linked Portland with the lower Snake at Grange City. Meanwhile, the Northern Pacific, with Villard temporarily in control, completed its line between Spokane and Ainsworth.

Henry Villard's dominance of the two railroads made possible a mutually profitable division of territory: the country south of the Snake went to the O.R. & N., while the Palouse was reserved for the Northern Pacific. Another throw of the Wall Street dice, however, soon cost Villard the N.P., and the Oregon Railway and Navigation Company eventually became a subsidiary of the Union Pacific. Intense competition resulted and within a few years the entire region was served by two networks, placing virtually every farmer in the Palouse within easy wagon haul of a railroad siding.

Throughout the 1880s, railroads extended through other portions of Eastern Washington. Jumping off in 1884 from Pasco, the Northern Pacific bridged the Columbia and built northwest through the Yakima Valley toward Stampede Pass and Puget Sound. To better control land sales, North Yakima was created as a rival to bypassed Yakima City. The surrounding countryside was opened to stockmen and farmers able to secure water from irrigation ditches. At the end of the decade, the N.P. built west from Spokane into the Big Bend, in hurried competition with a Seattle-financed rival. Before absorbing its competitor, the Northern Pacific reached the yawning chasm of Grand Coulee.

Three railroad corridors thus crossed Eastern Washington at statehood. One led due south from Spokane into the heart of the Palouse, passing through Spangle, Rosalia, and Colfax. The Northern Pacific mainline ran southwest from Spokane along the flank of the Big Bend country, serving Cheney, Sprague, and Ritzville, and swinging north from the Snake toward Yakima and the Cascades. The third axis reached west from Spokane across the Big Bend, opening that region to settlement and producing the towns of Davenport and Coulee City.

Railroading abruptly terminated the steamboat era east of the Cascades. Between Portland and Lewiston, regular river service was available only downstream from the Idaho border to Grange City, where the Oregon Railway and Navigation Company crossed the Snake. Moreover, eager to sell land and generate traffic, the railroads actively promoted settlement. Villard's Northern Pacific was noteworthy in this regard. A sales force of 831 agents penetrated Great Britain in 1882 and another 124 went to Northwestern Europe. Millions of circulars and other promotional tracts were mailed to interested parties in 1883 alone.

Readers accustomed to standard promotional materials, whose prose transformed barren waste into earthly paradise, might be taken aback by the Northern Pacific's literature. Would-be settlers were informed that they needed both money and a willingness to toil to succeed in Eastern Washington. Summers were hot and winters cold, it was admitted, and water scarce. The country as a whole was boosted, rather than specific holdings of the railroad. Accounts of the settler advance published in the Northern Pacific magazine, *The Northwest,* were only modestly inaccurate.

Whether stimulated by promotion or by the manifest attractions of the country, the settler influx was extraordinary. "Steamships arriving here each four days," reported a Portland observer in May 1882, "have of late been bringing three hundred to four hundred settlers on their way to the Upper Columbia country." Wagon upon wagon of immigrants lined up at ferry crossings on the south bank of the Snake. The beginning of the Palouse boom was reflected in mounting Columbia River wheat shipments, increasing in value from $595,000 in 1881 to three million dollars in 1882.

Movement into the Palouse was something of a shortened Oregon Trail in reverse, compressed into a few years. "The eye kindles," one writer noted of the settler enthusiasm, "the feet are swifter; the voice is clearer and the manner more resolute." Activity was greatest within a triangle bounded by Colfax on the west, Palouse City on the northeast, and Moscow, Idaho, on the southeast. Here the land was higher than elsewhere in the region—making for more rain and less exposure to killing frost—and closer to timber for buildings and fences. And the soil, according to a railroad surveyor, was "richer than any other portion of the Pacific Coast." As the decade progressed, settlement spread into less desirable parts of the Palouse, latecomers being unable to afford the inflated prices for land along the Idaho border.

Expansion along other railroad corridors was less impressive, primarily because of the relative scarcity of water. The southeastern fringe of the Big Bend, however, contained "islands" of amply watered rich soil and those quickly became important producers of wheat. Boom towns like those on all frontiers were built along the Northern Pacific mainline. "My eyes were greeted," noted a visitor to the most important of these island communities, "with a view that led me to ask, 'Where is Ritzville?' . . . There was only a station-house, a water tank, and one small dwelling and not a tree in sight." Yet a full plot of house lots "selling for fifty dollars apiece" had been laid out by speculators.

Conditions were least promising in the northern Big Bend, where the Northern Pacific built more to preempt a rival than to open the country. At first, enthusiasm was as great as in the Palouse. A traveler found "innumerable claim shanties" in the region. "Hundreds of men came in last fall, and this spring took claims, plowed from 50 to 200 feet square, built a shanty 6 feet by 10 feet, and went to the railroad or older farming districts to work until they are satisfied that wheat and other products can be raised without irrigation." Moreover, because the Northern Pacific reached only as far as the Grand Coulee, an inefficient and expensive haul east to Spokane was required of farmers.

Whether in the golden hills north of the Snake or on the dry plateau west of Spokane, wheat made Eastern Washington just as lumber did Western Washington. By the mid-1880s, production in the Palouse and in the Walla Walla Valley reached 7.5 million bushels a year. Shipments through Portland made up two-thirds of that city's export trade. Flour milling on Puget Sound, made possible by the Northern Pacific linkage, was second only to lumbering among Washington's industrial enterprises. In the year of statehood, the four leading counties of the wheat belt—Whitman, Lincoln, Walla Walla, and Adams—produced $28 million worth of grain and were firmly established as one of the nation's great farming regions.

Wheat ranching in Washington differed significantly from that of the Great Plains. Varying rainfall and topography forced farmers to experiment with varieties—Little Club, Pacific Bluestem, Forty-fold, Red Russian, and so on—to a greater extent than elsewhere. The constant search for the hardiest, most disease-resistant variety was aided by researchers at the State Agricultural College, established at Pullman in 1892. Hilly terrain affected the spread of mechanization. Combines, drawn by up to three dozen horses, required special adaptations to fit them for hillside work. Steam engines were of little use and only the development of gasoline-fueled caterpillar tractors early in the twentieth century permitted the replacement of horses.

Grain was stored and shipped in sacks, rather than in bulk form. To untutored observers this seemed wasteful and needlessly expensive. Columbia Basin farmers, though, believed that their method retarded the spread of smut spoilage. Much of the crop, moreover, went by sea to European markets. Stowage in bulk threatened vessel stability in heavy weather, a vital concern to captains plying the Cape Horn route. The use of sacks meant that elevators, those ubiquitous monuments of the Middle West, were rare in Eastern Washington. Rather, sacks of grain were neatly stacked in numerous railside warehouses.

Since all rail lines came together at Spokane, that unpromising town quickly became the dominant community in what came to be termed the Inland Empire. Claimed in 1879 by promoters interested in utilizing water power from the Spokane River, Spokane (or Spokan) Falls made little progress in the early years of the railroad era; nearby Sprague became the divisional headquarters of the Northern Pacific and Cheney was chosen as county seat.

But disappointment turned to euphoria by the end of the 1880s. Spokane's bankers were essential to wheat ranchers throughout the countryside, and the town's strategic location made it the supply center for the surrounding region. At the turn of the century, an electric railway even provided rural rapid transit as far as Moscow. As its population passed the hundred thousand mark, Spokane was established as the most important community in the vast northern tier between Seattle and Minneapolis–St. Paul.

Spokane's emergence owed as much to industry as to wheat. In the 1880s, enormous deposits of silver and lead were opened up in the Coeur d'Alenes east of the Idaho line. Tracts of valuable pine stretched northeast and east of Spokane. The arrival of Great Lakes lumbermen in the Pacific Northwest strengthened industrial enterprise in this tributary forest country. Railroads linked mines and mills to Spokane just as they did the Palouse. Financial and other services were as important to industrialists as to farmers.

Development of the wheat regions depended upon the juxtaposition of two factors: railroading and water. Trains brought farmers to land where rainfall was sufficient for the sowing of wheat, and carried away the harvest. Between the Columbia and the Cascades, however, the situation was not conducive to progress. The Northern Pacific built through the valley of the Yakima, but it could not ship in rain. The difference between ten and twenty inches of precipitation a year was the difference between sagebrush and wheat. East of the Columbia, the railroad builder and the wheat rancher symbolized the advance of agriculture; westward from the river to the mountains, the irrigation engineer assumed that role.

Until the late nineteenth century, Americans were driven by the comforting notion that new lands lay to the west, and that anyone seeking a fresh beginning could find opportunity on the frontier. The notion was threatened when the 1890 census revealed that a clear line no longer separated settled from unsettled territory. A national crisis appeared to be in the making, especially because many concerned observers somehow connected the depression of the 1890s to the end of the frontier.

But if the natural frontier was gone, why not create a new frontier by reclaiming the barren wastes in the American West? Two-fifths of the land area of the United States was categorized as arid, receiving less than twenty inches of rainfall per year. Irrigation was as old as human history and parts of the Southwest had received artificially provided water for years. But as a general national movement, reclamation grew out of the crisis of the 1890s.

Like developments in forestry, irrigation reflected the conservationist ethos gaining prominence at the turn of the century. National spokesmen like Theodore Roosevelt and Gifford Pinchot argued as vigorously for wiser water use as for improved timber management. Through application of human expertise, rivers might better serve the needs of Americans. Reclamation was also a social reform, promising to provide new farmland, vocations for the unemployed, and food for the world. "Homes for the homeless" was the captivating slogan of the movement.

Rarely has a slogan been more beguiling and less relevant. The truly homeless, as those familiar with irrigated country would attest, could not afford reclaimed land. Due to the cost of the water, such tracts were inordinately expensive. To afford a home, in other words, a settler needed an existing home to sell. Moreover, few of the homeless were likely to be experienced in the peculiar skills required of irrigation farmers. Settlers, finally, could never expect to become self-sufficient agriculturalists; instead, they would have to raise high-priced commercial crops in order to generate income for payment of water charges. The principal problem facing developers of reclamation projects was how to attract enough qualified land purchasers.

Whatever the perspective, myth or reality, the rivers of the Columbia Basin seemed ideally suited to irrigation agriculture. Expectations foundered, however, upon a natural obstacle: along much of its course, the Columbia River flowed hundreds of feet below the land needing water. Engineers might build the Brooklyn Bridge and confidently undertake a canal on the Central American isthmus, but they could not devise a workable way to move water from that stream up onto the plateau. "It will be the labor of some future generation," reflected William E. Smythe, reclamation's most prolific national publicist, "to utilize such opportunities when, with growing diversity of population and increase of land value, it will be economically profitable to do many things which are now unpracticable."

Attention focused instead on such tributaries as the Yakima River. Numerous mountain streams fed the Yakima as it flowed southeast toward the Columbia. The Northern Pacific bisected the region in 1883, making it possible to export agricultural products to Puget Sound. Because it was difficult to bring water to the land, however, local growth atrophied during the wheat boom east of the Columbia. Until the end of the nineteenth century, stockraising was the mainstay of the economy. Ellensburg, hoping to dominate the upper Columbia by means of a road to Wenatchee, was larger and more vigorous than somnolent Yakima.

Reclamation of the Yakima Valley passed through pioneer, corporate, and federal stages. The first commenced in 1868 with excavation of a ditch from the lower Naches River, a tributary of the Yakima. Many similar projects were subsequently undertaken by farm associations hoping to make landholdings productive. These modest canals required little engineering skill beyond the ability to recognize the force of gravity. By 1890, slightly over forty-thousand acres were irrigated in Yakima and Kittitas counties—a modest beginning, but four-fifths of the total for all Eastern Washington.

Ever anxious to profit from the sale of land, the Northern Pacific was drawn into the water business. Dry tracts sold for four dollars an acre, and the cost of reclamation averaged ten dollars an acre. But reclaimed land could bring up to fifty dollars an acre. In 1890 a Northern Pacific subsidiary was set up to develop the Sunnyside district along the river below Yakima. The concern fell victim to the Panic of 1893, but was subsequently reorganized as the Washington Irrigation Company. By 1904 the Sunnyside project included seven-hundred miles of canals and laterals irrigating thirty-six-thousand acres. It was, by all accounts, the largest reclamation system in the Pacific Northwest.

Railroading was also crucial to the development of irrigated country beyond the ridges northeast of Yakima. In 1892, James J. Hill's Great Northern Railway built across the central Big Bend to Wenatchee on the Columbia. That town, as division headquarters and a base for steamboats running to the Okanogan, became the dominant community of north central Washington. Constructed without benefit of a federal land grant, the Hill line energetically promoted development, including irrigation projects, in the so-called "Vale of Wenatchee." By the early twentieth century, the area was second only to the Yakima Valley in acreage under irrigation.

Conditions in the Yakima, meanwhile, reached crisis stage. Together, the Washington Irrigation Company and several dozen smaller ditch operators claimed more water than that carried by the Yakima River in normal years. Further reclamation, if not strictly impossible, could result in protracted legal disputes. To engineers, the solution was simple. The Yakima, like most streams, flowed at lowest stage when water was most needed and highest when water was least needed. Through storage in reservoirs, this troublesome equation could be reversed and valley residents would have sufficient water. The Washington Irrigation Company had the necessary expertise, but lacked the financial resources to assume the responsibility.

Even as they lauded rugged individualism, settlers and corporations clamored for government assistance in matters large and small. In the case of irrigation, the Yakima Valley had a fortunately situated champion in Wesley L. Jones, Eastern Washington's Republican congressman. Jones's long political career rested on two principles: provision of water to the dry and prohibition of strong drink to the wet. His constituency, for the moment, gave primacy to civil rather than social engineering. The congressman was a strong supporter of the

Reclamation Act of 1902, which authorized federal construction of irrigation projects and sale of reclaimed land to bona fide settlers.

As one of its first actions, the new United States Reclamation Service surveyed the Yakima Valley. Unexpectedly, however, federal engineers concluded that the region was unsuitable for the manifest purposes of the Reclamation Act. The tangled water claims were an insurmountable obstacle to orderly construction of a government project. Besides, benefits would accrue to existing private landholders, including the railroad, rather than to new settlers on the public domain. For the time being, the Reclamation Service shifted its attention to the Palouse and the Okanogan rivers, and to a visionary scheme for a canal between the lakes of northern Idaho and the Big Bend.

During this period, Representative Jones proved himself a tireless and adept behind-the-scenes operator on behalf of Yakima. His efforts bore fruit in a series of developments during 1905. The Department of the Interior ruled that the Reclamation Act did apply to areas already under settlement and that work could proceed in the Yakima Valley if water claims in excess of the river's normal flow were surrendered. The Washington Irrigation Company, previously opposed to the Reclamation Service, announced its willingness to sell the Sunnyside Project. A series of local rallies that featured emotional appeals persuaded valley residents to sign away excessive claims upon the Yakima.

On December 12, 1905, the Department of the Interior approved the initial elements of the Yakima Project: the Tieton unit, featuring a storage reservoir at the head of the Tieton River, and the Sunnyside acquisition. (A few days earlier, the Okanogan Project had been authorized.) Over the next two years, additional dams and canal systems were added for Kachess, Keechelus, and Cle Elum lakes. The aim, according to Yakima's newspaper, was to reclaim "from the desert . . . every acre which is available for cultivation." Planned for an eventual 350,000 acres, the project was the Reclamation Service's largest undertaking.

Over 200,000 acres were under irrigation in the Yakima Valley by 1910, two-thirds of the total irrigated lands in the state. It was the most expensive farmland in Washington, with values in Yakima County standing at $126 per acre compared to $47 in Whitman County, heart of the Palouse wheatbelt. Average farm size was correspondingly small, 96 acres in Yakima versus 384 in Whitman. The high cost of land forced farmers into commercial agriculture but small tracts made wheat ranching impracticable. Instead, Yakima and Wenatchee planted orchards on the irrigated lands. Washington apples, bright, firm, and attractively packaged, became as well known as Washington lumber and Washington grain. Orchardists were forced into dependence upon distant markets and upon the vagaries of freights and consumer taste. Instead of "homes for the homeless," reclamation encouraged domiciles for fruit businessmen with solid capital.

Eastern Washington's growth after 1880 was made possible by the rairoad, especially by the Northern Pacific. But the iron and steel linkages were also the bane of the country. "We have fought for railroads," went a standard refrain of the late nineteenth century. "Now we must fight against them." Freight rates were inflated beyond the decently profitable, it was charged, while distant and uncaring management assigned insufficient cars and equipment. The Grange and other farm organizations developed partly in response to the apparent need to curb the merciless railroads. Representatives from Eastern Washington fought the lines and their spokesmen in Olympia before, during, and after the Populist surge of the 1890s. The Northern Pacific, the Union Pacific, and the Great Northern were viewed by critics as wealthy and overbearing parents. Unable to live without them, settler offspring were nevertheless stifled by their unfeeling habits.

Nevertheless, the rail networks created a farm commonwealth in country once suited only to nomadic Indians or white cattlemen and sheepherders. Wheat dominated the vast belt stretching from Spokane south to Walla Walla and southwest and west into the Big Bend. Fruit, nurtured by engineered water, was equally important around Yakima and Wenatchee. Only a third of Washington's population lived east of the Cascades in 1910, but the region accounted for four of every five acres under cultivation in the state, 92 percent of Washington's wheat crop, and 95 percent of its acreage under irrigation. Matters of transportation and market dependency were of equal force on both sides of the mountains. There was still, however, a division of economic activity as sharply drawn as the lines on a meteorological chart: lumbering to the west and farming to the east.

~ 5 ~

The Era of Reform

$\mathbf{D}$aniel Cronin came to Seattle in
the summer of 1885 to seek work, leaving behind a wife and five
children in Eureka, California. The thirty-eight-year-old Irish carpenter was typical of the many men attracted to the Pacific Northwest
in the late nineteenth century. They were drawn by a lure that had
changed since the days of the Oregon Trail. These enthusiasts were
drawn to cities, not to wild frontiers; wage-earning opportunities in
industry meant more to them than the fertile soil and favorable growing
seasons that had attracted an earlier generation of pioneers. But there
was still something of the old magic in the real estate promotions
and railroad advertisements. "Pennsylvania of the Pacific," one slogan rhapsodized. A young Vermonter named Thomas Ripley thought
that the name Tacoma had a "musical" sound: "Tacoma! A new
city, carved out of the primeval forest, dipping its feet into the waters
of Puget Sound!" Seattle boasted a unique civic "spirit" that could
conquer all obstacles, and young Spokane already envisioned itself as
the center of an Inland Empire of minerals and wheat.

Population figures support the notion of a rapidly growing, increasingly urban region. In its last decade as a territory Washington's
population ballooned from 75,000 to 357,000, with most growth in
new urban areas. Seattle grew during that decade from 3,533 to
42,837, Tacoma from 1,098 to 36,006, and Spokane from only 350
to 19,922. Tiny Yakima increased almost sixfold in population,
Olympia nearly quadrupled, and Vancouver doubled; Walla Walla,
largest city in the territory in 1880, grew by only a third.

Opportunities were abundant, but many drawn to them suffered
disappointment. Daniel Cronin, among others, was unemployed,

frustrated, and angry. He, at least, knew what to do about the situation. He became—or possibly had been from the beginning—an organizer for the Noble and Holy Order of the Knights of Labor. That first nationwide labor union preached that all producing workers should be united. Slowly, local assemblies had formed in Northwest towns along the railroad and then in such coal-mining communities as Newcastle and Renton. But Cronin intended to heighten the activity. To bring workers together, he needed a cause and a specific target. Agitation against Chinese workers fit the bill.

In 1885, approximately 3,300 Chinese lived among the 123,00 white inhabitants of Washington Territory. Most had come to America to work in California mines, later heading north. Three or four hundred mined along the upper Columbia River and its tributaries in the late 1860s. Later, railroad construction provided jobs as the Northern Pacific and its competitors built across the territory. When such work gave out, some Chinese moved into fishing villages, coal-mining towns, lumber camps, and rural farming areas. But the majority headed for Tacoma and Seattle.

Compared with Cronin himself, or even Tacoma Mayor Jacob Robert Weisbach, many Chinese were old-timers in these urban areas. Chin Chun Hock, for instance, had come to Seattle in 1860, where he acquired wealth and prominence contracting labor and exporting produce. Most Chinese arriving during the 1880s, however, lived in small huts and quietly waited tables or did laundry. But suspicion surrounded them. Certain customs and eating habits struck whites as strange if not barbaric. Chinese were customarily viewed as slovenly heathens who wore peculiar clothing and smoked opium. Worse, they accepted incredibly low wages, competing with the white labor force.

Thus, the Chinese became convenient targets for all kinds of criticism and cruelty. One day Tacoma children stoned a Chinese resident. A literary society debated the issue: "Resolved, that Chinese immigration has been an injury to the United States." When local Chinese invited sympathetic businessmen to see their customs firsthand, newspapers ridiculed the effort at cultural understanding. From the vantage point of a later generation, Thomas Ripley recalled "John Chinaman, was, to be sure, a bit untidy and smelly in his wash house, but he was, on the whole, a peaceful, inoffensive sort of fellow. However, he was alien in speech and habit. It was enough." Enough, Ripley meant, to bring on the expulsion of Chinese from Tacoma and Seattle during the winter of 1885–86. Daniel Cronin was in the thick of it, arousing anti-Chinese sentiment to fuel the growth of his labor union.

Anti-Chinese agitation touched small communities throughout the territory. Harrassment and ridicule were more common than outright violence. Schoolchildren mocked these "Celestials" with crude rhymes. Everywhere during the autumn of 1885 speeches, newspaper editorials, and even cookies decorated by Tacoma matrons spread the slogan, "The Chinese Must Go."

No one matched the eloquence of "Jim Jams Jack" Comerford of the Tacoma *Ledger,* who bemoaned the town's decline after a Chinese laundry was built on the site of a burned-out whorehouse. Outraged by such indecency, Comerford cried out for action. Would good American citizens allow "an army of leprous, prosperity-sucking, progress-blasting Asiatics to befoul our thoroughfares, degrade the city, repel immigration, drive out our people, break up our homes, take employment from our countrymen, corrupt the morals of our youth, establish opium joints, buy or steal the babe of poverty or slave, and taint with their brothers the lives of our young men?"

Equally fervent was Tacoma's mayor. Forced out of his native Germany for anti-government activities, Jacob Robert Weisbach had prospered in Tacoma as merchant and politician. After hearing Daniel Cronin, in town to charter a Knights chapter in early September 1885, fire rhetoric to a crowd that included Weisbach and congressional delegate Charles Voorhees, Tacomans formed an Anti-Chinese League with the mayor as president. Using persuasion and threats, the league attempted to scare the Chinese out of town and compel sympathetic whites to dismiss their Asian servants. The few who dissented were drowned out by angry voices. Meanwhile, a city council ordinance required sleeping areas to have five hundred cubic feet of airspace, a rule clearly intended to outlaw the Chinese shacks along the waterfront.

Violent actions followed violent talk. Barely five days after an arson and shooting spree in Wyoming that took twenty-eight lives, violence struck Washington on September 7, 1885, near Issaquah, then called Squak Valley. The hop-farming Wold brothers employed both whites and Indians at harvest time. That fall, they paid Chinese ninety cents a box—more than Indians received, but less than whites. One evening, a gang of outraged whites and Indians together climbed a fence into the area where the Chinese lived and began shooting. Fung Wai and Mox Goat were killed in their beds, Ying Sun was fatally shot in the back while attempting to flee, and three others were wounded. Tents and possessions were piled high and burned. A few days later, Chinese at the nearby Coal Creek mine were similarly attacked, apparently without fatalities. Public approval of these acts was reflected in the acquittal of the Squak Valley conspirators, including one who had confessed involvement. Violence against Chinese, the verdict suggested, would be tolerated.

Meanwhile, Cronin and others were haranguing against the Chinese in Seattle, where social and economic class differences were clearly defined. Such civic leaders as Judge Thomas Burke openly expressed sympathy for the Chinese—or at least for cheap labor—while labor elements planned action. A mass meeting at Yesler's Hall, highlighted by an inflammatory Cronin speech, led to the formation of the Puget Sound Anti-Chinese Congress. The congress met in Seattle on September 28, drawing representatives from eight towns and seven labor unions. Almost a third of the delegates were from Tacoma and Mayor Weisbach was unanimously elected chairman. After a succession of speeches, the delegates set November 1 as the date by which all Chinese must leave, and they accepted no responsibility for "acts of violence which may arise from non-compliance." Seattle attorney George Venable Smith closed with a vivid expression of the prevailing attitude: "The Chinese must go at all hazards, peaceably if possible, but they must go."

On October 3, five hundred Tacomans paraded to a public meeting where they heard the usual rhetoric and appointed a Committee of Fifteen to deliver an ultimatum to local Chinese. Thus forewarned, most of the city's Chinese residents departed quietly. Whites who expressed sympathy for the outcasts were denounced. Clearly the agitators were in control.

Perhaps three hundred Chinese remained in Tacoma beyond the November 1 deadline. The few prosperous ones believed that their wealth and position would spare them, while servants expected protection from their employers. On November 3, a vigilante army of Tacomans, including the mayor, the sheriff, and other leading citizens, marched through the Chinese district, breaking down doors and forcing people from their homes. At the railroad station, most Chinese paid their own fares out of town. Victorious, the mob returned to torch the houses and property of the departed.

Throughout that autumn, local authorities kept assuring Territorial Governor Watson Squire that the situation was under control.

He did little. A grand jury indicted the Tacoma mayor and others involved in the expulsion, but the defendants were soon released to await trial and welcomed home by cheering townspeople. In time all charges were dismissed. The "Tacoma Method" of dealing with unwanted people was condemned in the national press, but Tacomans did not much care. They had succeeded in their immediate goal: the Chinese were gone and would not return for many years.

Thirty miles to the north, Daniel Cronin was orchestrating the expulsion of Seattle's Chinese. In that city there were businessmen supported by the mayor, the sheriff, and other officials who organized to resist the movement; yet even these opponents were willing to accept an orderly expulsion, one that would not besmirch the city's reputation. Representatives of the Knights of Labor, the business community, and the Chinese themselves met privately to assess the situation. Although the meeting was cordial, the Chinese realized they could not remain. The fragile harmony that ensued was broken during a public meeting on November 7 when Judge Thomas Burke, a businessman who pompously relished his Seattle heritage, delivered a harangue that reignited passions.

Governor Squire, hoping to avoid a repetition of the Tacoma incident, called for adherence to law and promised to prosecute violators. Soldiers from Fort Vancouver patrolled Seattle streets. The sheriff mobilized a local home guard, a revenue cutter anchored in Elliott Bay, and a grand jury indicted seventeen anti-Chinese leaders for conspiracy. Calm lingered over the city through the winter months, and the troops were withdrawn. Nevertheless, a committee of conspirators was plotting behind the scenes and inflammatory speeches were delivered at public meetings.

On the quiet Sunday morning of February 7, 1886, the anti-Chinese forces reemerged. Small parties of men circulated through the Chinese district, ostensibly checking violations of health regulations. They warned residents to leave aboard the *Queen of the Pacific,* soon departing for San Francisco. As tension mounted, many Chinese hurried aboard, with sympathetic whites assisting. It all happened so quickly and quietly that few city officials realized its significance and city police stood by helplessly. Governor Squire, who happened to be in town, requested federal assistance after the growing crowd ignored his demands to desist.

By noon, most of the city's three-hundred-fifty Chinese were at the dock. When the steamer's captain refused passage to those lacking the fare, whites passed the hat for funds. Then, as the ship prepared to sail, a local judge issued a writ of habeas corpus ordering the *Queen* to postpone its departure until he could determine whether any Chinese were being held on board illegally. Temporarily, the Chinese were removed to a warehouse and placed under guard.

In court the next morning, the judge promised protection to any Chinese wishing to remain in Seattle. Most, having no faith in this promise, returned to the ship. But with 196 passengers, the *Queen of the Pacific* had reached its capacity. Another ship was not due for a week, so half the Chinese remained behind when the *Queen* finally sailed. Observing the ship's departure and the return of some Chinese to their settlement, the crowd turned hostile. A pushing incident resulted in a fight and shots were fired. Five men were wounded and a full-blown riot erupted as the militia arrived on the scene. When warrants were issued for Judge Burke and others carrying guns, Governor Squire declared martial law to prevent their being served. The remaining Chinese eventually left Seattle, not to return for many years.

Tacoma and Seattle were not the only places where the Chinese encountered violence or expulsion. Individual incidents and expulsions occurred at smaller communities throughout the territory. But the events in the two largest towns made the area's reputation for vigilante action. The pronounced divisions between economic and social classes, reflected in the anti-Chinese movement, had long-term significance. This was especially evident in Seattle where workers and employers for the first time identified themselves as such and recognized differing needs and conflicting goals. The legendary time when men and women worked together in frontier towns with a sense of community was disappearing. Labor and business—the "lower" element and the "better" element—began to view themselves and each other from different perspectives. Even as the Knights of Labor vanished locally and nationally, it set the precedent for a distinctive Pacific Northwest labor movement. Daniel Cronin moved on to new ventures in Oregon, but he had performed his mission well.

In some cases, anti-Chinese agitation became the catalyst for more positive reform activities around Puget Sound. Attorney George Venable Smith, a leading Seattle agitator, drew upon its momentum to organize the Puget Sound Cooperative Colony, the first major communitarian venture in Washington. Envisioning a "model commonwealth," he founded a national organization and a weekly newspaper. Along Ennis Creek on the Strait of Juan de Fuca, a settlement of tents and rough-cut wood buildings housed up to three-hundred people. Gardens and orchards were planted, sawmills and shake mills opened, and stores and a hotel were established. The colony logged nearby hillsides, fished, and built a steamboat. The "model commonwealth" survived for several years despite infighting among its leaders and the increasing attraction of adjacent Port Angeles where colony members constructed buildings and provided much of the early social fabric. Smith himself withdrew early and became a force in Port Angeles. Less than a decade after its founding the colony died in a flurry of bitter recrimination and litigation.

Forces responsible for the anti-Chinese movement also created a People's Party, the first reformist political organization in the Northwest. Dissociating themselves from socialists, anarchists, and other extremists, party members nevertheless fought the business men who dominated Tacoma and Seattle. The narrow victory of their mayoral candidate in Seattle over pioneer Arthur Denny encouraged them to call a territorial convention in September 1886. The party condemned Republicans and Democrats alike for placing business interests above public interests and it charged the railroads with assorted injustices. A reform platform called for government control of corporations. Other planks opposed Oriental immigration, called for temperance legislation and increased educational expenditures, and demanded the direct election of U.S. senators. Except for minor victories in King and Pierce counties, the People's Party enjoyed little electoral success. Rather, it served as a rallying point for reformers and as an influence on succeeding movements.

By the time of the Depression of 1893—the suggestive term "panic" was used in those days—more than a few Washington citizens had grown disillusioned with the region. The famous scenery was unproductive, fertile land was harder to obtain than would-be farmers had anticipated, and harmonious social relations were illusory. Dissatisfied groups devised varied and conflicting responses toward the problems of the time. The depression of the 1890s brought many of these groups together in a broad-based political party that briefly influenced state and local affairs. The People's or Populist Party—not to be confused with the earlier People's Party—had a rural and agrarian emphasis, but it also had urban characteristics. It affiliated with the national organization of the same name.

Just a few years earlier, the Northern Pacific and other railroad lines had been welcomed into the developing region as they promised

Haying in Skagit County (photo by Bob and Ira Spring, Special Collections Division, University of Washington Libraries, neg. no. UW 392)

Spokane in the late nineteenth century (Eastern Washington Historical Society, no. 6212)

Left, *Chief Joseph;* right, *Chief Moses (Special Collections Division, University of Washington Libraries, negs. nos. NA 876 and NA 948)*

AN INJURY TO ONE IS THE CONCERN OF ALL
EMANCIPATION
EDUCATION
ORGANIZATION
WORKING CLASS
Boost for the 8 hour day
May 1st. 1912
Local No. 71
I.W.W.
One union
label
enemy
3
I·W·W·
Local
71
Boost for the 8 hour day.

The campaign for woman suffrage in Washington State (Special Collections Division, University of Washington Libraries)

Opposite page: *Local 71 of the International Workers of the World, the Wobblies. The poster calls for the eight-hour workday, still an unachieved goal when this picture was taken in 1912 (Special Collections Division, University of Washington Libraries, neg. no. 344).*

Chinese residents hastily prepare for departure during the attempted expulsion on February 7, 1886. There were incidents of violence in several cities. The drawing is from a series in West Shore *(Special Collections Division, University of Washington Libraries).*

Ruins surround the burned-out shell of the Occidental Hotel in Pioneer Place after Seattle's great fire on June 6, 1889 (Special Collection Division, University of Washington Libraries).

Downtown Seattle during the 1903 streetcar strike (photo by Asahel Curtis, Special Collections Division, University of Washington Libraries, neg. no. 3220)

to forge transportation links to eastern markets, to open land, and to bring in population and myriad blessings. But after a few years such promises turned sour. Railroad moguls flirted callously with places seeking service or selection as terminus points and held entire communities hostage to exorbitant rate structures. The rhetoric of disaffected farmers blasted the influence of railroads on the economy and on people's lives. But railroads were merely the most obvious villains. Other large corporations and property owners, often headquartered outside the region, distributed or withheld profits as if by whim and corrupted local leaders who catered to their wishes.

Just as many Western Washington townspeople rallied against the Chinese, farmers in Eastern Washington found common cause to oppose railroad dominance. Chapters of the Patrons of Husbandry, or Grange, organized in several counties, but proved ineffective. More substantial activity developed instead around the Farmers' Alliances, imported from the South and the Midwest, whose legislative program attracted dissident farmers.

It was one thing to recognize problems, but quite another to agree on solutions. During the 1890s, noted one socialist, Washington sprouted "more 'isms' and 'osophies' than any other state." Single taxers favored but one tax placed on land improvements; socialists would have government take over the production and distribution of goods; anarchists sought an end to government; and utopians dreamed of creating an ideal society. Some reformers were concerned with public and private morality while others dwelt on economic issues.

Alone, each group seemed small and ineffective, but if reformers could join forces, they might achieve political power. This the Populist Party sought to accomplish. Party chapters developed first in several states and then nationally in 1892. Washington state moved toward populism in July 1891 when several reformist groups sent representatives to meet in North Yakima. The thirty-eight delegates came mainly from labor organizations, and the platform reflected their interest in workers' issues, while planks advocating temperance and woman suffrage were rejected. The following year, however, delegates meeting in Ellensburg borrowed ideas directly from the recent national convention: free silver, public ownership of railroads, direct legislation, and a shorter workday. The Ellensburg platform also called for government-owned irrigation canals, changes in tax laws, regulation of railroad rates, and prohibition of Chinese immigration. Enthusiasm and a tour by presidential candidate James Weaver did not translate into electoral victory in 1892. Still, Weaver received twenty-thousand votes in Washington and eight populists went to the state legislature.

This was enough to build upon, especially in the depressed aftermath of the Panic of 1893. In that era no safeguards protected failed industries or assisted workers suddenly jobless. In Washington as elsewhere, distressed farmers and unemployed laborers joined with advocates of free silver to create a viable political force. Comprising varied dissatisfied groups, the Populists in 1896 were forced to choose between standing separate on principles alone and facing certain defeat, or cooperating with sympathetic Democrats and Silver Republicans to attain power—whether to pursue eventual long range change or immediate electoral victory. The question was answered nationally when the party seconded Democratic nominee William Jennings Bryan as its 1896 Presidential candidate. Bryan carried Washington, taking substantial majorities in both urban and rural areas. Within Washington, fusion with the Democrats proved successful with the election of John Rankin Rogers as governor and a fusionist-controlled legislature.

John R. Rogers was a thoroughgoing visionary. Like many of his generation, he had followed his star westward; born in Maine, he moved in his youth to Illinois and then to Kansas, there becoming involved in agrarian-based reform movements. Rogers wrote pamphlets and a utopian novel, *Looking Forward: the Story of An American Farm*, full of nostalgic rural Americanism. In 1889, Rogers completed his westward trek, taking up residence in Puyallup and plunging into the politics of the new state. Elected to the legislature in 1894, he championed an amendment to the state constitution exempting small farmers from property taxes. This popular if ill-conceived nostrum failed, but Rogers did secure enactment of the Barefoot Boy School Law, which guaranteed state funding for public schools and in effect established the state's educational system.

In a display of simplicity, Rogers walked part way to his inauguration, but he proved more a visionary than an effective administrator. He had immediate troubles over patronage. Despite a Populist majority in the house and a fusionist plurality in the senate, few Populist programs became law. A disruptive debate that finally sent Silver Republican George Turner to the United States Senate presaged the breakdown of fragile alliances. Legislation creating a railroad commission, long a major reform goal, was defeated in part due to fears that the commission would be controlled by the railroads them-selves. Some labor measures were passed, but other reform legislation died amid partisan infighting. Within two years, Washington voters restored control of the legislature to the Republicans. When Rogers won reelection in 1900, it was as a Democrat. He died early in his second term, and the governorship returned to Republican hands.

Populists won victories at the municipal as well as the state level. In Seattle, Tacoma, and Spokane, the state's three major cities by 1890, strong Populist movements focused on campaigns for public ownership of power plants and other utilities. Seattle Populists ad-vocated the single tax and led moral crusades against gambling and prostitution, finally splitting over fusionism. Spokane's Populist plat-form was broad. A campaign for municipal construction and own-ership of a hydroelectric power plant helped elect Populist Horatio N. Belt as mayor in 1894, but the forward-thinking Belt had trouble managing fusionist politics and dealing with conservative council members. Ultimately, fusion failed in Spokane, too. Populism in Washington thus followed patterns familiar elsewhere in America's agrarian regions, but it also had an urban orientation. Fusionism elected candidates but failed to enact enduring programs and permanently weld together contentious forces.

∽✺✺∾

Some who came to the Pacific Northwest near the turn of the cen-tury were utopians intent upon building the perfect society in a new setting. Following traditions that stretched back to colonial religious groups and embraced Brook Farmers and other dreamers of the mid-nineteenth century, their ideal communities would flourish in har-mony and cooperation between like-minded, well-meaning souls. They would live and work together, sharing in the work, joys, disappoint-ments, and miseries of communal effort. And they would point oth-ers toward the perfect life.

The earliest utopians came in response to the call from George Venable Smith of the Puget Sound Cooperative Colony. Later arriv-als were eastern socialists seeking a fresh start after Bryan's defeat in 1896. With a Socialist Party forming, one faction formed the Broth-erhood of the Cooperative Commonwealth. They sought to build homes and industries and promote socialist ideas in a sparsely pop-ulated, friendly state. They hoped that their success would attract others to form similar colonies and then swing the state to socialism, eventually creating a socialist America. But the emerging Socialist Party backed away from such tactics, favoring more conventional political activity.

Nevertheless the utopians proceeded, establishing their earthly paradise on 640 acres fronting Samish Bay in Skagit County. They called the place Equality. For several seasons they flourished, planting crops and an orchard, operating a dairy farm and a sawmill, and publishing a newspaper for their national organization. In the first few months, over three hundred persons arrived only to find an unfinished village of small log cabins and crude apartment barracks. Members established a democratic government and shared tasks communally. Equality Colony survived for almost a decade despite disturbances, frustrations, internal quarrels, the defection of several founders, and the accidental death of Ed Pelton, its strongest personality. The final months were marred, as utopians often are, with intense factionalism and an alteration of its character.

In its brightest hours, Equality spawned another, loosely united group of socialists at Freeland on Whidbey Island, and it shared aspirations with a like-minded group at Burley in Kitsap County. Burley was smaller, less intense, and more individualistic than the Equality experiment, and it died less painfully.

A few miles downsound, a trio of survivors of yet another socialist experiment established Washington's most exciting utopian venture. Home was a freewheeling community of individualists, including many anarchists. Eschewing doctrinaire practices and ignoring the contradiction between anarchy and communitarianism, Home grew to a population of several hundred, settled in divided two-acre tracts lining Von Geldern Cove and arching into the wooded valley beyond. Advocates of free love, atheists, anarchists, socialists, and wanderers created a strange potpourri of individuals who lived and raised families in relative freedom and harmony. Home was alive with discussions, debates, readings, lectures, and famous visitors from the radical world such as Emma Goldman and "Big Bill" Haywood.

But the peaceful life at Home could not endure. When a self-proclaimed "anarchist" assassinated President William McKinley in 1901, Tacoma's citizens turned their anger against the nearby community that openly professed anarchy. Newspapers, politicians, and preachers railed against it; postal authorities declared the colony's publications obscene and closed the Home post office. More moderate voices did emerge, and the immediate crisis was averted, but Home would no longer coexist quietly with the surrounding communities, though it continued to attract new members. A much-publicized dispute over, of all things, nude bathing foreshadowed its decline, as members began to challenge one another's beliefs. Incidents of provocation, once rare, began to occur, and the younger generation of colonists began to depart for wider horizons. The trend toward conformity that came with World War I sealed the fate of the community, and Home drifted into a somnolent existence not much different from that of other isolated settlements on Puget Sound.

Other communal efforts had more markedly religious or moralistic foundations, but for all their various conceptions, they represented turn-of-the-century efforts to establish the good life on Puget Sound. The communities and their people added a rich dimension to life in the Northwest, and they made distinct contributions. Yet they were outside the mainstream of liberal elements about to merge into what would become known as the progressive movement.

Various reform efforts culminated, in Washington and nationally, in the progressive movement, a loose assemblage of persons and programs that aspired to bring fundamental changes in a society recently industrialized and urban. Progressives believed in the inevitability of progress, that the world was destined to become a better place. Progress could be affirmed through laws and civic betterment. Blessed with the proper environment, all people would in turn be able to improve their individual lives and society as a whole would benefit. Progressives sought honest government, assuming that public affairs were best handled through the democratic process with minimal influence from special interests.

Loosely defined, the progressive movement lasted from 1900 until America's entrance into World War I in 1917. Progressives tended to be well informed members of the middle class, personally untouched by the problems they wished to correct. They were ministers, journalists, social workers, educators, politicians, and, in Washington more than elsewhere, labor leaders. Many Washington progressives were moving upward economically and socially in a mobile society. Their methods were generally acceptable to society; they partook of intelligent discussion, compulsively formed organizations, wrote books, and designed laws. Until Theodore Roosevelt left the Republicans to form a national Progressive Party in 1912, Washington progressives operated through the existing parties. Even in 1912, with Roosevelt running for president on his Bull Moose ticket, most Washington progressives remained loyal to the Republican and Democratic parties.

In Washington, no one better exemplified the progressive impulse than the Reverend Mark Allison Matthews of Seattle's First Presbyterian Church. From his arrival in 1902 until his death in 1940, Matthews was a dominant local personality and a churchman of national stature. Born into the post–Civil War poverty of northern Georgia, Matthews developed a puritanical respect for hard work and stern ethical standards. Swept into local evangelical revivals, he took up preaching as a youth, embraced the Social Gospel movement, and, after a half dozen years in Tennessee, moved to Seattle. Although sensitive to the needs of local farmers, Matthews believed, according to his biographer, "that the success of Christianity depended on the development of righteous urban environments," and he endeavored to create such an environment in Seattle.

A slender man of great height, he was an imposing figure in the pulpit, wielding tremendous oratorical skills and a graphic vocabulary. Under his direction, First Presbyterian became a major religious and social force in the city. To serve the wider community, Matthews opened a day nursery and started an employment bureau along with educational and physical fitness classes. He appointed a special minister to serve local Japanese. Urging his congregation into civic causes, he organized campaigns for a juvenile court, public hospitals, and parks and playgrounds. "It is cheaper to establish schools, parks, amusement halls, art galleries, libraries, and places of refinement, culture and morality," Matthews contended, "than it is to support a standing army, hundreds of policemen, jails, penitentiaries and asylums for inebriates."

Matthews railed against such moral evils as liquor, gambling, and prostitution, and he battled the alleged malignancies of machine politics. His most celebrated crusade was the successful recall campaign against Mayor Hiram Gill, whom he portrayed as an advocate of a city open to vice. Moral preoccupations eventually overshadowed the churchman's other civic interests, and he drifted toward narrow religious views and self-righteousness. He remained to his death a national figure and a local force, a conscience and a father figure for his congregation and the community beyond.

Other progressives also built enduring reputations. Matthews's Congregational counterpart, the Reverend Sydney Strong, also used the pulpit as a base to call for reform, and Rabbi Samuel Koch worked for social improvements that reached beyond his Jewish congregation. Joe Smith, journalist in Spokane and Seattle, delved into local and state politics in the best muckraking tradition. Professor J. Allen Smith of the University of Washington argued for democratic procedures at the local level—and was chastized for his willingness to associate with radicals. His colleague and one-time student Professor Teresa McMahon studied economic discrepancies. May Arkwright Hutton, a wealthy and flamboyant Spokane matron, engaged in social reforms and was a leader in the woman suffrage movement. And Ernest Lister, Tacoma foundry owner and political heir of John Rogers, was elected governor as a Democrat in 1912. In their variety, these individuals spanned the spectrum of Washington progressivism.

In 1910 Washington elected to the United States Senate a progressive who became more prominent nationally than any previous Washingtonian. Miles Poindexter, an attorney from Walla Walla and Spokane, admired Theodore Roosevelt and followed his hero into the short-lived Progressive Party in 1912. He balanced his progressivism with close attention to the practical needs of the state's small businessmen and farmers. During his two senate terms, Poindexter worked for the direct election of senators, and for woman suffrage, workers' compensation, low tariffs, antitrust laws, a graduated income tax, and the establishment of the Federal Trade Commission. Some of his ideas, such as an "industrial army" to create jobs for the unemployed, were ahead of their time. During World War I, Poindexter abandoned the sinking progressive ship and returned to the Republican Party, becoming increasingly conservative and isolationist.

Over the prewar years Washington, frequently influenced by neighboring Oregon where William S. U'Ren toiled in the interests of reform, was among the more progressive states in terms of legislation enacted. The initiative and the referendum allowed voters to pass legislation directly. The recall, which enabled voters to the remove public officials from office, was quickly put to use, deposing mayors Hiram Gill in Seattle and Angelo Fawcett in Tacoma. Washington legislators established commissions to regulate specific industries, including the long-sought railroad commission. Other major achievements included child labor laws, the eight-hour workday for women, worker's compensation, minimum wage scales for women and children, the direct primary, statewide prohibition, and woman suffrage. Many communities had local reform agenda. These often revolved around municipal ownership of utilities and transportation systems, moral issues, and governmental changes designed to increase participation and fix responsibility.

Perhaps the most significant progressive victory in Washington was voting rights for women. Washington women had voted in the late territorial days, until an unsympathetic court threw out that right. The authors of the state constitution denied women both the vote and jury duty, in the belief that such exalted responsibilities were best reserved for men. But, assisted by the vigorous efforts of Abigail Scott Duniway from Oregon, an active campaign got underway early in the new century. Leaders in Western Washington were Emma Smith DeVoe and Dr. Cora Eaton, with May Arkwright Hutton heading the eastern campaign.

More than geography divided these women. A Democrat with possible political ambitions of her own, Hutton worked among labor unions and buttonholed legislators with an aggressiveness that often embarrassed the more sedate, generally Republican women in the west of the state. But despite different styles and approaches, they managed to cooperate in pursuit of their common goal. They succeeded in 1910 when a state constitutional amendment allowed women to vote in state and local elections, serve on juries, and hold public office. Washington was the fifth state to so act, a decade before the national constitutional amendment. At the 1912 election two women were elected to the state legislature and Josephine Preston became state superintendent of public instruction—though the hope (or the dread) that a major influx of women would quickly engulf the male political world was never realized.

War traditionally thwarts major reform movements, and World War I was no exception. At the national level, President Woodrow Wilson, the scholarly exponent of progressive ideals, turned his focus from domestic to international issues. Demands for conformity and unquestioning patriotism weakened the energy of progressives. Aliens, suspect in the best of times, came under overt attack. Miles Poindexter, once the embodiment of reformist spirit, emerged from the war a conservative and bitterend isolationist. Postwar elections heralded the return of business dominance and the evaporation of the reform impulse. Yet many progressive achievements stayed in place as mainstays of twentieth-century Washington.

Most progressives desired to improve but not drastically alter the existing social and economic environment. More extreme activists attacked the capitalist system directly. Washington socialists organized their party in 1901, drawing members from the utopian communities, labor, the Populist Party, and a smattering of other groups. American socialists shared the goal of placing all means of production and distribution in the hands of the people, but there were pronounced divisions. A doctrinaire minority, consisting mainly of recent European immigrants, refused to modify views or tactics in their zeal to overturn society. Most American-born socialists sought to achieve their objectives within the context of existing political patterns; They relied on personal experience and the diluted theories expressed in the novels of Edward Bellamy and a Midwestern newspaper, *The Appeal to Reason*. They tended to stress the brotherhood of man rather than the theories of Marx and Engels.

Most Washington socialists fit the latter mold, but they were divided over shadings of theory and tactics. For many years, their most prominent leader was Dr. Hermon Titus of Seattle, a minister turned physician. Frustrated over the failure of conventional reforms to bring meaningful change, Titus moved to the left and launched *The Socialist*, a journal with wide regional circulation and some national influence. He urged socialists to avoid cooperation with other organizations and resist the lure of public office, remaining pure in their idealism and willing to accept defeat after defeat in the short run. They should agitate, propagandize, and organize, but never deviate. Titus did not speak for everyone, however. Moderate socialists were willing to accept limited objectives. Continuing factional struggles eventuated in the expulsion of Titus from the party in 1909.

Few Washington socialists were fiery hardliners who advocated violence. Most were laborers, craftsmen, small-town merchants, and farmers whose disillusion with existing conditions pushed them to the left of the larger reform movement. They were occasionally elected to school boards, town councils, and minor offices. Edmonds, Tukwila, and Burlington were among the small communities that elected socialist mayors, and Seattle Mayor Edwin "Doc" Brown had been an active socialist. The high point of formal Socialist Party success in Washington came in 1912 when presidential candidate Eugene V. Debs garnered forty thousand votes, 12 percent of the total, and Mason County elected William H. Kingery, a Shelton mill worker and farmer, to the state legislature. The only socialist ever elected as such to that body, Kingery lost party support when he was compelled to cooperate with other parties and concentrate on constituents' needs.

He was defeated in his bid for a second term. Thus electoral victory for specific individuals did not signify popular support of socialism or affect public policy.

World War I split the Socialist Party at national and state levels as members quarreled over whether to support or oppose the war effort. In Washington several leaders, including the state party chairman, were imprisoned for disloyal statements and actions. Once socialism had seemed alive and growing in Washington, a hope or a threat depending upon the perspective of the observer. After the war, it never regained its former vitality or support. Among other problems, socialists were often linked in the public mind with a more extreme group, the Industrial Workers of the World.

The IWW's emergence also altered the political balance of the developing labor movement. As early as the 1890s, with the decline of the Knights of Labor, the American Federation of Labor had begun to organize workers to seek shorter hours and higher wages; now, the AFL would be challenged by the IWW. By comparison with that outright radical union, the AFL was considered relatively safe, if not harmless; though hardly greeted with enthusiasm by employers, it posed no threat to the capitalist system. But, constrained by its policy of organizing workers according to their skills, the AFL made little headway in such industries as lumbering and mining. While this pleased employers, it was consequently in these very industries that the Industrial Workers of the World would present their most powerful challenge.

Organized in Chicago in 1905, the IWW brought together a mixed assemblage of labor leaders, socialists, and other radicals. Its aim was industrial unionism, joining all workers into one big, class-conscious union. Wobblies—the sobriquet is of uncertain origin—utilized strikes, propaganda, and sabotage to secure their goals. Sabotage, their spokesmen persisted, meant work slowdowns or inefficiency—"a poor day's work for a poor day's pay"—rather than outright destruction of property. This disclaimer failed to convince the public, which associated the Wobblies with bombings and killings, including the murder of a former Idaho governor, and harassment of peaceful citizens.

Their first organized effort in the Northwest, a Portland lumber strike in 1907, was easily put down, but it set the pattern of tactics that would be used by both the IWW and its adversaries. A favorite Wobbly device was the free-speech fight, perfected in Spokane in the spring of 1909. Spokane in its short history had become a respectable middle-class city where citizens proudly kept up homes, lawns, and appearances. Spokane was also an important hiring center for migrant laborers en route to nearby forests, fields, and mines, making it a natural target for union organizers. That spring IWW organizers set up soapboxes near downtown hiring halls, and harangued passers-by. Distraught city officials outlawed these demonstrations and arrested violators. But the Wobblies were prepared. When one speaker was pulled down by the police, replacements were ready, and the action spiraled. Over the weeks, Wobblies and sympathizers poured into Spokane from all over the West, professing a constitutional right to speak. As the number of arrests passed a thousand, jails overflowed and prisoners were placed in an abandoned schoolhouse. Those incarcerated complained of cold, crowded cells, beatings, water hosings, and general filth, but they kept spirits up by singing radical songs and ridiculing their captors with inventive taunts. Frustrated municipal officials began to negotiate and the free-speech fight ended with the Wobblies winning recognition of their speaking privileges. In victory they moved on to other places, but not before "Barbarous Spokane" was known across the nation. A viable organizing tactic was solidified for use in other cities and towns.

Everett, for instance, had survived cycles of dreams and disappointments since its founding in 1888. There had been the promise of silver, gold, and lead from mines in the hills east of town, of the Great Northern Railway, and of lumber mills and shipyards. Always anticipating large outside investment, Everett experienced more than the usual economic ups and downs of a frontier community. Although never living up to boosters' expectations, by 1916 Everett had a population of twenty-five thousand, dependent upon lumber mills and presided over by a few wealthy lumber barons.

In that year, a shingle weavers' strike developed into IWW free-speech agitation. According to pattern, street speaking was outlawed and outsiders poured into town. Citizen vigilantes, including businessmen and professionals led by an aggressive sheriff, organized to keep the Wobblies out. Each minor clash fed the next and the fear of violence mounted. One evening several demonstrators were taken to the outskirts of town and beaten with devil's club. Undeterred, a force of two hundred fifty Wobblies tried to reenter town aboard the steamer *Verona* on November 5. Several hundred townspeople gathered at the dock, determined to protect their community. From a source never established came a single shot and then a rash of gunfire. Minutes later two vigilantes and at least five Wobblies lay dead, and fifty people from both sides, including the sheriff, were wounded. No charges were filed against residents of the town, but seventy-five Wobblies were charged with murder. Tried in Seattle, the first defendant was acquitted, after which the others were released from prosecution. But the bitterness of sudden terror in a peaceful town lingered for years, and the "Everett Massacre" entered the lore of American labor history.

Labor unrest did not cease during World War I. Patriotic feelings were heightened, along with increasing hatred toward Wobblies and others suspected of disloyalty. Mobs destroyed IWW offices and publication plants. In such places as Cle Elum, Pasco, and Vancouver, men suspected of connections with the organization were jailed. Aliens were rounded up and deported. At least a hundred Wobbly leaders across the country, including some from Washington, served prison terms for opposing the war.

Thus, by war's end in November 1918, the Pacific Northwest had acquired a reputation for radicalism. As industries converted from wartime to peacetime operations, workers pressed for long-denied wage increases. Seattle shipyard workers launched a strike when the government agency supervising the yards appeared to be stalling. Other friendly unions voted a supportive work stoppage, creating the first general strike to hit any American city. Although the idea of a general strike was not new, the reality was frightening in its potential. Products might not be manufactured, nor goods sold and delivered, nor services available; businesses might be forced to close. Cumulative effects could paralyze a city.

Over the years, the Seattle Central Labor Council, local arm of the AFL, had grown increasingly independent of its parent body. Now the council called a general strike, with a walkout called for February 6, 1919. At ten o'clock that morning, sixty-five thousand men and women across the city left their jobs. Another forty thousand, many fearing what the day might bring, stayed home. Workplaces, stores, restaurants, and schools closed, and streetcars did not run. "The life stream of a great city has stopped," mourned Mayor Ole Hanson, former populist turned conservative. He was not altogether accurate, for strike leaders endeavored to maintain essential services. Hospitals stayed open and ambulances ran. Milk was distributed to children, electric power was generated, and newspapers published short editions. City streets were quiet, and the city was orderly.

Despite the peaceful nature of the strike, fear was widespread, reflecting the national mood. Little more than a year before, the Bolsheviks had come to power in Russia and many otherwise calm people feared a similar revolutionary upheaval in the United States. Might the Seattle strike be the first step toward revolution in America? However ominous the situation first appeared, the strike lasted only three days before it ended, a victim of exhaustion and unclear goals. An exultant Mayor Hanson, boasting that he had foiled a plot against America, resigned in order to tour the country and offer himself as a candidate for the presidency. The episode neither boosted the mayor toward higher office nor brought improved working conditions for laborers in Seattle.

Later in the year, fears of radicalism revived when a dramatic incident a hundred miles south disrupted a community celebration. On November 11, 1919, parades and other festivities were held throughout the state to celebrate the first anniversary of the armistice. As in many towns, the American Legion, a new and energetic organization of veterans, eagerly led the celebration at Centralia, a logging and farming community of seventy-five hundred. Patriotic and proud, Centralia had a strong labor tradition and was a target of IWW organizers. After being run out of town a few months earlier, Wobblies had returned to open headquarters in the Roderick Hotel. Rumors circulated that marchers would finish off the Armistice Day parade with an attack on the building, and Wobblies armed in self-defense.

Townspeople cheered as Warren O. Grimm, a popular local war hero, led uniformed Legionnaires down Tower Avenue. They circled the block around the Roderick and then marched back, where Grimm ordered a halt. A shot was fired and gunfire erupted from several directions. Within minutes, Grimm and three other veterans were dead, and a fifth later died of wounds. Ten Wobblies and Elmer Smith, a sympathetic lawyer, were promptly arrested and charged with murder. That evening, masked citizens broke into the jail, dragged Wobbly Wesley Everest from his cell, and killed him, hanging his body from a bridge over the Skookumchuk River.

News of the "Centralia Massacre" spread across the nation. At their trial in Montesano, the Wobbly defendants claimed they only fired in self-defense, a reasonable argument that fell on deaf juror ears. Although three were acquitted, the seven convicted received long prison terms. For many years, supporters waged a campaign to reduce the sentences, especially of those probably not involved in the actual killings. No one was ever charged with the murder of Everest nor was there a serious investigation of his death.

By the time of the Centralia Massacre, the IWW in Washington was in serious decline. Eventually many of its goals would be realized, but by other groups. Few historians today would argue that the Wobblies sought to overthrow the government, or that they were much more violent that their opponents. Yet, taken together, such events as the Everett and Centralia violence and the Seattle General Strike fixed the state's reputation as a hotbed of radicalism. The Red Scare, a reaction against aliens and radicals following World War I, was national in scope, but much activity centered in the Northwest where the government arrested and sometimes deported persons of doubtful loyalty.

Two very different individuals whose careers were touched by such events were Anna Louise Strong and Albert Johnson. An intellectual, energetic young woman with a doctorate in social work, Strong moved to Seattle in 1915 where her father and brother were active in civic betterment. Welcomed at first by women's groups, she soon became well known and was the first woman elected to the Seattle School Board. But contracts and funding issues bored Strong and she turned to openly sympathizing with Wobblies and others she believed were being mistreated. She opposed American entry into World War I and published articles and poems in the labor daily that expressed views antithetical to those standard in the community. All this was bad enough, but her open support for Louise Olivereau, an admitted anarchist convicted for distributing antiwar literature, sealed her fate. Criticism mounted until she was recalled from the school board. Leaving Seattle after the General Strike, Strong lived in and defended the policies of the Soviet Union and later the People's Republic of China, always maintaining close ties to her Seattle home. She died an honored figure in China in 1970.

At the opposite end of the political spectrum was U.S. Representative Albert Johnson. As a Hoquiam newspaper publisher, Johnson fought the IWW from its early days. Elected to Congress in 1912, he gained power as chairman of the House Subcommittee on Immigration. After the war, Johnson steered through major revisions of immigration laws that effectively limited the number of immigrants allowed to enter the United States and excluded the Japanese altogether. After twenty years in Congress, Johnson was defeated in the Democratic landslide of 1932.

Neither reforms nor radicalism disappeared completely during the 1920s, but in Washington as elsewhere, major concerns turned elsewhere. For a decade, the reformist impulse was quieted. But soon the Great Depression produced new circumstances and an altered political atmosphere.

∼ 6 ∼

From Great War
to Great Depression

Appearing before an extraordinary session of Congress on April 2, 1917, President Woodrow Wilson requested a declaration of war against Germany. Disillusioned by three years of unsuccessful diplomatic effort, Wilson had cast aside his progressive idealism. He had come to realize that America, as a great world power, was dependent upon maritime commerce and must take responsibility for its safety. Four days of heated debate followed Wilson's request. Despite two and a half years of German provocation, the country's attitude toward the Great War was divided; when Congress passed the resolution of war, fifty representatives and six senators voted against it. Many Americans felt that their democracy should be aloof, avoiding contamination from contact with corrupt European societies and political regimes. Others considered the declaration of war to be a repugnant move to protect Wall Street's loans to the Allies. Though opponents of the war were in the minority, they were vocal and many were prestigious. This divisiveness in large part prompted the government's frenzied efforts, assisted by volunteer watchdogs, to stifle dissent through censorship, propaganda, and prosecution.

Although far distant from both the nation's capitol and the European front, Washington State quickly felt the effects of the war. Opposition to Wilson was widespread before and after April 1917. Such well-known figures as Anna Louise Strong of the Seattle School Board and Seattle *Union Record* publisher Harry E. B. Ault were eventually indicted for conspiring to obstruct the bureaucratic machinery of wartime. Hysteria also gripped many respectable and patriotic Americans. Previously moderate persons declared the teaching of German in secondary schools and colleges to be a treasonable activity. After the Bolshevik revolution in the fall of 1917, American dissenters were accused, improbably enough, of being simultaneously paid agents of Lenin and the Kaiser.

History, like the evening news, inevitably emphasizes the most colorful events. Thus, the massacres at Everett and Centralia, bracketing the Seattle General Strike, have come to epitomize wartime Washington, while other formative developments have been neglected. The nation took note when vigilante gunmen killed Wobblies at Everett and Centralia, but the greatest damage done to the IWW itself occurred during the great lumber strike of 1917 and 1918. Through unspectacular methods, industrialists achieved what mindless mobs could not. In the process, the war introduced to Washington what would eventually be known as the military-industrial complex.

World War I revealed that the Pacific Northwest was fully integrated into the American nation; the region was no longer aloof from political conflicts generated in eastern states. But the realization came slowly. When the European war erupted in August 1914, Washington residents generally considered themselves immune. Preoccupied with the happy return of prosperity to lumbering regions west of the Cascades, manufacturers failed to recognize that good times resulted from sales to the Allies and the Central Powers. Transcontinental railroads, steamship connections with Europe, and the Panama Canal tied Washingtonians to the fortunes of war.

This vital linkage was still unrecognized in April 1917, when the United States entered the conflict. Executives of Washington mill companies concentrated on securing draft exemptions for themselves: making money took precedence over winning the war. Only Weyerhaeuser's chief George S. Long took an active part in the early mobilization effort, and he withdrew abruptly from involvement when a mindless congressman questioned the loyalty of the German-born Weyerhaeusers. For several months, lumbermen refused to sell to the government, preferring the more lucrative civilian market. With great reluctance they finally agreed to provide lumber for cantonments, ships, and airplanes.

Transportation also enabled Washington to become a training center and a producer of finished war products. After frenzied construction on land donated by local patriots, Camp Lewis south of Tacoma opened in the summer of 1917. The seventy-thousand-acre post was the largest homefront cantonment built during the war and, with the older Bremerton naval yard, made Puget Sound a vital part of America's defense infrastructure. Meanwhile, established individuals and institutions undertook new endeavors.

Timber investor William E. Boeing, an early aviation enthusiast, found in the war the vital impetus for his fledgling airplane factory. The Skinner and Eddy Corporation, owner of the giant Port Blakely Mill Company, opened the largest shipyard in the Pacific Northwest at Seattle. Puget Sound became a center of American shipbuilding for the first time. The Emergency Fleet Corporation, established as a preparedness measure in 1916, expended $2.8 billion during the war to build up the nation's merchant marine. By 1918, five companies on the Sound were engaged in construction of steel-hulled vessels, and a dozen more concentrated on wooden ships. Patriots too old or infirm for military duty satisfied their yearning for service by working, part or full time, in the yards.

Western Washington's involvement with airplane production was of particular significance. Although one observer quipped that the "usefulness of aeroplanes in war depends on whether or not the enemy can be induced to use them," their value was quickly proven on the Western Front. Spruce timber, from the rain-drenched coast of the Olympic Peninsula, became a strategic raw material because its strength and lightness made it ideal for use in airplanes. Before the United States entered the war, lumbermen sent hundreds of thousands of feet of spruce a month to England and France. Smaller amounts were sold to Germany, the ratio having more to do with the Allied blockade than with reluctance to do business with the Kaiser. After America's declaration of war, the focus shifted to domestic consumption.

Management is enriched by modern war and so too is labor. Military enlistment reduces the work force, while employment opportunities increase. Wages inevitably spiral upward, particularly where the work force is unionized. This scenario was played out in the shipbuilding and lumbering industries of Western Washington. In the former, employers were protected against wage demands by the terms of their government contracts and the American Federation of Labor's reluctance to take unfair advantage of the war. Until after the armistice, employee earnings mounted without resort to strikes.

In camps and mills, however, the only active union was the Industrial Workers of the World, which was hostile toward the war. Beginning in early July 1917, the Pacific Northwest was convulsed by a dramatic wartime strike against what had become a vital defense industry. Spearheaded by the IWW, strikers halted an estimated 75 percent of the lumber output of Washington, Oregon, and Idaho. Of the major operators, only the Puget Mill Company, isolated at Ports Gamble and Ludlow, maintained a semblance of normal production. With local variations, the walkout focused on a call for the eight-hour day. Hardly a revolutionary goal, this was sufficient to produce six months of deadlock.

Although many employers likened a reduced workday to "practicing philanthropy with . . . stockholders' money," others did not oppose the concept. Logging was already restricted to the eight hours or less of day light through much of the year. Prior to the war, moreover, many industrialists had sought to cut back hours in order to reduce production and stiffen prices. But all agreed in July 1917 that they must not appear to be making concessions to the IWW. "You can no more meet them half way," contended George Long, "than you can meet a burglar half way who enters your house and insists on looting all the valuables." To hold fast against the Wobblies, a hurried Seattle meeting of alarmed employers formed the regional Lumbermen's Protective Association.

Professor Carleton Parker of the University of Washington, the government's mediator, advocated improved working conditions and was a suspect figure to many lumbermen because of his Berkeley background. The Puget Mill Company even employed a private detective to unearth his alleged radical connections. Nevertheless, Parker established cordial relations with thoughtful employers, especially because he sympathized with their basic position, and nearly secured a victory for the industry. In a tentative accord, employers granted the eight-hour day in return for a federal crackdown on the IWW. The Wilson Administration, though, declined at this time to take blatant action against organized labor.

Nevertheless, management held firm, confident that the government would eventually accept the abortive agreement. Pressing its battle of appearances, the Lumbermen's Protective Association broadcast lurid propaganda, accusing Wobbly arsonists of starting forest fires and burning mills. Actually, strikers pitched in to fight fires ignited by lightning or carelessness, but officials in distant

Washington, D.C., understandably miscomprehended the state of affairs. The LPA's campaign mounted, despite the lack of evidence for its allegations.

The association was even more successful in manipulating the shortfall in spruce production, which occurred when the Wilson Administration called for a 200 percent increase in airplane production. Because spruce tended to grow in isolated areas, exploiting the timber required time-consuming construction of railroads and other logging facilities. Since government officials were ignorant of this cause, employers were able to blame the Wobbly strike for the delays while exaggerating the urgency of the shortage, thus painting a picture of a treasonous conspiracy to deprive America of strategic raw material.

Before the industry campaign could bear repressive fruit, strikers unexpectedly returned to work in early September. Rather than giving in, however, the Wobblies had switched to a sophisticated "strike on the job" strategy. Detailed safety regulations were for the first time followed to the letter, reducing production. Wherever possible, workers blew mill whistles at the end of eight hours, a tactic successfully countered only by the Puget Mill Company, which ordered guards to shoot anyone making the attempt. Ironically, the wages paid out actually served to subsidize the strike. Understandably, there was an immediate acceleration in anti-Wobbly propaganda efforts.

Circumstances began to favor lumbermen in October, when Colonel Brice Disque of the Army signal corps arrived to end the strike and stimulate spruce production. A career military man and former prison warden, Disque was an energetic and impatient type who believed that reformed working conditions could resolve discontent. But he was also highly susceptible to flattery; shrewd lumbermen lost no time cultivating him and promoting him as "czar" of their industry. Disque was easily convinced that employers were genuinely interested in reform and that only the IWW stood in the way of a better life for workers and increased output of spruce.

Two startling homefront organizations emerged from Colonel Disque's initial conferences with leaders of the industry. The Army's Spruce Production Division directed all aspects of the spruce lumber program, building sawmills and railroads and relieving labor shortages with soldiers. The Loyal Legion of Loggers and Lumbermen was a government-sponsored union for all persons involved in the industry: employers, workers, and soldiers alike. The mission of the Four-L—as the legion was immediately dubbed—was to improve morale through patriotic exercises and serious efforts to better working and living conditions.

From November 1917 to the end of the war, Disque's organizations were enormously successful. Despite Army bungling, spruce production reached an all-time high. The Four-L virtually destroyed IWW strength in the industry by requiring all employees to join. Known Wobblies were barred from joining, and any who joined surreptitiously found their activities effectively nullified by daily flag-raising ceremonies, ever-present soldiers, and military discipline. Sanitary conditions and logging camp food were raised to the standard enjoyed by Army privates. By the end of the war, an estimated seventy-five thousand Northwesterners were carried on the rolls of the Four-L.

Despite his enormous energy in launching these two organizations, Disque was cautious in his approach to the central issue of the dispute, the eight-hour day. He and key advisers in the industry supported the reduction, but recalcitrant lumbermen threatened to shut down if pressed too hard. Thus Disque held back while such prestigious figures as George Long and Mark Reed of the Simpson Logging Company spent the winter quietly cultivating holdouts. At last, an arrangement was reached. At a mass meeting of the industry in Portland in late February 1918, Colonel Disque urged implementation of the eight-hour day in the national interest, thus avoiding any imputation that management had given in to labor. The assembled lumbermen reluctantly agreed, as a gesture of patriotic self-sacrifice, and eight hours became the standard workday in the Pacific Northwest.

In return for the eight-hour day, the industry received Army assistance in eliminating the IWW in Northwest camps and mills. The Wobblies were never as strong as in July 1917, when they closed down the region's lumber industry; six months later, the organization was for all practical purposes moribund. Employers had skillfully capitalized on wartime hysteria and on the Wilson Administration's ignorance to win a pivotal labor dispute. For good or for ill, the handling of the strike involved the exercise of intelligence by management. Thoughtful if cynical action distinguished the affair from the mindless violence of the Everett and Centralia massacres.

A pause in the course of Washington history followed the war, a taking of stock more calm than the post-statehood era and the drama of wartime conflict. The government dropped its sponsorship of the Loyal Legion of Loggers and Lumbermen, but employers perpetuated the 4L in truncated form in the camps and mills. Although the military-industrial complex declined in importance, the components remained in place for expansion in the event of new international crises. The Army retained Camp Lewis as its principal installation in the Pacific Northwest. William E. Boeing struggled to keep his airplane company in business in the uncertain early world of civilian aviation.

Washington's political life in the 1920s was almost completely under the direction of the Republican Party, and dealt mainly with the popular topic of cost reduction. In the first years of the decade, Governor Louis F. Hart and his key supporter, lumberman Mark Reed, endeavored to reorganize state government in the interest of efficiency. This was a realistic if less than dramatic course. After his election in 1924, Governor Roland H. Hartley adopted the alternative of destroying governmental departments and functions that could not be brought under his own grasping control. His most audacious effort, the dismissal of Henry Suzzallo as president of the University of Washington, prompted an unsuccessful recall campaign against the governor sponsored by the Seattle *Times* and other "better" elements of Republicanism. Politics was increasingly embroiled in the emotional struggle between Hartley and his enemies, so much so that the long era of G.O.P. dominance was imperiled.

The federal census of 1920 revealed that over half the American people lived in urban areas, defined as places with a population of more than 2,500. The United States had evolved from its rural heritage to become an urban nation. For the state of Washington, the transition had come a decade earlier. In 1910, 53 percent of the state's 1.1 million residents lived in urban areas; the percentage would remain fairly constant during the next half-century. The state's three largest cities failed to match their frenetic growth of earlier decades. To the dismay of its energetic promoters, for instance, Spokane grew by only thirty-five new residents between 1910 and 1920.

Mythology tells us that the 1920s were a time of economic prosperity and unrelenting optimism. Critics respond that this is not so: the decade was a stagnant era between the progressive period and the New Deal. Perhaps it was neither a time of prosperity nor stagnation so much as one of consolidation. The decade was a stopping point, a breathing time to consolidate and modernize. As elsewhere, Washington cities reshaped themselves even if they failed to grow rapidly. They improved their downtowns with new buildings, department stores, widened streets, and transportation and utility networks. Electricity had not yet reached some farms or isolated logging camps, but it was commonplace in the cities. Typical homes enjoyed the benefits of electric light, heat, and appliances. The radio, as much as anything, drew Washington into the heart of national life.

The automobile also broke down barriers to communication. It was a national phenomenon with local implications. A Good Roads Association actively promoted construction of an extensive highway network in Washington. No one was more active in this area than Samuel Hill, who promoted roads with the same zeal that his father-in-law, James J. Hill, had expended upon railroads. Automobiles and highways led to other needs and in 1921 the state established a motorcycle highway patrol; the first arrest was of a speeder doing 45 miles an hour on the outskirts of Olympia.

Newspaper readers seeking diversion followed the latest developments in the bizarre saga of prohibition. Thanks to the influence of its large rural population, Washington went dry by vote of the electorate in 1916. On the national level, decades of effort by the enemies of alcohol came to sudden fruition during the war. Draftees were the purest of American manhood, it was argued, and must be protected from sin. Men sent to kill and be killed could not be exposed to strong drink and sex. To stiffen soldierly resolve, those at home must also adhere to the pure life. In bedazzling succession, the eighteenth amendment to the U.S. constitution passed through congress and was ratified by the states in 1919; the manufacture, sale, and possession of alcoholic beverages became illegal throughout the United States, from the most backward hayseed hamlet to the most sophisticated urban thoroughfare; and stern penalties for violation and a superficially impressive apparatus to enforce the law were provided in the Volstead Act.

Few great acts of government have been approved with such blindness to the consequences. Prohibition, boosted as the penultimate social reform, was instead an immediate and abysmal failure. According to some calculations, consumption of alcohol actually increased during the 1920s. Elimination of the saloon, the brewery, and the distillery—the devil's triad—was intended to reduce or even eliminate corruption in public life. Illegal sales of liquor, though, required and obtained the acquiescence of police, federal agents, and the judiciary. Crime was thus encouraged rather than discouraged and, given the force of consumer demand, became semirespectable. Depending upon location, the caliber of government enforcement ranged from the incompetent to the dishonest, with an overall aura of sleaziness.

In urban Washington, as across the nation, prohibition was dead almost before the ink dried on the documents. As early as the 1850s, liquor traders among Indians had demonstrated how well suited the numerous inlets of Puget Sound and the San Juan Islands were for smuggling. After 1919, the nearby wet haven of British Columbia offered an unparalleled source of supply. The most famous rumrunner, Seattle police lieutenant Roy Olmstead, supposedly directed his fleet of fast boats to unguarded landing places by transmitting coded messages during a children's radio program. Although Olmstead was eventually imprisoned—undone by the overly blatant conduct of his affairs—a sufficient number of competitors remained in the trade. Years before legal repeal in 1933, the electorate abandoned prohibition, a victim of thirst and dollars. Vestiges of the ignoble experiment remained, however, in Washington State's monopoly of liquor sales, and strict licensing of drinking establishments.

The 1920s were essentially backward-looking years. The decade's politics involved efforts to come to grips with the fiscal implications of progressive-era programs. The saga of prohibition reflected a lingering respect for old-fashioned rural values and finally the declining force of those values. More important developments of the 1920s were found in the arrival of new, forward-looking tendencies.

Important changes were underway in the forest industry west of the Cascades. Washington remained the nation's leading lumber producer, but its bellwether enterprise was depressed after the early 1920s. Even with the opening of a new Atlantic coast market via the Panama Canal, more lumber was produced than could be sold at a profit. Overproduction was exacerbated when Weyerhaeuser expanded into large-scale manufacturing on Puget Sound and at Longview. That Columbia River town proved an enduring obstacle to industry recovery. Created from whole cloth in 1924 as a model community by R. A. Long of Kansas City, one of America's most famous timbermen, it was soon home of the Long-Bell Lumber Company, the largest sawmill in the Pacific Northwest. Together, the massive output of Weyerhaeuser and Long-Bell oversupplied the new trade outlets, depressing prices throughout the industry.

During the decade, Washington also emerged as a major supplier of pulp and paper. Abundant timber and fresh water, needed for chemical processes and waste disposal, combined to make the western part of the state ideal for manufacturing these forest products. Mills at Camas on the lower Columbia and at Everett opened before World War I. Afterward, things changed rapidly. Extensive tracts of hemlock, a "weed tree" unsuitable for lumber but well-suited to the production of pulp and paper, attracted investors to the Olympic Peninsula. The Panama Canal made it economically practicable to sell to the Atlantic coast.

Edward M. Mills and Isadore Zellerbach introduced large-scale pulp and paper manufacturing to Washington. Mills, a Chicago investment broker, had come west during the war to rescue the fiscally troubled Elwha River power project near Port Angeles. Zellerbach's San Francisco paper distribution business needed a dependable source of materials. Mills, whose prime genius was salesmanship, persuaded Zellerbach to join him in purchasing the Elwha dam as the centerpiece of a new industrial enterprise. Their Washington Pulp and Paper Company commenced business in 1919.

Loggers on the Olympic Peninsula, happy to dispose of their hemlock holdings, were quick to invest in the new industry. In 1927 Mark Reed, Mills, and the Zellerbachs opened the Rainier Pulp and Paper Company at Shelton. In the 1930s it merged with two newer companies to become Rayonier, Incorporated. Other Zellerbach interests joined with an Oregon and California manufacturer to form the giant Crown Zellerbach pulp and paper enterprise. Washington was clearly entering what one trade journal termed the "pulp age."

By 1928, two dozen pulp and paper plants operated in Washington. That year the state produced 89 percent of the sulphate pulp and 68 percent of the sulphite pulp on the Pacific coast. But water pollution from the mills destroyed valuable oyster beds on the southern Sound. Washington's environment, this suggested, might be incapable of accommodating all economic exploitation. Other problems also plagued the new pulp and paper enterprise. Unfavorable international currency relationships made for heavy competition from Canada and Scandinavia. Manufacturers, moreover, were as likely to undermine prices by overproduction as were lumbermen.

Like industry, agriculture prospered mightily during the war. With world supplies depleted and Europe in need, the price of wheat reached $2.06 a bushel, two and a half times the 1914 figure. Farmers, forgetting that prices can go down as readily as up, reacted in typical fashion. Expecting the boom to last forever—or at least long enough to pay off loans—they borrowed money to buy acreage and purchase additional equipment. By 1921, however, grain was again in over-supply and prices dropped by more than half. Throughout the United States, depression in agriculture began eight years before the Wall Street crash. In Eastern Washington only the strong and the fortunate could withstand the downward pressure.

Behind the battles of politics and prohibition, the real story of Washington in the 1920s was reflected in the cold and harsh statistics of economic nonperformance in lumbering and agriculture. While most of the nation dizzily staggered through the speculative boom of the Roaring Twenties, Washington's depression foreshadowed the Great Depression. Lumbermen and wheat ranchers alike shrank before their bankers. Workers in camps and mills, supposedly protected by the Four-L, endured wage cuts and layoffs. Viewed in long perspective, however, the decade's major legacy was the inauguration of planning for the development of the Columbia River.

In 1923, an obscure civil engineer named M. J. Lorraine completed a remarkable and foolhardy journey. Setting out alone in a rowboat from the Canadian headwaters of the Columbia River, he passed down the entire course of the mighty stream to the Pacific at Astoria. He rowed in fearless solitude through many rapids, hauling his vessel around only the most awesome obstacles. Lorraine subsequently published a detailed account of his feat in *The Columbia Unveiled,* boasting truthfully that he was only the second person ever to navi-gate the complete open river. (Canadian explorer David Thompson had been first in 1811.) Thanks to massive changes soon to occur, Lorraine was also the last person to make that passage.

By the end of the Great War, engineering technique had vastly progressed. The concept of taking water from the Columbia River to irrigate Eastern Washington was no longer fantastic. Thus was born the greatest of all speculative ventures in state history: the Columbia Basin Irrigation Project. If the idea was theoretically practicable, however, the vision was far from sound. With the nation's farmers mired in the deflationary muck of oversupply, it made little sense to bring a million or more new acres of farmland into production. Farm organizations, ironically, opposed an undertaking ostensibly designed to benefit agriculture. Sponsorship came instead from contractors, bankers, politicians, and other seekers of wealth and acclaim. The Columbia Basin project was an urban venture—a reclamation cru-sade transformed into a grandiose real estate scheme.

A new element had recently entered the Eastern Washington developmental scene. One of the most significant booms of the 1920s involved the utilization of electricity. Nationally, energy production doubled during the decade and power industry revenues increased from $882 million in 1920 to $2.1 billion in 1929. The phenomenon was particularly evident on the Pacific coast, where per capita consumption was 50 percent greater than the national figure. Descending 1,300 feet between the Canadian border and the Pacific, the Columbia River was admirably suited to generating hydroelectricity. In 1921, two dozen power plants were engaged in the basin above the mouth of the Snake. Only one tiny irrigation facility at Priest Rapids was on the Columbia proper, but other projects were in preparation and electricity soon joined reclamation to lead full-scale exploitation of the Columbia.

Potential developers of the Columbia Basin could choose between two alternatives. The gravity plan, promoted out of Spokane, involved construction of a storage dam on the Pend Oreille River at Albeni Falls, on the Washington-Idaho border. A canal would carry water from the reservoir to the Big Bend country, where a system of supplementary works would distribute water to farming and ranching territory. Between 1.2 and 1.7 million acres would be irrigated, and the wealth of the newly reclaimed land would gravitate toward Spokane just as earlier riches had come in on the railroad lines.

On the other hand, residents of Wenatchee and north central Washington, led by Rufus Woods and James O'Sullivan, favored a dam on the Columbia at Grand Coulee. That geologic marvel would be transformed into a huge reservoir, filled with water pumped from behind the dam. A notable feature of the plan involved generation of hydroelectricity to operate the pumping machinery. Sale of surplus power might subsidize the entire project, reducing the cost of the reclaimed land.

The mounting importance of energy eventually gave the Grand Coulee plan a marked advantage over the Albeni Falls plan, which lacked—in large part because of pressure from Spokane's Washington Water Power Company—an electricity component. At first, however, the gravity plan appeared close to implementation. The Columbia Basin Survey Commission, created by the state legislature in 1919, carried out a supposedly unbiased investigation of the rival proposals. But the study was controlled by Spokane interests and, to the surprise of few, reported in favor of Albeni Falls. It recommended immediate construction of the project at an estimated cost of $300 million.

One significant problem remained: only the federal government was capable of constructing a project of such magnitude. But Reclamation Service engineers who had cooperated with the state investigation were convinced that the study was rigged. Officials in the nation's capital pointed out that the Columbia Basin Commission did not even address the vital issue of how to attract qualified settlers to the project. The endorsement of Albeni Falls, moreover, appeared to rest upon a deliberate underestimate of the expense and difficulty involved, while the cost and problems of the Grand Coulee alternative seemed grossly exaggerated.

Attempting to shore up its standing with the Reclamation Service, the Columbia Basin Commission in 1921 secured funding for an on-the-spot study of Grand Coulee by Seattle engineer Willis T. Batcheller. Privately instructed, as he later recalled, "to turn in an adverse report," Batcheller disappointed his superiors. He concluded that Grand Coulee would be less expensive and easier to build than Albeni Falls. Batcheller was promptly dismissed, his draft report suppressed, and his expense vouchers rejected. His opinions, though, reached friends in the Reclamation Service, where mistrust of the commission mounted.

When facts are unsatisfactory, it becomes necessary to resort to public relations. Thus, in December 1921, the state hired General George W. Goethals, famed as the builder of the Panama Canal, to prepare the definitive report on the Columbia Basin. The retired general-turned-consulting-engineer lacked expertise in reclamation matters, and Albeni Falls backers expected him to be susceptible to their manipulations. Goethals spent two weeks in Spokane in February 1922, conferring with project supporters and examining the extensive data gathered by the Columbia Basin Commission. Over the agency's protest, he also met with Batcheller and other critics.

Many who knew the general's reputation for integrity were surprised at the tenor of his report, issued with fanfare in March. The document asserted that Albeni Falls would cost even less than earlier estimated. Although costs for Grand Coulee were comparable, it would irrigate fewer acres. Conversations with private power executives convinced Goethals that no market existed for electricity generated at a Columbia River dam. Not surprisingly, his report strongly endorsed the Albeni Falls plan, comparing its importance to that of the

Panama Canal. Reclamation Service engineers observed that the general had simply sold his name to the Columbia Basin Commission.

Meanwhile, a more thorough study was undertaken by the Federal Power Commission, which appointed Colonel James Cavanaugh of the Army Corps of Engineers to investigate the Columbia River. The colonel, a canal builder like Goethals, had completed Seattle's Lake Washington Ship Canal, but he was also on active duty. Over the protest of state officials, who insisted that Goethals had uttered the final and authoritative word, Cavanaugh's investigation focused on Grand Coulee. The report, published in June 1922, contended that a dam there was technically and economically feasible and that major revenue could be anticipated from sale of power. Additional detailed studies and actual construction, however, awaited future growth and the determination of demand for electricity.

With contradictory reports in hand, attention shifted to Washington, D.C. Between 1922 and 1929, Senator Wesley Jones fought for a full-scale government study of the Columbia Basin as preliminary to federal construction. Although Jones was a powerful member of the Republican hierarchy, first as chairman of the commerce committee and by 1929 as chair of appropriations, he faced enormous obstacles. With the agricultural depression deepening yearly, farm organizations offered heated and effective arguments against the creation of new farmland. The great cost of the project was another obstacle, for congressmen of that era were still devoted to the rhetoric of public economy. And the Bureau of Reclamation (so renamed in 1923), preoccupied with its Boulder Dam project on the Colorado River and disgusted by the flimflam in Washington State, did not step forward to accept the chore.

But Senator Jones, while often unaggressive in his leadership role, was a shrewd observer of government. He recalled an earlier, relatively obscure congressional action: in March 1925 the Army Corps of Engineers was authorized to study multipurpose development of all the nation's river basins in the interest of flood control, irrigation, navigation, and power generation. At that time, investigations in Washington State concentrated on Western Washington's Skagit River, and study of the Columbia was assigned a low priority in deference to the Reclamation Service. But Wesley Jones realized that "we will probably get a report through the army service sooner than we might otherwise get it," and the Army, accustomed to catering to influential legislators, became the key developmental agent in the process.

By the fall of 1929, against the backdrop of the Stock Market crash and the beginning of the Great Depression nation-wide, several dozen Army engineers were at work in Seattle and Portland under the leadership of Major John Butler, while survey parties examined dam sites. Reports were submitted in July 1932, and complete findings, including additional testimony and exhibits, were transmitted to Congress in 1932.

The final "308 Report" presented in 1,800 pages a comprehensive plan for development of the Columbia Basin, and—most important—it resolved the Grand Coulee–Albeni Falls debate. The report concluded that the Spokane-centered gravity canal plan would cost $750 million (twice the state's estimate). The Grand Coulee pumping project would cost only $341 million, of which a significant part could be subsidized by the sale of power. Assuming orderly settlement of twenty-five thousand acres a year, the project would pay for itself in sixty-eight years. Faced with official, convincing endorsement of the Grand Coulee project, Spokane interests accepted the outcome as preferable to no development of the Columbia Basin.

Power generation had been growing in importance since the various studies of the early 1920s, and it now became the focus of overall regional planning. Installed hydroelectric capacity in the Pacific Northwest exceeded 1.1 million kilowatts by 1930. East of the Cascades that year, the Puget Sound Power and Light Company began construction of its Rock Island project, first of the great Columbia River dams. Electricity was essential to all other development on the stream. The Grand Coulee irrigation scheme, flood control dams, and navigation locks were financially practicable only if subsidized by the sale of electricity to homes and factories.

The 308 Report recommended eight dams, including the Puget Power project: Grand Coulee, Foster Creek, Chelan, Rocky Reach, Rock Island, Priest Rapids, The Dalles, and Warrendale. These structures, once in place, would utilize 96 percent of the river's normal low-water volume. "Each dam as planned," the Army engineers noted, "will back water practically up to the next dam above, thus making available for power production about all the head that can be obtained at each site without interference with the next." Except for the stretch between Priest Rapids and the Snake, where suitable dam sites were lacking, the Columbia would be brought completely under control.

Designs for the most imposing of the dams, Grand Coulee, were published with the report. The Army offered plans for both a "low" and a "high" structure. The former would be 360 feet high and cost $114 million. The bigger of the two was projected for a height of 490 feet and a length of over 4,000 feet, and would cost $181 million. Each consisted of a fifteen-unit powerhouse, with turbines to be installed at regular intervals over a decade, and ten pumps to lift water into the coulee. The Columbia above Grand Coulee would be transformed into a 151-mile-long lake stretching to the Canadian border.

Aside from the enormous cost involved, two factors determined whether the plan could be implemented: the method of moving power to market, and the market itself. Most of the dams, including Grand Coulee, were to be built far from urban centers. Although some industries, notably chemical plants and smelters, might locate near the dams, these would never be sufficient for absorption of power. Electricity would have to be sold on Puget Sound and in the Willamette Valley of Oregon. To reach those places, the Army sketched out a 250-mile transmission network expected to cost $10 million.

Close to a fifth of the 308 Report discussed whether sale to Seattle, Tacoma, and other metropolitan centers would be profitable. One startling observation was that household consumption had actually increased since the onset of the Great Depression, the result of unemployed persons spending more time at home. Industrial usage, in contrast, had fallen off since 1929. Over the decade since the end of World War I, the Army calculated that electricity output in the Northwest had increased at an average annual rate of 9.5 percent. Not to be overly optimistic, the report assumed a gradual decrease in future growth; projecting that by 1960, the rate of increase would be half of the 1930 level and that usage would level off by 1990. Even so, the engineers concluded, all eight dams would eventually be required in order to meet demand.

An awesome undertaking, rivaling the Panama Canal and dwarfing Boulder Dam, was detailed in the 308 Report. The engineering problems were capable of resolution, but the $711 million total cost of the dams gave pause. Engineers in the Pacific Northwest were enthusiastic, but their superiors viewed matters from the perspective of a federal government pressed to the wall by the Great Depression. They advised Congress that the United States "would not be justified at the present time" in developing the Columbia River, and added only that any private concern foolish enough to build a dam should be required to provide for navigation locks in the structure.

President Herbert Hoover, the "Great Engineer" of the 1920s, was left in a somewhat embarrassing position. As Secretary of Commerce under Harding and Coolidge, he had championed the Columbia Basin Project and lent his name to its promotion. At a November 1931 meeting in the White House with a delegation from Eastern Washington, Hoover explained his recantation. There were no customers for power, farm prices would be further undermined. Even if approved, construction would come too late to aid Northwest Republicans in the elections of 1932. From this perspective, Hoover could not justify massive public works in hard times, so the dams and large-scale reclamation work must await the eventual return of prosperity.

Nevertheless, long before the nation emerged from the Great Depression, the 308 Report became the guiding light of regional history. In 1933, the year of its official appearance, work started on the dams deemed most essential, Grand Coulee and Bonneville (which was found to have better foundations than nearby Warrendale). As it happened, these structures were completed in time to provide electricity for the atomic works at Hanford and the new aluminum industry that arose during World War II—endeavors that would otherwise have been impossible. The report's elaborate transmission network became the basis for the Bonneville Power Administration system, and other dams were undertaken by federal and local agencies. Subsequent studies of the Columbia and its tributaries were officially regarded as revisions of the 308 Report. In only one respect was the report repudiated: demand for power after the war did not taper off, but accelerated beyond the most fantastic predictions.

Government had always been a vital presence in the Pacific Northwest. Settlers and their entrepreneurial progeny might think of themselves as self-reliant and independent from public assistance, but the reality was otherwise. During World War I and the 1920s, the federal role became more direct and more pervasive. Military installations were erected and major industries subsidized. The Army intervened in a great labor dispute, destroying the vitality of the Industrial Workers of the World. After the war, the federally developed 308

FULL Leased Wire of the United Press Association.

COMPLETE Service of the News-paper Enterprise Association.

The Seattle Star

THE GREATEST DAILY CIRCULATION OF ANY PAPER IN THE PACIFIC NORTHWEST

FINAL EDITION

TWO CENTS IN SEATTLE

VOLUME 21. NO. 290. SEATTLE, WASH., TUESDAY, FEBRUARY 4, 1919. Weather Forecast:

STOP BEFORE
IT'S TOO LATE

This is plain talk to the common-sense union men of Seattle.

You are being rushed pell-mell into a general strike. You are being urged to use a dangerous weapon---the general strike, which you have never used before---which, in fact, has never been used anywhere in the United States.

It isn't too late to avert the tragic results that are sure to come from its use.

You men know better than any one else that public sentiment in Seattle--that is, the sentiment of the ninety per cent of the people who are not directly involved in the wage dispute of the shipworkers---*is against a general strike.* You know that the general public doesn't think the situation demands the use of that drastic, disaster-breeding move. *You know, too, that you cannot club public sentiment into line, and you know, too, that no strike has ever been won without the moral support of the public.*

The people know that there is a decent solution of the issue at stake. And the issue at stake is merely a better wage to the average unskilled worker in the shipyards. To a large extent public opinion is with these unskilled workers now, but public opinion will turn against them if their wage issue brings chaos and disaster upon the whole community unnecessarily. Seattle today is awake to the fact that she is on the brink of a disaster, *and Seattle is getting fighting mad.* The people are beginning to visualize the horrors that a general tie-up will bring. They see the suffering that is bound to come and *they don't propose to be silent sufferers.*

Today Seattle resents this whole miserable mess. Seattle resents the insolent attitude of the shipyard owners; Seattle resents the verbosity of Director General Piez, whose explanation does not explain, and just as emphatically resents the high-handed "rule or ruin" tactics of the labor leaders who propose to lay the whole city prostrate in a vain attempt to show their power. Let us not mince words. A general strike cannot win unless one of two things happens. Either the ship owners and Piez must yield or else the workers must be able to control the situation by *force.* The latter method no doubt would be welcomed by the agitators and the babblers of Bolshevikism. But the latter method is bound to be squelched without much ado, and you decent union men of Seattle will be the sufferers then. *A revolt--and some of your leaders are talking of a revolution--*to be successful must have a country-wide application. There isn't a chance to spread it east of the mountains. There isn't a chance to spread it south of Tacoma *and today fifty per cent of the unions of Tacoma have turned down the proposition for a general strike.*

Confined to Seattle or even confined to the whole Pacific coast, the use of force by Bolsheviks would be, and should be, quickly dealt with by the army of the United States. These false Bolshevik leaders haven't a chance on earth to win anything for you in this country, *because this country is America--not Russia.*

The Star *warns "union men of Seattle" that a strike will turn public sentiment against unskilled shipyard workers, February 4, 1919 (Special Collections Division, University of Washington Libraries, neg. no. 345).*

"The Red Barn" on the Duwamish where Boeing's early planes were built (Boeing Company Archives)

*Governor Roland Hartley, whose political maneuvering delayed and compli-
cated the construction of the new state capitol, nevertheless took a center
position on the dome at the topping-out ceremony on October 13, 1926
(Wilder and White files, Special Collections Division, University of Washington Libraries, neg. no. UW 7506).*

Indians feared that the Columbia Basin project would destroy traditional fishing sites; dam builders called this "superstitious." Here, Indians spear fish at Celilo Falls on the Columbia River, a site which has since been flooded by construction of The Dalles Dam (photo by A. M. Prentiss, Special Collections Division, University of Washington Libraries, neg. no. NA 745).

Facing page: Grand Coulee Dam (U.S. Bureau of Reclamation)

Like other American cities, Seattle acquired a "Hooverville" during the Depression. This photograph was taken on June 10, 1937 (photo by James Lee, Special Collections Division, University of Washington Libraries).

The B reactor at Hanford, after completion (DOE, Richland, no. 85385-5a)

Overleaf: *Spokane* Spokesman-Review, *August 7, 1945. The headline perpetuates a common misunderstanding about the actual manufacture of the bomb.*

THE SPOKESMAN-REVIEW

ATOM BOMB, MADE AT HANFORD, PRODUCT OF COSTLY GAMBLE

Powerful Force Unveiled to Army, Scientists in First Test.

(See full page of pictures on page 14.)

By Associated Press.

WASHINGTON, Aug. 6.—The text of the war department statement describing the first test of the atomic bomb, said that experiment, which culminated the efforts to create the bomb, was conducted in July on July 16, 1945, before the eyes of a few score of renowned scientists and military men gathered in the desert lands of New Mexico to witness the first end results of their $2,000,000,000 effort.

Here in a remote section of the Alamogordo air base 120 miles southeast of Albuquerque, the first man-made atomic explosion, the first time on earth that the tremendous forces of nature as set free in the sun had been tapped and utilized by man, was set off with all intensity that was the most ambitious and perhaps the most terrifying scientific experiment in history.

"IKE" GIVES NAZIS WIDER FREEDOM

Permits Setting Up of Trade Unions and Political Groups.

By Associated Press.

BERLIN, Aug. 6.—The United States and Britain today gave the conquered Germans the right to form local trade unions and local political parties, but Gen. Eisenhower warned that full freedom only after they proved themselves willing to build democracy.

One of the Industrial Building Groups on the Hanford Bomb Project

Above is a group of the industrial buildings on the huge Hanford project where chemical elements for the new atomic bomb are being produced. The purpose of the project was one of the best kept secrets of the war. Thousands of workers were kept in the dark. Press reports were said one of the bombs was used on a Jap city yesterday. (Official army photo.)

G. O. P. EYES SEAT OF IDAHO SOLON

JET PLANE BLAST KILLS ACE BONG

Private Line Far From It

KANSAS CITY, Aug. 6.—(AP)—After waiting patiently for three

RAIN FIRE BOMBS ON KYUSHU CITY

$2,000,000,000 Weapon Is Likely to Shorten War; Already Hits Japan.

By Associated Press.

WASHINGTON, Aug. 6.—The most terrible destructive force ever harnessed by man—atomic energy—is now being turned on the islands of Japan by United State bombers.

Existence of the great new weapon was announced personally by President Truman through the White House at 11 a. m., eastern war time. He said the first atomic bomb had been dropped on the Japanese army base of Hiroshima 16 hours before.

BOMB OFFSPRING OF CLEVER GUESS

Woman Set Science on Trail of Terrible Power of Atom.

By Associated Press.

NEW YORK, Aug. 6.—The atomic bomb, by official description, is perhaps the nearest thing to a spectacular and not the terrific thing the size of a football or maybe a stove, that could wipe out New York off the map in one explosion.

New Era at Hand.

Scientists armed for work in both war and peace use upon this newly conceived energy, the official report says.

Report proposed a plan to reorder the natural environment in the valley of the Columbia River. The implications of these expanding government activities became fully evident in the New Deal and in a second world war.

~ 7 ~

Washington's New Deal

On a warm and bright October Saturday in 1937, the President of the United States, with two rambunctious grandchildren in tow, disembarked from his train in the dry-lands town of Ephrata. Entering a yellow Lincoln touring car. Franklin D. Roosevelt set out on the sixty-mile drive northeastward to the Grand Coulee Dam construction site. Three years before, he had made this same journey in searing August heat. Then the route had been a dirt road, specially oiled to protect the presidential party from choking dust, and Roosevelt had dined on fried hamburger at a remote greasy spoon. Now the forty-car motorcade and its state patrol escort sped along a hard-surfaced highway. Stops were made so that local dignitaries, including Governor Clarence D. Martin and the state's congressmen, could change places and each ride for a time with the President.

Greater change became evident at the river. In 1934, excavation had just begun and only five hundred workers were on hand. By October 1937, the dam's foundation was nearly complete and in places its concrete wall soared fourteen stories high. Six thousand men and women labored at various tasks and, where a few hundred settlers had recently lived in outback solitude, over sixteen thousand resided in construction towns. "The famous Roosevelt jaw," claimed a reporter, "dropped appreciably as he drank in the scene of vast change before him." This was hack bombast, for the presidential jawline remained resolute, but there was no doubt that the transformation was great.

The motorcade stopped first at a view tower, where Roosevelt was greeted by Frank Banks, resident manager for the Bureau of Reclamation. The President, his gray suit rumpled from the automobile ride, studied a model of the project and then compared it to the partially completed real thing, spreading across the Columbia before him. Daughter Anna Boettiger bustled about like any mink-attired tourist, shooting home movies. Fifteen news cameramen energetically recorded the sort of happening that would one day be termed a photo opportunity. "Flash bulbs puffed regularly," wrote an observer, "and a veritable shower of used bulbs poured out the open window."

Returning to his car, Roosevelt was driven to the riverside and onto an elevated platform erected for the occasion. A crowd estimated at seventy-five hundred, including ceremonially clad Shriners gathered at Grand Coulee in convention, had assembled to hear his remarks. Using a loudspeaker placed in the Lincoln's back seat, the President detailed the benefits of completion of the dam. "My head is full of figures," he confessed, "and the easiest way to describe the figures is that this is the largest structure so far as anybody knows that has ever been undertaken by man." After a bologna sandwich lunch provided by the principal government contractor, the motorcade departed down a street lined with schoolchildren waving flags and presidential photographs. Ninety minutes had elapsed between arrival and departure.

In his remarks, barely audible over the rumble of nearby conveyor belts, Roosevelt promised to "come back . . . in two or three years and see this dam pretty nearly completed." Although he remained in the White House another seven and a half years, he never redeemed that pledge. Still, among the political, economic, and environmental achievements of the New Deal in Washington State, Grand Coulee stood out as the most breathtaking. It was, as a Spokane newspaper asserted that October, the "world's greatest dam" and "the new deal's biggest baby."

During the final week of October 1929, the newspapers of Western Washington featured, along with the football scores, four big stories. On Puget Sound, the ferry *Hyak* rammed a fishing boat in morning fog. Nationally, former Interior Secretary Albert Fall was convicted of taking bribes in the Teapot Dome scandal. In Los Angeles, theater magnate Alexander Pantages was judged guilty of indecent assault upon a teenage girl. And on October 24—the blackest of all Black Thursdays—stock prices plummeted on Wall Street. "You had to stand in line to get a window to jump out of," Will Rogers quipped, "and speculators were selling space for bodies in the East River."

Due to the time difference between the Atlantic and Pacific coasts, the crash was well advanced when exchanges and brokerages in Washington State opened their doors. Men and women jammed offices and gathered at curbsides awaiting news, only to find that tickers were unable to keep up with the avalanche of sales. Long-distance telephone calls to New York set a new record. Five hours after the market closed on Wall Street, final figures were still unavailable. On Friday the early edition of the Seattle *Post-Intelligencer* was held back for hours awaiting complete quotations.

Locally, restraint rather than panic was the order of the day. The Tacoma *News Tribune* headlined its report from Wall Street, "Conditions Almost Panicky as Millions of Values Vanish Every Minute." The Seattle *Star* observed that "nothing has been lost but some hot air." Andrew Price, president of Seattle's Marine Bancorporation, reported that his clients had avoided eastern investments and were thus "not particularly concerned with the fluctuations of the stock market." A prominent broker announced that he spent Black Thursday acquiring a "moderate amount of attractive securities." Hearst columnist Arthur Brisbane suggested on the *Post-Intelligencer's* front page that the only people worried were "women speculators" who in the fiscal ignorance of their sex were "amazed to learn that prices can go down."

American business clearly was sound in the most fundamental sense. "There were just as many dollars in the United States after the crash as there were before," pointed out Colonel C. B. Blethen, publisher of the Seattle *Times,* in the first of a series of dispatches from New York. All that was happening, claimed the *Star,* was a necessary and healthful readjustment of stocks "that the gamblers have skyrocketed to ridiculous, impossible levels." The American people were "composedly at work and business as usual," noted the Spokane *Spokesman-Review.* "Their faces bear no anxious look; they lose no sleep at night, but will awake this morning, as in the past, refreshed and ready to carry on the industries and commerce of the nation."

Widespread opinion held that the crash would actually prove beneficial to the Pacific Northwest. "There are many people," observed Colonel Blethen, "that have put off home building and delayed investing in real estate as long as there was a possibility of big, quick profits in stocks." The *Spokesman-Review* agreed that "hundreds of millions of dollars heretofore used unproductively in New York will go into legitimate development work at home and abroad." New homes and new real-estate developments would lift the region's vital lumbering industry out of its economic doldrums and make Washington a solid centerpiece of genuine national prosperity.

Newspaper editorials predicted good times. On the Sunday after Black Thursday, the *Post-Intelligencer* urged readers to invest in stocks: "The country is prosperous, business is sound and the average sound stock is worth more than it is selling for today." Blethen seconded his journalistic rival. "It has become certain already," he insisted, "that there can be neither a panic nor a business depression to follow." The fortuituous end to mad speculation on Wall Street, observed the *Spokesman-Review,* cleared "the way for the Hoover administration to proceed with its comprehensive program for a wider dissemination of prosperity." These confident prognostications, a mere sample of the faith offerings, soon proved devastatingly wrong.

Despite the optimistic forecasts of eminent economic thinkers, the stock market crash signalled the beginning of the long nightmare known with appropriate capitalization as the Great Depression. In the next three years, approximately twelve million Americans lost their jobs, five thousand banks failed, and the gross national product was halved. Corporate profit, that heady indicator of the 1920s boom, was extinguished with a vengeance, losses for 1932 alone totalling $12 billion.

The Pacific Northwest was not sheltered from the collapse. Per capita consumption of lumber in the United States declined by two-thirds between 1929 and 1932, spelling disaster for the already depressed sawmills of Washington. The state's annual lumber production dropped from 7.3 billion feet to 2.2 billion feet during those three years. According to trade journals, the industry operated nationally at only a fifth of its normal capacity, and overall industrial employment in Washington at the end of 1932 was less than half the level of the late 1920s. Following a succession of wage reductions, payrolls were only 36 percent of the earlier rate. "There are . . . few in the world," lamented Grays Harbor timberman Alex Polson, "who have escaped Old Man Depression's oppressive methods."

Conditions were no better in farm country east of the Cascades. Wheat prices already had fallen from $1.83 a bushel in 1920 to sixty-seven cents at the end of the decade, then dropped to a miniscule thirty-eight cents by 1932. Farmers, pressed to the wall before the stock market crash, were pulverized in its aftermath. In the fifteen years after 1920, the value of Washington farmland and buildings dropped from $920 million to $551 million. Over the same period, moreover, acreage under cultivation increased as operators sought to compensate for falling prices with added production. The average value per farm by 1935, in unhappy confirmation of the heartless verities of supply and demand, was less than half that of 1920.

Those who live in an age when unemployment insurance, welfare, and federally insured bank deposits are taken for granted can never truly grasp the awful nature of the Great Depression. Until 1933, neither the state nor the federal government provided direct assistance to the unemployed and dispossessed. Under the most fortunate circumstances, only pennies on the dollar might be returned to depositors by bankrupt financial institutions. In Olympia, Governor Roland Hartley steadfastly resisted pressure to summon a special legislative session to deal with the economic crisis. Repudiated by his party in the 1932 Republican primary, the governor maintained to his final controversial day in office that "we must stop multiplying government activities." President Hoover, on the other hand, was neither uncaring nor irresponsible, but he too was unable to take effective action.

According to precepts of an earlier uncomplicated era, relief was best left to private charity and local government. That such tenets were unsuited to a crisis of unprecedented magnitude was soon and amply demonstrated. County debt in Washington State increased 300 percent in 1932 alone, through issuance of bonds for modest public works ventures. Although the city of Seattle was advised in the fall of 1931 that a minimal appropriation of one million dollars was essential for relief, falling revenue and various legal complications reduced the amount actually provided to less than a fifth of a million.

Individual initiative, as Roland Hartley and other rugged believers in public frugality averred, remained the prime means of salvation for many caught in the grasp of the Depression. Communities of the self-reliant homeless became commonplace on the outskirts of cities and larger towns. The most famous of these "Hoovervilles" was south of Yesler Street near the Seattle waterfront, where in 1934 an investigator found 632 men and seven women eking out a hand-to-mouth existence in ramshackle habitations. Also in Seattle, the Unemployed Citizens League, a self-help organization, was created to provide food, fuel, and services to its several thousand members through bartering. It was, in the view of one admirer, "the most striking social and economic experiment that has come out of these troubled times." Thousands joined similar cooperatives throughout the state.

A political revolution was the first major product of the economic crisis. Since the turn of the century, Washington had for all practical purposes been a Republican satrapy; at one point in the early 1920s only two Democrats served in the state legislature. Nationally, Republicans had dominated presidential politics since the Civil War. But by 1932 things had changed. Governor Hartley, once entertainingly stubborn, was out of touch and embarrassing. Hoover had once promised a chicken in every pot and a car in every garage; the car, it was now observed, had since been repossessed, the garage had been foreclosed upon, and the pot stood empty.

In 1928 Washingtonians had favored Hoover by a ratio of two to one, even better than his national performance. Four years later, they rejected him just as decisively, his tally barely reaching 34 percent. New York Governor Franklin D. Roosevelt garnered 57 percent of the vote, double the Democratic returns of 1928. (In addition, one in ten Washingtonians voted for Socialist Norman Thomas or some other independent candidate.)

While voter turnout improved nationwide, in Washington State the increase was an amazing 23 percent. This was due to more than just eagerness to throw the Republicans out of the White House. At home, Democrat Clarence D. Martin, a conservative mill owner from Cheney, won the governorship. Wesley Jones lost his bid for a fifth Senate term to Homer T. Bone, a Democrat whose political odyssey had included periods in the Socialist, Progressive, and Republican parties. Democrats won three-fourths of the seats in the state house of representatives, increasing their numbers from eight to seventy overnight. Only the overlapping four-year terms of the state senate prevented a similar landslide there.

Washington politics took a sensational turn. Seattle danceband leader Vic Meyers, elected lieutenant governor in 1932, built a career by entertaining voters with larkish acts. After a promising start, Representative Marion Zionchek's career descended into alcoholism and mental illness, his bizarre and much-publicized behavior ending with a suicide leap in 1936. The Washington Commonwealth Federation, a union of assorted radical groups, became a power within the Democratic Party on the basis of its public ownership platform. The liberal Oregon journalist Richard Neuberger penned a widely held assessment: "In addition to being the country's storehouse of timber, Chinook salmon, apples, and hydroelectric power, the Evergreen state is also the citadel of cockeyed and fantastic politics."

According to a quip attributed to James A. Farley, Roosevelt's Postmaster General, the nation consisted of forty-seven states and the soviet of Washington. This much-quoted remark failed to recognize the relative conservatism behind the newspaper headlines that attacked the radical fringe. The principal politicians produced by the New Deal, after all, were Clarence Martin and Warren G. Magnuson, who were neither radical nor irresponsible. The main innovation in state government was the sales tax—hardly an assault upon the wealthy. And truly significant developments were taking place outside the political arena.

Roosevelt's principal weapon against America's industrial depression was the National Industrial Recovery Act, passed by Congress in June 1933. The legislation empowered individual industries to devise and operate under "codes of fair competition," devices to legally control production and prices. The act's original champions included the lumbermen of the Pacific Northwest, who had conspired for decades—informally and through trade associations—to attain the same end. They had unanimously supported Hoover in 1932; now they became fair-weather converts to the New Deal.

Work on a code for the lumber industry began even before Congress completed action on the Recovery Act. Two principles dominated the drafting process. Under "birth control," building new sawmills would be prohibited; in the "soup bowl," individual operators were to be allocated specific portions of an overall national production quota. The Weyerhaeuser Timber Company and other large firms, however, opposed anything that would forestall plans for expansion. The code, as finally signed by President Roosevelt in August, retained the quota system but did not include the "birth control" device.

This omission doomed the code. On the one hand, lumber markets at home and abroad continued to stagnate, forcing successive reductions in quarterly production quotas. At the same time, artificially stiffened prices brought hundreds of new sawmills into operation across the country. The result was smaller "soup bowl" servings for all. In Washington State, the government's failure to vigorously prosecute blatant violators fueled growing discontent within the industry. Sensing this, Weyerhaeuser was by 1934 prepared to throw its weight behind a campaign to abolish the code. Long before the Supreme

Court declared the NIRA unconstitutional in 1935, the code was a dead letter in the Pacific Northwest. Lumbermen, learning from this experience that Roosevelt was after all the devil on earth, reverted to the former Republican faith.

The NIRA typified Roosevelt methodology in a grandiose way, grafting diverse interests and objectives. If the lumber code failed in its nominal main purpose, certain clauses did have long-term significance. In Article X, timbermen agreed to implement selective logging, sustained yield, and other forward-looking strategies. Even though these clauses were not mandatory, they did encourage improved forest management.

Furthermore, in return for federally sponsored industrial self-government, business swallowed a bitter pill. Section 7a of the act recognized labor's right to organize and management's obligation to bargain with employees. This provision, common to all the NIRA codes, was mandatory. However noncontroversial it may seem today, Section 7a overturned traditional management-labor relations, and the solidification of Washington's labor movement was the direct result and greatest legacy of the New Deal in the Pacific Northwest.

Organized labor in Washington stagnated in the years after World War I, especially in lumbering. The Industrial Workers of the World, once a conservative nightmare, was moribund and the American Federation of Labor was only a minor irritant to management. Organization in camps and mills amounted to little more than the remnant Loyal Legion of Loggers and Lumbermen, its membership a fraction of the wartime level. Employers, no longer fearing the IWW, avoided involvement with the Four-L whenever possible.

Employment conditions worsened after the stock market crash. At least half of those normally employed in camps and mills were out of work altogether by the end of 1931, while workers retaining jobs endured sharp reductions in hours and pay. The minimum daily wage was cut to $2.60 by late 1932. Rallies organized by communists and other radicals attracted sizeable audiences from among displaced laborers. Wildcat strikes disrupted production and the lives of prominent timbermen were threatened. Arson was practiced by people who hoped to be hired to fight the fires. Facing upheavel in the industry and in society at large, management attempted to reinvigorate the Four-L as a bulwark against radicalism; that organization lingered until 1937, when the National Labor Relations Act, commonly called the Wagner Act, outlawed company unions.

Nationwide, union membership increased by a third in the year following passage of the National Industrial Recovery Act. Although a few AFL locals were formed in late 1933, expansion was not rapid in the Northwest lumber industry, and the national organization extended little or no assistance. The AFL's craft orientation, organizing member unions according to skilled trades, limited enrollment in camps and mills, where few workers were skilled.

On Pacific Coast docks, the notorious shape-up system, under which employers daily hired laborers of their choice, was the norm. The International Longshoremen's Association, led by Australian-born radical Harry Bridges, focused its organizing campaign on abolition of this practice. Major coastal ports from Puget Sound to Southern California were closed by the ILA in the spring of 1934. The situation quickly deteriorated, became violent, and culminated in a general strike in San Francisco. By midsummer, management was forced to accept the union-controlled hiring hall in order to reopen the docks.

If Bridges was radical, rumpled, and lean, Seattle teamster Dave Beck was conservative, natty, and squat. Beck, too, sought to organize Seattle dock workers, and he was at least as tough and shrewd as his great antagonist. "I run this place just like a business—just like the Standard Oil Company or the Northern Pacific Railway," Beck succinctly admitted. Dealing with employers man to man, he concluded agreements that gave his members high wages, while management got security against disruption. Teamsters, true to their leader's code, crossed picket lines to honor contracts, making them effective strikebreakers.

Beck fought the emerging lumber industry union and became the AFL's point man against industrial unionism on the west coast. Establishment conservatives joined with liberals and radicals to denounce him. Editorializing between the lines, a *Life* magazine photo essay portrayed Beck as "an aggressive, two-fisted man, beefy, red-faced and gimlet-eyed," and lasciviously noted that he employed "a pretty blonde, smart, efficient and statuesque" secretary, whom he addressed "by her first name." Journalists and subsequent historians agreed that Beck and Bridges made good copy.

Back in the lumber camps and mills, orgnization rushed ahead amid widespread turbulence. By early 1935, AFL timber locals in Washington and Oregon united under the banner of the Northwest Council of Sawmill and Timber Workers. As part of a campaign to organize the unskilled and semiskilled, the AFL placed the timber workers under the jurisdiction of the United Brotherhood of Carpenters and Joiners. Rarely has there been a more improbable and unwholesome marriage. The Carpenters, one of the most conservative unions in the AFL, was devoted to the sanctity of the craft principle. Timber union leaders in the Northwest, in contrast, supported the New Deal and advocated industrial unionization, which would cut across craft lines to unite all workers in a given industry. Over the protest of Carpenters representative A. W. Muir, the Northwest Council called a regional strike for May 1935. They made three demands: a thirty-hour work week, a seventy-five-cent hourly minimum wage, and recognition of the union as sole bargaining agent for all employees. Most sawmills on Puget Sound and Grays Harbor and those south of the Columbia closed in the first week of May.

At Longview, work continued briefly while Muir negotiated with Weyerhaeuser and Long-Bell. A compromise announced on May 9 provided a forty-hour week, a fifty-cent minimum wage, and limitation of union representation to members only. Repudiating their nominal leader, the rank and file promptly walked off the job, closing the Longview plants. With ninety percent of the industry in Washington and Oregon shut down, a strike reminiscent of 1917 was underway. Employers sought to reopen the mills on Longview terms. Concentrating on Tacoma, Weyerhaeuser executives convinced Governor Martin that only intimidation by radicals prevented workmen from returning to work. On June 24, the National Guard and the state patrol were sent in to protect strikebreakers crossing the picket lines. The next day, fixed bayonets and tear gas helped break up demonstrations and intimidate strikers. Soon, production was back to 70 percent of normal. Similar displays of force at Longview and Everett and on Grays Harbor brought the strike to an end by late August.

This meant no end for the labor movement, however, because lumbermen had conceded the union's right to speak for its members. While Muir unsuccessfully demanded obedience to Carpenter leadership, most timber workers leaned toward the Committee for Industrial Organization, formed nationally in November 1935 by John L. Lewis and other champions of industry-wide unionization. During the next year, the anti-Carpenter forces formed their own organization and allied with timber workers in British Columbia. In July 1937, the new International Woodworkers of America became an affiliate of the CIO.

Responding with unprecedented vigor, the Carpenters set up the Oregon-Washington Council of Lumber and Sawmill Workers. Until the eve of Pearl Harbor, work in the region was disrupted by jurisdictional disputes having little to do with traditional worker-management issues. Employers who dealt with one union risked closure by the other. "The problem of what will satisfy the CIO and not put the A.F. of L.'s nose out of joint (and vice versa)," lamented Phil Weyerhaeuser, head of the family business, "is completely baffling."

Labor dissipated much of its energy in these jurisdictional struggles, and the International Woodworkers of America suffered from the radical image of its leadership. Nonetheless, the union movement triumphed in camps and mills. By 1940 the IWA claimed a hundred thousand members on both sides of the Canadian-American border, while the Carpenters carried thirty-five thousand on their rolls. Despite slumping markets, pay scales increased. The average hourly wage in Washington sawmills rose from fifty-seven cents in 1935 to seventy-three cents in 1938, and the logging camp rate reached eighty-four cents that year. Lumbermen could no longer arbitrarily slash wages in hard times. The new power of labor was a major New Deal achievement.

Another achievement all but boggled the minds of observers along the Columbia River. The 308 Report, plotting a series of dams to harness the stream for hydroelectricity and irrigation, had been prepared during the Hoover Administration. But Hoover, preoccupied with the Depression, had rejected its recommendations, arguing that the dams were too costly, there was no market for the power, and reclaimed land would further depress farm prices. The same sorry economic circumstances prevailed at the outset of the Roosevelt Administration, but a different vision prevailed.

Campaigning through the Pacific Northwest in September 1932, Franklin Roosevelt delivered a major address in Portland. Government projects along the St. Lawrence River, at Muscle Shoals on the Tennessee, and at Boulder Dam on the Colorado created "a national yardstick to prevent extortion against the public and to encourage the wider use of that servant of the people—electric power." By voting the Democrats in, he continued, the electorate would protect Washington and Oregon against the greed of the private power industry. "The next great hydroelectric development to be undertaken by the Federal Government," Roosevelt vowed, "must be that on the Columbia River." In redemption of this pledge, the 308 Report was resurrected to guide the New Deal's greatest contribution to the region.

Four months elapsed between the defeat of Hoover and the March 4 inauguration of Roosevelt. Over this winter of despair, Oregon's congressional delegation, led by the influential Senator Charles McNary, lobbied for the dam farthest downstream, now known as Bonneville. In addition to providing hydroelectricity and thousands of construction jobs, the project's navigation lock would reinvigorate the old river trade oriented toward Portland.

Oregon's campaign alarmed Eastern Washington advocates of the Columbia Basin project. If Bonneville was approved, they feared, worry over cost and lack of power markets would prevent federal action on Grand Coulee. Unsure of Roosevelt, Grand Coulee backers looked to Olympia where Clarence D. Martin and the Democrats assumed the reins of state government in January 1933. Among his first actions, the new governor appointed a Columbia Basin development commission and the legislature debated a bill for state construction of a dam at Grand Coulee. Reflecting the values of hard times, the measure's explicit purpose was to provide work for unemployed residents and business for in-state engineers and contractors. After passing the senate, the legislation failed in the house, supposedly due to private power lobbying.

Attention reverted to the national capital, where New Deal willingness to expend public funds brought unexpected approval of both Bonneville and Grand Coulee dams. Between 1933 and 1939, Washington ranked first in per capita federal spending among states with populations over a million. By the end of the decade, one-fourth of all government expenditures on water projects went to Washington. Dams were the key to the broad New Deal goals of relief, recovery, and reform. Tens of thousands of workers were employed, millions of dollars were pumped into the economy, and efficient utilization of natural resources was advanced. Roosevelt's campaign promise had been honored.

With little controversy, the Bonneville project was authorized in mid-1933 and assigned to the Army Corps of Engineers, the federal agency responsible for navigation improvements. Grand Coulee, on the other hand, was highly controversial. Clarence C. Dill, a Washington Democrat who had served in the United States Senate through most of the Republican twenties, campaigned in the first months of the New Deal for funding. "We simply must get this started," he informed Governor Martin, "while the President has the money and will help us." The question, though, was whether Roosevelt had the money and whether he could, whatever his personal inclination, aid the project.

Critics' assertions notwithstanding, Roosevelt was at heart a fiscal conservative, especially early in his presidency. And Secretary of the Interior Harold Ickes, who doubled as administrator of major public works projects, was even more devoted to careful calculation of cost and benefit. The administration's farm policy, moreover, sought to raise commodity prices by reducing agricultural surpluses. Concern was also voiced that Bonneville alone would produce more power than existing markets could absorb. Building Grand Coulee, with a projected hydroelectric capacity four times that of Bonneville, might be irresponsible if not criminal.

Conferences among interested parties resulted in significant alterations in the project. At Roosevelt's suggestion, it was decided to build a low dam at Grand Coulee, reducing both cost and power capacity; later on, this structure could serve as foundation for the originally planned high dam. The reclamation component was postponed, moreover, to avoid conflict with the New Deal's farm program. (Work on the Columbia Basin Project finally began in the mid-1940s.) With these changes, the first funds for Grand Coulee Dam were approved in the summer of 1933. In a bureaucratic balancing act, construction responsibility was given, over Army objection, to the Bureau of Reclamation.

Actual work began at Bonneville, four miles above the original Warrendale site, in June 1934. Laborers resided in the rugged new community of North Bonneville on the Washington shore. There, wrote a visitor, " a boom town typical of those which have spring up near construction camps" featured the customary saloons and grubby streets that turned to mud in winter and dust in summer. The construction design pivoted on a mid-channel island. A spillway 1,090 feet long and 175 feet high—in technical terms the dam was a "concrete gravity, ogee crest, gate-controlled structure"—stretched from the island to the northern bank. The 1,027-foot-long powerhouse, with space for ten generators, reached to the Oregon side of the river.

On his visit in the fall of 1937, President Roosevelt dedicated the completed dam structure. The first electricity was produced the next spring and by Pearl Harbor five generators were turning out enough energy to meet the needs of Portland. The single-lift navigation lock, the largest such device built up to that time, was opened in July 1938, and waterborne commerce on the Columbia increased fivefold within five years. But these impressive achievements paled alongside the work underway far upriver in northeastern Washington.

With construction of Grand Coulee Dam underway in October 1934, Bureau of Reclamation Director Elwood Mead pressed for a return to the original high dam concept. Postponement of the Columbia Basin Project and the lack of navigational facilities, he pointed out, meant that the cost of construction would have to be recouped through power sales. Unsubsidized high prices would place Grand Coulee at a competitive disadvantage with Bonneville. A high dam, though, would produce more hydroelectricity, thereby reducing prices. "From being a dubious enterprise," Mead argued, "it becomes an attractive one." The soundness of this argument was convincing and the plan was approved in 1935. With this decision, projected expenditures tripled to a figure of $181 million.

Grand Coulee Dam was, in Richard Neuberger's much-quoted description, "the biggest thing on earth." The final plan, for a dam 550 feet high and 4,173 feet long, required fifteen million cubic yards of earth and rock for construction. Planned power capacity was five times that of Bonneville and greater than the combined total for all Tennessee Valley Authority dams. The free-flowing Columbia would be transformed into a vast reservoir lake for 150 miles east and north to the Canadian border. Each pump lifting the river's flow into the coulee for storage was sufficient to handle the water needs of a city the size of New York.

Work on the original low dam foundation was completed in early 1938, at which time a new contract permitted immediate work to begin on the complete high structure. The spillway was finished in May 1939 and attention then turned to powerhouse construction. Generation of hydroelectricity began in the third week of March 1941. Considering that the newly formed lake flooded a famous Indian fishing site at Kettle Falls, it was ironic that the first energy produced went to a Colville tribal cooperative. And the time, eight months before Pearl Harbor, would have great importance for the history of Washington.

Chemical plants and pulp mills, expected to become the prime customers for the dam's power, were not likely to locate in such remote areas, so the government carefully planned to transmit and market the power. Because neither the Corps of Engineers nor the Bureau of

Reclamation would tolerate having its rival assume those responsibilities, Congress created the Bonneville Power Administration in 1937. By the early 1940s, the BPA completed a network of transmission lines linking the dams with Puget Sound and the Willamette Valley. Existing public and private utilities were patched into its grid and the agency became a permanent and potent influence on the region.

Amid the celebration over Grand Coulee and Bonneville, two potential problems haunted careful observers. The dams tripled the amount of hydroelectric power available for Northwest consumption. But unless a market could be found for this output, worried Richard Neuberger, "the rest of the energy in the continent's greatest treasure-trove of hydroelectricity will not be developed during the lifetime of any man now living." Although engineers drafted plans for new dams upstream from Bonneville to Lewiston on the Snake, a generation was expected to pass before additional construction was required. In the immediate future, there was a fear that the New Deal's great engineering triumphs would become embarrassing white elephants.

Planning for the Columbia River, moreover, all but ignored a major factor in regional life. Millions of salmon returned each year to make the long swim up the Columbia to their spawning grounds. Historically, Indians from ocean mouth to remote headwaters depended upon these ceaseless runs for physical and cultural sustenance; in more recent times, extensive non-Indian commercial and recreational fishing flourished on the river and its tributaries. Sixty years of thoughtless exploitation, pollution, and early dam building had reduced the annual catch by 50 percent.

All fishing interests reacted with alarm to authorization of Bonneville and Grand Coulee dams in 1933. At Bonneville, the Army planned a rudimentary fish ladder but then, under pressure, cooperated with fisheries scientists to build an elaborate apparatus; nevertheless, salmon migrating upstream there suffered a 15 percent mortality rate. Grand Coulee's height was too great for such engineering, and salmon became extinct above the dam. In an attempt to make up for the loss, the Department of the Interior transplanted runs to such downriver tributaries of the Columbia as the Okanogan, Methow, Entiat, and Wenatchee rivers. Still, these results proved to all thinking persons that salmon and dams were incompatible. A paradox emerged: the power projects epitomized the conservationist vision for efficient use of natural resources, while at the same time spurring the development of a new conservationist ethos, this one demanding preservation of those resources.

Just as Grand Coulee and Bonneville dams were permanent New Deal engineering monuments, the Olympic National Park was an enduring legacy of New Deal environmentalism. The tangle of mountain peaks, high alpine meadows, and dripping rain forest valleys on the Olympic Peninsula had undergone several administrative reorganizations since the 1890s. President Grover Cleveland originally created a 1.5-million-acre forest reserve. In early 1909, Theodore Roosevelt set aside 615,000 of these acres as Mount Olympus National Monument. To free up timber for the world war, Woodrow Wilson returned half this acreage to the Olympic National Forest. In the 1930s, preservationists sought to combine what was left of the monument with extensive national forest lands to create a new national park.

Invariably, America's national parks were created out of so-called "worthless land," unsuited by remoteness and rugged topography to economic development. For instance, Mount Rainier National Park, opened in 1899, was enthusiastically endorsed by Washington lumbermen as there was no way to commercially exploit timber within its bounds. In the Olympics, however, one specific timber species was neither valueless nor distant from milling centers. Vast stands of hemlock, the raw material used for pulp and paper manufacture, spread across the western reaches of the Olympic National Forest to the ocean. Long-range Forest Service plans called for logging these stands to support manufacturing on the peninsula.

Environmentalists assumed that Washington's lumber industry opposed creating the national park, but the actual struggle was over the boundaries of the preserve. No responsible person or organization objected to a park that took in the existing monument and other isolated areas, but pulp and paper interests contended that including the hemlock stand would wreck the peninsula's economy. That, contended one timber owner, "would sound the death knell to any possible increase in the pulp industry." Port Angeles and Grays Harbor manufacturers, backed by the Forest Service, were the principal opponents of a large park.

Battle was joined in March 1935, when Washington Representative Monrad C. Wallgren introduced legislation to include four hundred thousand National Forest acres in a Mount Olympus National Park. Pulp-mill owners, state government officials, and foresters from the

University of Washington charged that park proponents wanted to sacrifice the jobs and fortunes of peninsula residents in order to provide scenic attractions for affluent and sissified tourists. The main support for the bill, indeed, came from the Emergency Conservation Committee, a creation of eastern environmentalists who distrusted Roosevelt, regarded National Park Service officials as mediocrities, and doubted that Washingtonians had the commitment or know-how to win the park.

Congressman Wallgren, hoping for a compromise, submitted a revised bill in February 1937 for a 648,000-acre park excluding the lush Hoh, Bogachiel, and Queets valleys, as well as other pulpwood areas. Neither the pulp industry nor large park advocates were satisfied with the effort. Wallgren had made, according to journalist Irving Brant of the Emergency Conservation Committee, "a shocking retreat" and "a capitulation" to the lumbering interests. Both sides expected the President, who planned to tour the Olympic Peninsula during his fall 1937 visit to the Northwest, to resolve the dispute. The Forest Service, in charge of the presidential itinerary, attempted to bar its critics from joining the tour, and removed national forest signs from offensive logged-over tracts. Park supporters gleefully informed their White House contacts of these clumsy manipulations.

In fog and rain, Roosevelt spent September 30 and October 1 on the peninsula, traveling by car from Port Angeles via Lake Crescent to Aberdeen and Hoquiam. Passing through the heavily timbered Quinault Indian Reservation, just south of the national forest, he expressed horror at what he later termed "criminal devastation" by "lumber interests" logging on that reserve. Popular accounts of doubtful reliability had him exclaiming, "I hope the lumberman who is responsible for this is roasting in hell." The President concluded the tour with a personal declaration in favor of the large park.

After further negotiations in the national capital, a third Wallgren bill in March 1938 proposed an 898,000-acre national park. Opponents chose this moment to play their final and supposedly strongest card, sending Governor Clarence D. Martin on a mission to the White House. Meeting with Roosevelt in late April, Martin, "considered pretty much of a nitwit" by the Emergency Conservation Committee, secured an apparent compromise. The President agreed to initial creation of a small park, provided that he was also given authority to enlarge it upon "consultation" with the state. Celebration of the governor's accomplishment was brief, for it was soon noticed that "consultation" was a vague term offering less than foolproof protection for pulp and paper.

The final Wallgren bill, creating what was renamed Olympic National Park, passed Congress in the late spring of 1936 and was signed into law on June 16. A 648,000-acre park was established, with the President authorized to expand its bounds to a total of 898,000 acres. (A clerical error would have allowed an *additional* 898,000 acres!) A year and a half of bitter investigations and hearings over inclusion of the disputed hemlock tracts followed. "After all," noted one environmentalist, "the whole fight was really over timber in the west, and to lose that is to accept defeat." These airings of antagonistic opinions constituted the promised "consultation."

In January 1940 President Roosevelt added 187,000 acres to Olympic National Park, including the Hoh and Bogachiel river valleys. The addition, he assured Governor Martin, "would not harm the established pulp industries of the peninsula." It would, however, prevent expansion of those industries. Angry manufacturers, deprived of a future source of raw material, shelved plans for new mills. It was a moment of great symbolic importance in Washington history. For nearly a century the needs of the forest products industry had been paramount. Now, with the creation of a large wilderness preserve on the Olympic Peninsula, preservation of the environment achieved equivalent importance.

To paraphrase Jim Farley, there were by 1940 forty-seven states and a *new* Washington. Organized labor was fastened upon the lumber industry and advanced in other sectors of the economy. Grand Coulee and Bonneville dams harnessed for the first time the mighty current of the Columbia River and began the process of changing that stream into a series of unnatural lakes. And Olympic National Park, vitiating the old "worthless lands" criteria, was formed out of the wondrous core of the peninsula west of Puget Sound. But the New Deal failed in its central aim of restoring economic prosperity nationally and in the state.

Despite the many public works jobs, from Grand Coulee to construction of local post offices, male employment in Washington actually decreased between 1930 and 1940; more men had worked under Hoover than under Roosevelt. There was, on the other hand, a slight increase in female employment, quite likely because employers in those times of casual pay discrimination found women cheaper to hire than men. Per capita income for the state fell from $749 to

$655 during the decade. Things would have been worse without the programs of the Roosevelt Administration, but the New Deal did not bring recovery. That would come in on the aftermath of Japanese bombers descending in sudden fury out of Hawaiian skies.

～ 8 ～

Homefront Washington

The news came over the radio just after eight o'clock on the morning of August 6, 1945. Astounded listeners learned that an atomic bomb, America's shattering wonder weapon, had obliterated Hiroshima in the Japanese home islands. That afternoon, dozens of reporters reached the heavily guarded outskirts of the Army's secret installation near Richland in Eastern Washington. "All of the wire services, practically all of the local radio stations and the principal radio networks have been represented," the base commander, Colonel Franklin T. Matthias, noted in his top secret diary. A delegation of congressmen was traveling to the scene. For two and a half years, amid countless rumors out of the desert— most false and some dangerously close to the truth—journalists and members of Congress had been denied admittance. Although thousands of men and women had labored inside the mysterious Columbia River reservation, only a select few had known the purpose of their work.

Over the next several days, reporters and government dignitaries were escorted through the project. Broad details were given about the production of "material"—the euphemism required by security regulations—for shipment to "Y" in New Mexico. As visitors prepared broadcasts and reports, federal officials awaited the final result of their secretive effort. Finally, on August 14, after a second atomic attack had hit Nagasaki, President Harry Truman announced that Japan had surrendered to the United States and its allies. "The statement quickly spread over the job," wrote Colonel Matthias, "and resulted in rejoicing among all of us here who have been sweating it out at this project for these long months and years." Every employee "at the Hanford Engineer Works," he continued in this moment of self-congratulation, "feels that he or she has really done his part in ending this war." The world, the nation, and the State of Washington had stepped over a threshold into the uncertainties of the nuclear age.

Almost four years earlier, on the first Sunday in December 1941, Washingtonians scanning their thick morning newspapers found the usual mix of the important and the trivial. There was news of war, present and impending. President Roosevelt had dispatched a personal plea for peace to Emperor Hirohito of Japan. The immediate threat, however, did not seem to be directed at the United States; Japanese troop concentrations and convoy movements were clearly aimed at British and Dutch colonies on Asia's Pacific rim. In the Libyan desert, British forces were rolling up Axis armored columns, and on the Russian front a million German troops neared Moscow. But there were happier items as well. Texas A & M had just triumphed over Washington State College in the annual Evergreen Bowl thanks to suspect officiating. There were wedding announcements and the first holiday season features. Movie buffs could read previews of the new W. C. Fields comedy.

Those dallying over late morning coffee were suddenly roused by crisp radio bulletins—or by the exclamations of neighbors with radios on. Three thousand miles to the southwest, Japanese planes were bombing America's Pacific fleet in its bastion at Pearl Harbor. Days passed before details of the devastation were published, but it was instantly clear that the United States faced a treacherous foe.

Amateur and professional strategists alike perceived that nothing stood in the way of an enemy attack upon the poorly defended coast of Washington State. The Boeing plant made Seattle seem a target to follow the Hawaiian attack. Boarding a plane for the nation's capital, Representative Henry Jackson voiced "surprise . . . that a bombing assault was not made in this area at the same time as Pearl Harbor." That very night, three thousand volunteer airwardens stood on alert in and around Seattle. Civil defense was compromised, however, by the lack of air-raid warning sirens, and the four hundred members of a home defense regiment, guarding the streets against parachutists and saboteurs, were prohibited from carrying arms.

Tension rose the next night, amid rumors that a Japanese carrier force was off the Aleutian Islands and that an enemy air armada had been sighted west of California's Golden Gate. Representative

Warren G. Magnuson, an expert on naval matters, warned that submarines lay in wait to sink merchant ships between Puget Sound and Alaska. (Despite a hurried flight east, Magnuson arrived in Washington, D.C., too late to vote for the declaration of war the next day.) Governor Arthur Langlie's office announced that fifth columnists on the Olympic Peninsula had ignited "flaming arrows" to guide attacking pilots toward Seattle. The story made headlines, but the subsequent revelation that the beacons were merely slash burns set by loggers was buried on a back page.

Blackout regulations were imposed in urban areas on Puget Sound. Ironically, Boeing, the prime target, was exempted because it needed to continue around-the-clock production. From ten at night until daybreak, buildings and homes were darkened and vehicle headlights visored. (At first, these driving conditions caused an increase in auto accidents, and one hapless mugger tried to hold up a uniformed policeman.) In hope of confusing enemy pilots, radio stations as far east as Spokane and Boise were ordered off the air, except for Seattle's KIRO, which was designated to transmit official government announcements.

Fear-driven irrationality was abundant in the immediate days after Pearl Harbor. The first night of the blackout, an inebriated mob broke out the windows and looted Seattle businesses showing lights. The city council remained in stalwart twenty-four-hour session to prevent sabotage of Seattle government by the dreaded fifth column. A War Department official warned air wardens not to relax their vigil because "a typical totalitarian maneuver" was to wait several days before attacking at an unexpected moment. Women skywatchers, for some unspecified reason, were thought to be especially susceptible to the fatal relaxation.

Nerves calmed in time, as even the most paranoid realized that the Pacific Coast was not seriously threatened. Instead of laying waste to new targets, Japan's Pearl Harbor task force steamed toward home, its commanders ecstatic with their success but regretting their failure to catch American aircraft carriers in port. The prevailing mood among Americans was one of grim confidence. Even with the war effort concentrated on defeating Germany first, the United States would certainly triumph over a tiny island that depended for raw materials upon its distant and unreliable empire.

The conflict was, in a tangible sense, "the good war." Except for the bombing and occupation of small Aleutian Islands, incendiary attacks on Northwest forests, and isolated coastal shellings, the United States—alone among the major participants—never suffered direct attack. Home life was disrupted and families dispersed, work routines were broken, and many supposed essentials were in short supply. But loss of American lives in the theater of war, however devastating for the families touched, was modest compared to the fatalities suffered by the other combatants. And the war effort brought economic health.

For the Northwest, as for other parts of the country, triumph over the Great Depression came long before victory over Germany and Japan. Unheard-of levels of federal spending restored economic health. The $95.2 billion allocated in the 1945 fiscal year was ten times the last peacetime budget of the supposedly profligate New Deal. Between 1941 and 1946, the government expended $378 billion and the federal debt increased fivefold to $260 billion. These funds for the military and defense production effectively wiped out unemployment; virtually every able-bodied adult was at work.

What a Seattle newspaper described as "the narcotic effect of war contracts" was evident in Washington State. Personal income tripled between 1940 and 1948 and per capita income more than doubled, even with rapid population growth (from 1.7 million to 2.4 million) factored in. The impact was concentrated in urban areas. Six hundred thousand migrants took up residence in the cities and towns of Washington. Seattle grew from 368,000 to 530,000 between 1940 and 1944. A ferry ride away, Bremerton, home of the Puget Sound Navy Yard, grew out of control from 15,000 to 75,000.

Three factors combined to make Washington both a prime contributor to, and beneficiary of, the war effort. The federal government expended at least $40 billion on the Pacific coast, stoking regional economic fires. The Roosevelt Administration dispersed American industrial enterprise through construction of war plants in the coastal states. Finally, and most important, vast quantities of cheap hydroelectric power were available from Grand Coulee and Bonneville dams. "Low-cost power from the Columbia," noted the Northwest Planning Commission in mid-1943, was "having a revolutionary effect upon the industrial development of the region."

That revolution transformed industrial activity in Washington. In 1940, as in decades past, most wage earners toiled in woods and sawmills. Learned commentators portrayed the state as a backward raw material colony, dependent upon manufacture and export of lumber, pulp, and paper. Boeing's Seattle employee force of four thousand was impressive by contemporary airplane industry standards, but modest compared to lumbering. Throughout the Northwest, fewer than two thousand persons worked in shipyards. And until 1939 there was not a single aluminum plant north of California.

Aluminum became the great new industry of the wartime Pacific Northwest. Light, strong, and resistant to decay, the metal was ideal for use in airplanes. Monopolized by the Aluminum Corporation of America (ALCOA), prewar production was located close to bauxite mining areas in the southeastern United States. Aluminum plants were enormous consumers of energy, requiring seventeen thousand kilowatt-hours of electricity to turn out one ton of finished product. Defense bureaucrats planning to expand and disperse this strategic industrial enterprise naturally looked to the power-rich Northwest. Long-distance transport of bauxite, however inconvenient and expensive, was more than offset by the low cost of hydroelectricity.

National output of aluminum soared from 163,000 tons in 1939 to a record 920,000 tons in 1943. The basin of the Columbia River, where the government financed construction of five manufacturing plants, accounted for much of this increase. Giant mills were built at Spokane, Longview, and Tacoma. Federal financing was also a trust-busting wedge that forced ALCOA to surrender its monopoly and admit new producers like Reynolds and Kaiser to the industry. By the end of the war, between 37 percent and 45 percent of America's aluminum (depending upon the source consulted) came from Washington and Oregon.

Much of the aluminum turned out along the Columbia went to Seattle, where Boeing all but instantaneously became a major national business enterprise. Beneath ingenious camouflage netting that made its chief plant appear from above to be a quiet residential neighborhood, Boeing turned out thousands of airplanes. Additional plants were built nearby along the Duwamish River and at Renton south of Lake Washington. Boeing's B-17 Flying Fortress, the so-called "tank in the sky," was the main Allied weapon in the air offensive against Germany. The B-29 "superfortress," which was developed later in the war and was the most advanced bomber of its time, played a similar role in the assault on Japan. By 1944, fifty thousand people worked for the company on Puget Sound and sales exceeded $600 million, ten times the figure for all Seattle industry in 1939.

Modern warfare, as the events of the first world war had demonstrated, required that ships be built faster than enemy submarines and surface raiders could destroy them. Thus, the shipyards of the Pacific Northwest, in decay since the earlier conflict, enjoyed a highly profitable resurgence in the new war. Over a hundred thousand men and women toiled in dozens of yards around the Sound, from giants like Todd in Seattle to small family-operated concerns. Thirty-six thousand worked directly for the government at Bremerton. Henry J. Kaiser, who had garnered national fame for his work on Boulder, Bonneville, and Grand Coulee dams and the San Francisco Bay Bridge, opened a massive plant alongside the Columbia River at Vancouver. There, rapidly assembled merchant vessels known as Liberty ships poured forth in assembly-line fashion.

Between Pearl Harbor and V-J Day in August 1945, the industrial framework of Washington took its modern form. Lumbering, the pioneer mainstay, lost predominance to aluminum, airplanes, and ships. Employees of sawmills and logging camps declined from 46 percent of the work force in 1939 to 17 percent in 1944. In revealing contrast, shipyard employment increased from 1 percent to 32 percent. One in every seven industrial workers worked for Boeing in 1944. Planners expected a reversion to former conditions after the war, but continued international tension following the conflict made the alteration permanent.

For centuries, warfare had been conducted with discretion. Combat was performed by small armies, while noncombatants carried on their normal affairs with moderate inconvenience and occasional interruption. Industrialization, with modern transportation and communication, changed everything. Now entire domestic economies could be geared to organizing and supplying huge armies. War production and actual military service involved almost every citizen. The airplane and the submarine carried death and destruction far from the front lines. Civilians experienced social and economic dislocation.

Americans of Japanese ancestry were the victims of the grossest dislocation on the World War II homefront. Most of the nation's 125,000 Japanese Americans lived in California, but 14,000 resided in Washington State. Of these, 8,900 were native-born U.S. citizens. Three-fourths lived in the Seattle and Tacoma metropolitan areas, including the agricultural valleys of the Green and Puyallup rivers. Half the farmland in King County and a third in Pierce County was operated by Japanese truck farmers. (Seattle's Pike Place Market nearly shut down the day after Pearl Harbor because produce growers stayed home, fearing attack.)

Prejudice directed against immigrants from Japan had been a Pacific Coast commonplace since the late nineteenth century. Respectable middle-class whites employed Japanese even as they lampooned their manner and culture. White laborers complained about their willingness to work hard for low pay. Discrimination in California produced diplomatic embarrassment for the United States and led to the Gentlemen's Agreement of 1907, which barred importation of so-called "coolie" labor. The Immigration Act of 1924 appealed to nativism by denying naturalization to the Issei, immigrants born in Japan. Washington State joined in the bigotry during the 1920s by prohibiting alien ownership of land in a law explicitly directed against Japanese farmers.

Despite this benighted tradition, there was little hysteria immediately following Pearl Harbor. Newspapers from Puget Sound to the Inland Empire cautioned against holding the Nisei (first-generation Americans enjoying the full protection of citizenship) responsible for the actions of Tokyo's war lords. John Boettiger, the *Post-Intelligencer's* publisher and President Roosevelt's son-in-law, reminded readers that citizens of Japanese ancestry were "as loyal as any white Americans." The Seattle *Times* denounced the "premeditated, treacherous and murderous assault" on Pearl Harbor, but also applauded the "devotion" of Japanese Americans "to the land of their birth." East of the Cascades, the Spokane *Spokesman-Review* urged that "the shameful cruelties of ostracism" inflicted upon persons of foreign background in 1917 be avoided in the new conflict.

Although assaults against Japanese Americans were rare, there were unsettling signs. Within hours of the Pearl Harbor attack, the FBI, busily justifying years of peacetime surveillance, rounded up 156 suspected persons, of whom 122 were of Japanese descent. One was a retail clerk suspected of being both a "camera fiend" and a relative of Japan's ambassador to the United States. When the beheaded corpse of a Chinese educator was discovered in Seattle's International District, the *Times* immediately concluded that the murder was the work of enemy agents. And the *Spokesman-Review,* despite its laudable concern about "ostracism," recommended that Japanese who were ineligible for naturalization be "placed in concentration camps for the duration of the war."

Events on the battlefront eventually made the position of Japanese Americans untenable. Defeat followed upon defeat for America in the Pacific. Japan invaded and quickly captured the Philippines, and the Imperial Navy destroyed a fleet of Allied warships in the Java Sea, opening the invasion route to Australia. Prisoner-of-war listings, printed alongside accounts of Japanese atrocities, began to appear in local papers early in 1942, and some Americans' thoughts turned to revenge. Rumors of homefront spying and sabotage received full press coverage, and subsequent FBI arrests lent credence to the stories. Even previously moderate Americans began to suspect that the Japanese American community might harbor actively disloyal individuals.

As fear of Japanese attack along the Pacific coast increased, military leaders there confronted a difficult situation. Plans had to be devised and implemented for protection against attack and sabotage on a front extending from the Aleutians to San Diego. With regard to Japanese Americans, the Army could either allow the FBI to pursue the disloyal, or lump them all together as potential enemies. In this time of heightened emotions, the choice seemed clear. General John DeWitt of the Western Defense Command eloquently summed up the prevailing mood: "A Jap's a Jap."

On February 19, 1942, President Roosevelt signed Executive Order 9066, authorizing exclusion of suspect persons from war zones designated by the military. Although the document did not specify any ethnic group, the White House announced that it was aimed at the Japanese. A short, one-sided public debate ensued over the wisdom and legality of exclusion, and a congressional committee chaired by Representative John Tolan of California held hearings on the "evacuation of certain groups."

Political leaders pressed for action. Most of his constituents, asserted Governor Arthur B. Langlie, wanted Japanese Americans removed from Washington. "The people feel this is no time to worry about hurting feelings," he informed the Tolan committee. "Being nearest to possible attack, and having a large number of shipyards, airplane factories, machine shops, steel works and lumber mills, we have a grave responsibility." According to Seattle Mayor Earl Milliken, "the most disloyal" elements were actually found among native-born citizens. As for the alien Japanese, the mayor insisted, in a tortured argument bereft of evidence, that virtually all were trustworthy. Even so, a few dozen "could burn this city, let in the Jap airplanes and raise havoc that would dwarf Pearl Harbor."

Federal authorities had waited too long to take the only practicable action, observed Senator Mon Wallgren. "We can't consider ourselves safe from sabotage until the aliens and certain others the army thinks ought to get out are removed." Washington timbermen predicted an epidemic of forest arson fires if the Japanese were allowed to remain. Miller Freeman, prominent publisher and occasional public official, contended that fifth-column machinations permeated Japanese life in the United States. "Through fraud, deception and collusion," he contended, Japan had "accomplished the miraculous feat of permanently planting 300,000 of her people in this country, quadrupling the original number since the [Gentlemen's] agreement was entered into in 1907, limiting the Japanese influx."

Virtually everyone agreed that removal would benefit the Japanese. Without such steps, Washington Attorney General Smith Troy pointed out, the innocent and the guilty alike would be slaughtered by justly outraged white neighbors. Newspaper opinion mirrored these sentiments. The Seattle *Post-Intelligencer,* abandoning its earlier support for Nisei rights, applauded the "vigorous, yet sensible steps" taken by the Army; "waiting until evidence shows an individual directly connected with a disloyal undertaking. . . . might be too late for national safety," and "sensible Japanese" would cheerfully submit to removal as part of their patriotic contribution. On a bombastic note, the Seattle *Star* suggested that it was "preferable that they lose a few freedoms than for traitors among them to blast war plants, air fields or guide invading forces." The Tacoma *News-Tribune* viewed events of the day from a historic perspective, linking removal to the uprooting of the Acadians and Loyalists in colonial times. The Japanese "lot" emerged as "far easier" than the miseries endured in these "previous mass evacuations."

One widely voiced concern involved neither legality nor morality. How would urban residents feed themselves without produce raised by Japanese truck farmers? White growers in the Green River Valley eagerly volunteered to take over the abandoned land. The *Post-Intelligencer* launched a campaign to encourage the planting of backyard gardens. But food shortages, noted the *Times,* were preferable to the alternative. "There would be little to gain in leaving thousands of Jap farmers on these farms for the sake of a crop of vegetables" if, as a result, Boeing was attacked.

Finally, on March 2, General DeWitt, in the most notorious act of his career, ordered removal of all persons of Japanese descent from coastal areas, including Washington west of the Cascades. Evacuation of Japanese Americans from Western Washington began in late March when two hundred persons were removed from the vicinity of the Bremerton Navy Yard. These and others that followed were taken first to an Army assembly center at the fairground in Puyallup. Residents of that community were angered that their profitable state fair might have to be canceled. Eventually, detainees were dispersed to permanent camps in remote areas of California and Idaho until revocation of Executive Order 9066 in December 1944 allowed them to return, often to a hostile reception.

Public relations and patriotism dictated that even the most unsavory governmental actions be whitewashed, and a host of euphemisms were adopted to mask the ugliness of the action. Japanese were "evacuated" or "relocated" rather than forced from their homes and farms. The Puyallup assembly ground was officially named "Camp Harmony." Detention camps were "relocation centers" or even "Japanese colonies."

Most of the Japanese Americans bore their sufferings with dignity. Even before issuance of Executive Order 9066, they voluntarily surrendered cameras, radios, and weapons to federal authorities. Evacuees organized their own registration system so that relatives and friends could locate and keep track of one another in far-flung camps. A car pool was even set up in case the government failed to provide transportation to detention centers. Protest against exclusion took the form of legal challenges rather than overt resistance. In the principal suit, brought by University of Washington student Gordon Hirabayashi who was imprisoned for his failure to report, the Supreme Court upheld the legality of relocation; the Court's decision was reversed over four decades later.

While the war brought oppression to Japanese Americans, women and other minorities found unprecedented economic opportunity in the job markets traditionally filled by white males. "Rosie the Riveter" became a popular cultural symbol reflecting reality; women made up at least a third of the work force in the airplane factories and shipbuilding establishments of the Pacific coast and one-fifth of the work force at the Puget Sound Navy Yard. Although many of these women lost their jobs or chose to leave the work force when the soldiers came back, the position of women in the labor market was permanently enhanced. Between 1940 and 1950, female employment in Washington increased by two-thirds, compared to a 35 percent gain for men.

Burgeoning defense industries also enabled black Americans to make substantial progress. In 1940, prior to the wartime boom, fewer blacks than Japanese Americans lived in Seattle. Boeing had a whites-only hiring policy, which it managed to blame on the Jim Crow charter of the Aero-Mechanics Union. Housing discrimination confined blacks to the city's Central Area. Public facilities were legally color-blind, but among other informal injustices, minorities endured harrassment from drivers and white patrons on the municipal transit line.

During the war, increasing numbers of blacks moved into the region from the American South and from eastern cities. Labor needs and sporadic federal efforts to enforce nondiscrimination in defense contracts considerably changed conditions. Government pressure forced the Aero-Mechanics Union to abandon its racist stance, enabling blacks to make a modest inroad—3 percent of the work force—at Boeing. Discrimination, especially of the de facto variety, did not end, but blacks established, in terminology appropriate for the time, a beachhead from which to expand in the postwar era.

In hindsight, the advances made by women and blacks might seem minuscule. Viewed in context, however, such is not the case. In 1940, thinking Americans realistically anticipated American entrance into the war, but few would have predicted the social consequences of this step. The imprisonment without cause of thousands of citizens, the taking over of traditionally male jobs by women and of whites-only positions by blacks would have been all but unthinkable. The most fantastic consequence of all was the birth of what journalist John Gunther described as the "apocalyptic, demonic child of the Columbia," the atomic bomb.

Of the many self-defeating acts of Nazism, perhaps the ultimate was the expulsion of scientific talent from the European continent. During the 1920s and 1930s, refugee pioneers of nuclear physics such as Albert Einstein, Enrico Fermi, and Leo Szilard uncovered the secrets of the atom. With money and time, they theorized, enormous energy could be released by a nuclear chain reaction—for either military or peaceful purposes. In September 1939, just after the outbreak of war in Europe, a letter signed by Einstein was delivered to President Roosevelt. The letter stated that there was nothing to prevent Hitler from becoming the first to wield atomic weapons.

In response to this ominous prospect, the federal government initiated a top-secret research effort. Scientists at Columbia, Chicago, and other universities received funding for research into the atom. By 1942, it was concluded that plutonium, a manufactured element derived from enriched uranium, was a key to production of an atomic bomb. That December, Enrico Fermi created the world's first controlled chain reaction, in a pile (later called a reactor) beneath the University of Chicago football stadium.

Earlier in 1942, the Roosevelt administration had decided to proceed full speed on building an atomic bomb. Responsibility was assigned to the specially created Manhattan Engineer District of the U.S. Army Corps of Engineers, with General Leslie R. Groves, a former University of Washington student who had just overseen construction of the Pentagon, in command. A decision was quickly made to establish facilities at three locations. The main laboratory and testing grounds were located in the high desert near Los Alamos, New Mexico, and a giant uranium separation complex at Oak Ridge, Tennessee. The third plant, located in the Eastern Washington wastelands, would manufacture plutonium.

The area had obvious advantages. Its isolation would ensure both security and public safety; General Groves had ruled out Oak Ridge for the plutonium facility because an accident there would expose nearby Knoxville to radiation, but here only few settlers ran irrigated orchards and peppermint ranches, and the population center, a half-abandoned ferry station called Hanford, had only a hundred residents. Reactors required large quantities of fresh water for cooling, and a vast, dependable supply of electricity was essential; as if made to order, the recently completed Grand Coulee Dam stood ready to provide the power, and the Columbia River itself flowed past the site selected.

In January 1943, the government and its chief contractor, the DuPont Company, acquired an eight-hundred-square-mile tract west of the Columbia and north of the mouth of the Yakima River. The small local population was hurriedly bought out and removed. The half-dozen installations were constructed some distance apart, to minimize the impact of possible accidents. Three water-cooled graphite reactors transmuted plutonium from uranium slugs loaded into aluminum tubes. Miles away, three chemical separation plants, known as "Queen Mary's" because each was nearly as long as the famed passenger liner, handled final processing. There, workers carried out the complicated process separating plutonium from uranium, using remote control devices to avoid exposure to radiation.

The highly technical procedures were fully understood only by a handful of persons, but construction problems were those common to all large engineering projects. To overcome labor shortages, Hanford was given the highest priority. Nevertheless, the War Manpower Commission, antagonized by the Army's refusal to provide details about the Manhattan Project, refused to expedite assignment of workers. Many laborers detested the isolation and absence of diversions, and decamped whenever they could for urban defense plants.

Because of the Army's policy of racial discrimination, time and money were poured into erecting segregated housing facilities for blacks and whites. Since males and females were housed apart, four separate developments were required. Despite a near emergency shortfall in available workers by early 1944, threatening the entire bomb program, the Manhattan District declined to bring Hispanic laborers from the Southwest. Funds, it seemed, were not available for two more Jim Crow camps.

Given the nature of the project and the likelihood that the Axis powers were also working on an atomic bomb, strict security measures were essential. Thousands of men and women and countless trainloads of equipment could not disappear into the wastes of Eastern Washington without arousing notice. Rumor, hearsay, and occasional fact appeared for a time in regional newspapers. After meeting with Hanford commandant Colonel Franklin Matthias, publishers agreed to voluntary censorship for the duration of the war. More persistent were the efforts of congressmen—especially the special investigative committee chaired by Missouri Senator Harry Truman—to find out what was happening on the Columbia. Despite hurt feelings and bruised political egos, such inquiries were firmly rebuffed. General Groves even labelled Warren Magnuson a security risk for mentioning Hanford in a 1945 speech.

With little knowledge of the effects of radiation, a contract was entered into with the University of Washington to investigate "the Use of X-rays in the Treatment of Fungoid-Infections in Salmonid Fishes." Fisheries researchers were told that their purpose was to find a cure for jungle rot and other maladies suffered by soldiers in the South Pacific. The real concerns were more sinister. What would happen, the Manhattan District hoped to discover, to Columbia River salmon exposed to heated and radiated water released from the reactors? What would happen to human beings exposed to radiation from an atomic explosion?

The projects at Hanford, Los Alamos, and Oak Ridge were as expensive and complex as a top secret re-creation of the American automobile industry. Twenty-five million cubic yards of earth were moved and eight thousand pieces of construction equipment employed at Hanford alone. Two hundred and twenty-one carloads of stainless steel, 748,000 cubic yards of concrete, and 160 million feet of lumber were used. The largest bus system in Washington carried workers between housing and construction sites. In the process, the town was simply removed to make way for what subsequently became the Hanford Site Richland Operations of the Office of the Secretary of the Department of Energy. In mid-1944, Hanford was the fifth largest town in the state, with a population of 41,269; by February 1945, it had all but vanished as a result of the completion of the plant and the evacuation of all but technical and security personnel.

The first Hanford reactor began operation on September 26, 1944, with Enrico Fermi present. Plutonium production commenced by the end of the year. Early in 1945, Colonel Matthias personally carried the first flask of plutonium to California for handing over to a delegation from Los Alamos; although less than 100 grams, this was virtually the world's entire supply. Heavily guarded ambulance convoys transported the material over interior highways to the Southwest. On July 16, 1945, a mysterious flash of light was seen over the New Mexico desert. The Army announced that an ammunition dump had exploded, but insiders at Hanford realized that a bomb had been tested successfully.

Three weeks later, on August 6, the awful secret was revealed at Hiroshima. Washington newspapers stressed the local connection in breathless reports. Headlines announced: "Hanford's Mystery Cleared!" and "Ingredients for Missile Made in State"—though in fact plutonium from Eastern Washington was used only in the second bomb, dropped on Japan several days later. Other headlines showed a common misunderstanding: "Hanford-Made Atomic Bomb Unleashed on Japan," and "Atomic Bomb, Made at Hanford, Product of Costly Gamble."

Over the next several days, firsthand accounts from correspondents touring Hanford appeared alongside descriptions of the bomb's dreadful impact. Unhappy reporters were not allowed even a glance at the reactors or the separation plants, so their stories were either innocuous or inaccurate. The *Post-Intelligencer* ran a gushing portrait of Mrs. Matthias, the "first lady of Hanford," depicting her "gay mood as she describes the unveiling of the atomic bomb mystery."

After a second bomb was dropped on Nagasaki, several days of suspense and speculation passed before Japan announced a cease-fire on August 14. Revellers danced and whooped through the streets of downtown Seattle. Students at the University of Washington, some in formal attire and some in pajamas, climbed lampposts and cavorted across campus. The Bon Marche department store captured the public mood with a full-page newspaper advertisement carrying the single word, "Hallelujah!"

A cartoon in the *Post-Intelligencer* showed a scowling Uncle Sam raining down thunderbolts labeled "atomic bomb attack" against a cowering and defenseless Japan. In Spokane, the *Spokesman-Review* cartoonist portrayed a bucktoothed and bespectacled Japanese militarist being knocked senseless by a giant fist inscribed "Utter Destruction." The Seattle *Times* ran a witticism of comedienne Gracie Allen on its front page: "There is a rumor that Japanese generals refer to it as the Atom's Apple. Guess this is because they get a lump in the throat every time they think about it."

Amid the general euphoria, some public debate focused on the bomb. Among the few prominent Washingtonians to speak wholeheartedly in its defense was Rabbi Raphael Levine of Seattle's Temple de Hirsch. Militarily, he pointed out, the atomic bomb was "no different in principle than a large force of B-29s." Moreover, the weapon would actually "save, rather than destroy, lives" by ending the war without an invasion of Japan. The rabbi's points were valid, in that incendiary raids upon Japan's wooden cities killed more people than died at Hiroshima and Nagasaki.

One editorial line reasoned that Japan's fanaticism had made use of the bomb necessary. "The Japanese nation, having chosen to live by the sword," the *Post-Intelligencer* pointed out just after Hiroshima, "is being visited by the implacable penalty of such a course— and will eventually and inexorably die by the same means, if it persists in its fanatical and suicidal resistance." The *Times* contrasted the irrationality of Japan's leaders with Hitler's inner circle. They, at least, "knew when time had come to quit. The war lords of Tokyo have been carrying on long past the reasonable quitting time. They have literally asked for more and heavier blows." But the editorials also recognized that "the new atomic bomb is a frightening and fearful thing to contemplate," and expressed "regret that such a weapon must be used." And they were pessimistic about the implications of the new weapon. One of the nation's stated war objectives, a world free of war, was shattered in the moment of victory: "This terrific force makes man's place on the planet more insecure than ever." Scientists had "let the mighty genie out of the bottle"; now the diplomats had to somehow control the uncontrollable. In winning the war, many feared, the United States might have lost the world.

The control and use of this awesome new weapon was grist for decades of national and international discussion. Such issues had an immediacy in Eastern Washington. All hoped that peaceful applications would determine the future of Hanford. "Material would be useful for civilian purposes as it is for military," Colonel Matthias pointed out in his first post-Hiroshima interview. Regional newspapers speculated that Hanford might become an atomic-powered industrial complex specializing in production of fertilizer, plastics, and synthetic fabrics, or atomic airplanes and trains that would "streak to New York with less than a scoopful of fuel in the tender." Such ideas smacked of science fiction, yet only a few days earlier, the atomic bomb itself seemed even more fantastic.

But Matthias warned that practicable civil applications "will probably take a long time to figure out." The Manhattan Project had succeeded only because the government kept "the best scientists in the world at work for two and a half years figuring out the use of this energy for just one purpose." The colonel's personal pride was in contributing to the secret weapon that had ended the war. The accomplishment at Hanford, whether considered evil or benign, was the most significant undertaking ever to occur within Washington State.

In historical perspective, the New Deal's key contribution to Washington history was the building at Grand Coulee and Bonneville of an energy-producing infrastructure. Without that, neither the aluminum plants nor Hanford would have been viable and Boeing's growth would have been restricted. With these two dams on line, World War II became the epochal event of the state's twentieth-century history. Supplanting the traditional economy oriented toward lumber, wheat, and little else, a modern high-technology machine for metals, aircraft, and atomic energy was built up east and west of the

Cascades. And the relationship between these activities and national defense gave the state strategic national importance. The Washington of 1945 was closer to the Washington of today than it was to the Washington of 1940.

~ 9 ~

Postwar Washington

$\mathbf{F}$or Washington State's economy, World War II ended and the postwar era began not at Hiroshima or Nagasaki or aboard the battleship *Missouri,* but in the board room at the Boeing Company. The date was September 5, 1945. War had elevated Boeing from a significant employer in the Puget Sound area to the state's's major manufacturer. Earlier years of struggle had been overcome with the help of government contracts, but the wartime success of the B-17 and B-29, the Flying Fortress and the Super Fortress that became legendary over European and Japanese skies, dramatized the rise of this company. Boeing's success illustrated the importance of federal moneys to the Northwest economy.

But the war was over and preliminary efforts to convert warplanes to commercial use proved unsuccessful. The sudden death of Boeing President Philip Johnson, who had guided the company during the war years, prompted this meeting at which William Allen was selected as the new company president. Unlike his predecessors, Allen had little engineering background; he was a methodical Seattle attorney. The meeting held yet another moment of import: as it was closing, word arrived that the government was drastically cutting B-29 contracts.

Allen was forced to make major adjustments almost immediately. The work force, recently over forty thousand, was sliced to eleven thousand and sales in the first peacetime year fell to $14 million. The company was rescued when renewed international conflict—the Cold War in general and the Korean conflict in particular—created new demand. The B-47 and the B-52 were developed and commentators observed that Seattle's economic health depended largely on war production. On the other hand, the war-born aluminum industry, using abundant inexpensive electric power and imported raw bauxite, grew rapidly and by 1950 provided about half of the aluminum produced in the United States; during the next decade a decline would set in.

Indeed, Boeing's own success proved a mixed blessing. Seattle, and to a large extent the state, became dependent upon the success of this single company. The slightest loss had serious repercussions for the region and its people. Thus when the commercial market was temporarily saturated and the company's supersonic transport contract was cancelled in 1971, the area experienced a recession. But Boeing learned to recoup, experimenting with such innovations as hydrofoils and people movers. Seattle and environs sought new economic activities that were not directly linked to the aerospace industry. Such efforts at diversification marked yet another phase of the economic maturity of Washington.

The war also altered irrevocably a remote spot in Eastern Washington. To the world, the dropping of atomic bombs over Japan ushered in the nuclear age, but for the desert area surrounding the final hairpin bend of the Columbia, it foreshadowed a new urban environment. Under the Manhattan Project, a construction camp reminiscent of the Wild West, with gambling, drinking, and brawling, was hastily thrown together. Meanwhile, twenty-five miles south of Hanford, a permanent town was replacing the dusty farming village Nelson Rich had begun half a century earlier with irrigation waters from the Yakima River. At Richland work crews demolished older houses and buildings and laid out four thousand prefabricated clapboard houses in several models and furnished with government issue furniture. Fast-growing trees and lawns planted along new streets gave the appearance of a settled community. Rapid growth meant scarce supplies and services, and there were long lines for almost everything. Newcomers reached out to one another to develop instant friendships. Many who could not bear the isolation and hardships soon left, but those who stayed developed an uncommon sense of commitment and unity.

The construction frenzy ended with the war, and the area's population dropped from a one-time high of fifty thousand to a mere fifteen thousand. Despite speculation that the Hanford works might close, fear of a confrontation with the Soviets and new weapons technology combined with the search for peacetime uses of atomic energy to ensure its survival. The Atomic Energy Commission replaced the Army Corps of Engineers as the supervising government agency and DuPont turned its operations over to General Electric. After plans were announced for new reactors and related facilities at Hanford, two thousand additional homes and a large trailer park were added at Richland. By 1950 the city had twenty two thousand residents and anticipated steady long-term growth.

Yet Richland remained an unusual company town dependent upon a unique industry. For fifteen years it was owned by the federal government, with people occupying homes that did not actually belong to them. Changes were supposed to be approved by bureaucrats, but many people ignored this and enclosed garages, excavated basements, built additions, and added decorative touches. Manicured lawns and gardens gave Richland a pleasant appearance of stability. Many early residents who had planned to leave after the war stayed on and made Richland home. Bridge and golf clubs, service organizations, and churches proliferated. Mothers rarely worked outside the home, contributing to the image of a secure community that cherished family life. The populace was white, middle class, highly paid, and well educated—Richland allegedly had the highest percentage of Ph.D.s of any American city—with few divisions save that line eternally separating workers and managers.

Such outward appearances could not alter the truth that Richland remained a company town under federal and GE control. Only Hanford employees and their families lived there. Neither self-government nor privately owned homes were allowed. Change came slowly. In 1955, ten years after the war ended, Congress finally permitted residents to purchase land and buildings. Within three years most property was privately owned and Richland incorporated as a full-fledged town free to run its own affairs. *Look* magazine and the National Municipal League selected Richland as an All-American city in 1961. New firms arrived during the 1960s, including subsidiaries of Douglas Aircraft and ITT, and a Battelle Institute "think tank." And there were local entrepreneurs, many of them former Hanford employees.

But Richland remained the "Atomic City," and its major industry permeated civic life. The local high school, a state leader scholastically and athletically, adopted "Bombers" as its nickname and the mushroom cloud as its emblem. A major hydroplane race held each year on the Columbia River was dubbed the Atomic Cup, and an ecumenical congregation beckoned, "Where the atom is split, the church unites." In 1971, Richland sent one of its own, nuclear physicist Mike McCormack, to Congress.

When outside public opinion began to question the safety and advisability of nuclear power, Richland maintained pride in its industry. The Tri-Cities area—Richland, Kennewick, and Pasco—welcomed construction of three Washington Public Power Supply System plants in the 1970s. Local residents were pleased when Hanford was selected as a possible site for a major nuclear waste facility, even though most state leaders fought the proposal. As voters statewide opposed the site selection in a 1986 referendum, strong support came from Richland and its environs. Its elimination from consideration as a major repository the next year alarmed residents and state officials concerned for the area's economic future.

Neighboring Pasco and Kennewick were affected differently by these events. Pasco, an early railroad center, remained a town of blue-collar workers, including black and Chicano newcomers, while Kennewick retained a strong sense of its agricultural past. Yet both grew to complete the urban atmosphere of the tri-cities area. By the 1970s, Kennewick had become a stable middle-class community attracting young workers from the WPPSS plant, complete with shopping malls characteristic of contemporary urban growth. Indeed, while Richland's population hovered in the middle thirty thousands and even declined, Kennewick's slowly rose to surpass the more glamorous "Atomic City."

Meanwhile, older cities were bulging. The development of suburbs following World War II is customarily viewed as a flight from cities grown old and overwhelmed with unsolvable problems. In the Pacific Northwest, where cities were comparatively young and still offered many attractions, there was another motivation: the American dream of a private home with two-car garage, backyard, barbecue pit, and basketball hoop—a nice place to raise a family, close to work but away from the heart of the city. Suburban growth was not a new phenomenon; American cities had always expanded and persons who could afford it frequently followed streetcar lines and highways to the outskirts. The suburban craze of modern times, though, was telescoped into a few frantic years.

War on the heels of depression had left a vacuum in many aspects of daily life, a vacuum people were anxious to fill. Wartime deprivation and separation ended as veterans returned home to start new families and careers. The GI Bill helped many veterans obtain schooling and loans to purchase homes. Little new housing was available in central cities, while construction of new highways and the availability of automobiles after wartime curtailment accelerated the movement to the outlying areas. The trend began slowly and then grew as prosperity and economic opportunity increased during the 1950s. Around Spokane people moved west into the valley and east toward the Idaho border. The move across the Columbia River from Portland enveloped Vancouver and its rural environs. Tacoma spread south into the Lakes area and also drew established towns such as Fife, Puyallup, and Sumner into its net. That city's suburbs inched north, meeting those of Seattle moving south, and Federal Way became a sprawling bridge connecting Puget Sound's two major cities.

By the 1960s, the term "Pugetopolis" was describing the populated area that stretched along the east side of Puget Sound from Bellingham, or at least from Marysville, to Tumwater south of Olympia, and occasionally reaching across the Sound. It was a gigantic metropolis made up of many cities and populated areas. The well-established towns of Marysville, Edmonds, Burien, and Des Moines mushroomed while such new places as Lynnwood, Shoreline, and Highline emerged. One community preplanned in its entirety was Mountlake Terrace in southern Snohomish County, where street after street of cinder-block houses attracted low-income families. The opening of Northgate Shopping Center in Seattle's north end in 1950, heralded as the nation's first modern suburban mall, foreshadowed a coming trend. Construction of the Interstate Five freeway, reducing Highway 99 to a business street interrupted by countless stop lights, both confirmed and contributed to growth in progress.

Nowhere was suburban growth more dramatic than around Lake Washington. Old highways around the lake became enclosed by housing developments, restaurants, gas stations, and burgeoning neighborhood shopping complexes. Older communities like Lake Forest Park, Bothell, Kirkland, Redmond, Bellevue, Mercer Island, and Renton grew and were absorbed into the metropolis. Kirkland and Renton were affected, respectively, by a wartime shipyard and a Boeing plant. Another catalyst for growth was the four-lane floating bridge that stretched across Lake Washington, built just before the war began. It affected the entire east side, but mainly Bellevue, which expanded in a few years from a bucolic lakeside community to a sophisticated suburb and the fourth largest city in Washington.

Bellevue's history began in 1869 when William Meydenbauer, a prosperous Seattle baker, acquired property on the eastern shore of Lake Washington. On weekends he rowed two miles across the lake to work on his holding amid the natural beauty and a quiet atmosphere. In time other Seattleites and a few eastern investors acquired acreage nearby. Around Meydenbauer Bay, the community of Bellevue slowly emerged as lots were cleared and homes built.

By the late 1930s, Bellevue was a pleasant little town set among hills, truck farms, and berry patches. Along the two blocks called Main Street, a handful of merchants operated shops. A small whaling fleet wintered in the bay. Wealthy Seattle families built stately lakefront homes with extensive gardens. Some residents spent almost an hour each way crossing the lake to Seattle aboard ferries or small passenger launches and then took streetcars to downtown Seattle. The drive by automobile around either end of the lake took more than an hour. It was a peaceful life, highlighted by the annual strawberry festival which attracted several thousand visitors.

Some East Side residents talked of replacing the ferries with a bridge, but a conventional structure was impractical on such a deep lake. Visionary engineers and state highway director Lacey V. Murrow developed a plan for a bridge made of hollow concrete pontoons, lined up and floating on the water. Although skeptics were many, support grew. For one, Governor Clarence D. Martin, a Cheney flour-mill owner, recognized the advantages to Eastern Washington of a more direct highway route into Seattle. Enthusiastic support came from Bellevue, where townspeople helped put out a special bridge edition of the weekly *Bellevue American,* aimed at influential politicians and civic leaders. Ultimately, bridge champions secured sufficient legislative support and construction was approved. In the summer of 1940, the first major floating bridge in America connected Seattle with Mercer Island, which was already linked to the eastern shore by a more conventional bridge.

World War II delayed the East Side boom, but by 1950 it was well underway. New neighborhoods grew up around Bellevue, many on hillsides with views of Lake Washington and the Olympics. Typically, new residents were young adults starting families and professional careers. A strong sense of community spirit focused on social and service clubs and a consolidated school system. The new Bellevue was not an inexpensive place to live. Its aspirations were reflected in golf courses, a yacht club, a community theater, and an annual arts and crafts fair that was destined to serve as a model for others. Incorporated as a city in 1953, with a population approaching six thousand, it was one of the fastest-growing places in the state. By the 1980s it had over eighty thousand residents—it was now a complex urban center with its own cluster of suburbs. The East Side life style was characterized by acres of split-level homes, sleek condominiums, and high-rise office buildings along slopes where berries had grown a generation earlier.

But the suburban life style brought its own problems. With rapid growth arose contentious issues of zoning, utilities construction, water quality, and education. Critics declared the suburban "good life" to be illusory. People sacrificed human ties and the sense of community found in older urban neighborhoods, they said, for a plastic and artificial life style obsessed with competition for material possessions. Parents burdened their children with goals and expectations, while lavishing upon them unearned and unappreciated gifts that confused their sense of values. Suburban consciousness was limited, it was said, to the most immediate personal environment. A professor observing postwar Seattle, assigned his college freshmen "to write about their surroundings, working out from their homes and stopping as soon as the landscape became unfamiliar. Well over half were from north-end [Seattle] high schools, and almost all had no place they could clearly name as familiar between their homes and the mountains. No sense of street or meeting place, no image of school worth remembering, no sense of Seattle as a city." Critics viewed suburbs as so safe, secure, and middle class they were inevitably dull and vapid. Clusters of similar ranch-style homes occupied ubiquitous cul-de-sacs, and undistinguished thoroughfares became lined with gas stations, fast-food outlets, and asphalt parking lots.

Moreover, the rise of suburbia meant the decline of the downtown areas of cities left behind. Seattle, Spokane, and Tacoma gained population during the late 1940s and the 1950s, but their rates of growth slowed as surrounding areas burgeoned dramatically. This was not so much a drain from the city as the failure of central cities to keep pace with suburban growth. As more stores, offices, theaters, and restaurants opened in the suburbs, it became less necessary for anyone to venture downtown.

Nor did downtown remain the workplace it had customarily been. Meticulously landscaped "business parks" sprang up in suburban settings. Warehouses and workplaces of new "clean" industries such as electronics soon followed. The trend was graphically demonstrated in the 1960s when the Weyerhaeuser Company forsook Tacoma to open its new multi-million-dollar headquarters complex alongside Interstate Five at Federal Way. South of Tacoma, middle-class residents of Lakewood told an interviewer how such changes affected them. "Numerous breadwinners," he noted, "bypass Tacoma each morning on their way to Boeing, while another sizeable group works either at Fort Lewis, just southwest of Lakewood, or at McChord Air Force Base, located to the southeast. For housewives in Lakewood as well, little reason exists to visit downtown Tacoma; on a regular shopping day, they can more easily do business at the huge new Tacoma Mall or, as in the past, at Villa Plaza or Lakewood Center."

Urban centers were also plagued by transportation and parking problems. Buildings decayed and facilities deteriorated. Those best able to afford civic amenities tended to move to the suburbs, where their taxes financed new schools, sewer systems, parks, and civic centers. Paradoxically, this meant that the people left behind during the suburban exodus were those most in need of services and least able to pay for them: those with little education, the poor, the elderly, and minorities.

Meanwhile, Lake Washington had become the victim of its own attractiveness. Long prized for its beauty and clear water, it was now encircled by city and suburbs. Sewage and runoff from homes and businesses nearby and from highways circling and crossing it so polluted Lake Washington that it was virtually unable to support life. Its beaches were closed to swimming and other recreational activities were limited. Yet no existing agency had the authority to effect significant changes. Although Seattle lined almost half the shore, the problem was shared by a dozen or more incorporated and unincorporated areas of King County. Further complicating matters, several hundred sewer, water, and fire districts created a hodgepodge of tiny governmental units competing for tax dollars and public attention. Their boundaries crisscrossed in a complicated maze.

The solution was the creation of the Municipality of Metropolitan Seattle, or METRO. Devised by a group of Seattle and Bellevue civic leaders, its moving force was James Ellis, a Bellevue resident and regular over-lake commuter. As originally proposed, METRO would be controlled by a council of fifteen members, eight from Seattle and seven from the suburbs, and would have three tasks: to build sewers, develop a rapid-transit system, and establish area-wide planning. In a March 1958 election, the proposal was soundly rejected by voters, apparently because of suburban fears that Seattle would dominate the organization. Although pollution problems were obvious, rapid transit and planning evoked little enthusiasm. Ellis and his cohorts, regrouping after this initial defeat, scaled down their proposal to conform with public feeling and realistic cost estimates. The transit and planning features were eliminated and communities further from the lake were excluded. Resubmitted to the voters, METRO's focus on cleaning up Lake Washington won it approval. Results were apparent within a few years. New sewer lines fed into modern treatment plants at Renton and at Seattle's West Point. Once more Lake Washington became noted for swimming, boating, fishing, and sheer beauty. Now it was also a model of how inventive civic leadership could resolve public problems.

꒛ꋵꙻꋷ꒛

The optimism that marked the end of World War II was shattered by the rising conflict between the Soviet and Western blocs, soon labelled the Cold War. Touching many aspects of national life, the Cold War had a significant impact upon the Pacific Northwest. The region pondered its proximity to the Soviet Union. Local war industries retooled and defense installations, scheduled to be dismantled, remained operative. Boeing engineers rapidly developed the B-47 and then the B-52. The military occupation of Japan and the Korean War reconfirmed the Pacific Northwest's importance as a shipping point for goods and personnel. The world war had barely subsided before Seattle, Bremerton, and other militarily significant places again came alive with war related activities.

Cold War tension also affected domestic affairs and local politics. Anti-communist fervor spread throughout the United States, intensified by Wisconsin Senator Joseph McCarthy's exposures of alleged conspiracies to subvert the government. Washington State, with its heritage of radicalism, was ripe for such investigations even before McCarthy. It was easy to find admitted former Communists and sympathizers; during the 1930s, some had been active in the Democratic Party. Several important politicians were particularly vulnerable to attack, including U.S. Representative Hugh DeLacy, shortly defeated for reelection by a former commander of the state American Legion. Conservative Republicans who controlled the state legislature and traditional Democrats seeking to purge their party supported a legislative investigation of communist influence in Washington.

The 1947 legislature approved a loyalty oath for state employees and then, a day before adjournment, established a "Joint Legislative Fact-Finding Committee on Un-American Activities." Commonly called the Canwell Committee after its chairman, Albert Canwell, a freshman legislator from Spokane and onetime sheriff's investigator, the panel was assigned wide-ranging authority to investigate individuals and organizations. Composed of stern-minded legislators, the Canwell Committee held hearings throughout the state, the most notorious focusing on the Washington Pension Union, a left-wing remnant of the Great Depression, and on University of Washington faculty members. The university was thrown into debate and turmoil for months over past communist activities of several professors, the meaning of academic freedom, the willingness of individuals to cooperate with the committee, and the fear that alleged communists on the public payroll would harm impressionable students. Professors Joseph Butterworth, Ralph Gundlach, and Herbert Phillips were fired and other reputations were shattered as a result of the investigations. A residue of bitterness hung over the campus for years.

"Redbaiting" became a standard feature of Washington politics in this frenzied period. During his 1948 reelection campaign, Governor Arthur B. Langlie, long respected for his personal integrity, changed tactics to accuse his opponent, U.S. Senator Hugh B. Mitchell, of being soft on communism. Superintendent of Public Instruction Pearl Wanamaker, defeated for reelection, won a substantial lawsuit against syndicated columnist Fulton Lewis, Jr., who had accused her of communist sympathies. In the early 1960s, a prominent legislator from Okanogan County and his wife, John and Sally Goldmark, won a libel suit against a local newspaper publisher who had accused them of communist activities. The zealous warfare between extremists of the left and the right continued, even as mainstream Washington politics settled near the center of the ideological spectrum.

World War II significantly transformed the racial composition of towns and cities in the Northwest. The first blacks in Washington were for the most part individuals from western states who found discrimination in Oregon and moved north of the Columbia. Some played significant roles in settling Washington, including George Bush, a leader of the first immigrant party to reach Puget Sound, and his contemporary, George Washington, founder of Centralia. Among later arrivals, Seattle hotelkeeper William Grose became wealthy from property holdings east of town, which would be the nucleus of the city's Central Area in later generations. Grose, publisher Horace Cayton, and other black Seattleites were accepted and respected by friends and business associates of both races.

The Cayton's "lived in a large, two-story house on Capitol Hill, the most wealthy residential area of Seattle," wrote Horace Cayton, Jr., born in 1903. "It faced a broad avenue with a garden area in the center, which led directly to the water tower in Volunteer Park. We were the only Negro family in that part of town; all of our neighbors were white and wealthy. . . . my father was known and respected in the community, and though we were not warm social friends, our neighbors were pleasant and respectful." If the Caytons lived better than most, other blacks also had rising expectations. Horace, Jr., recalled his father telling Booker T. Washington, who visited their home in 1909, that "here in the Northwest we are striking out in every direction. Negroes in this town have become small businessmen or skilled mechanics and live a good life. Their children are getting educations and will be able to stand up and compete with other men. Here the race is to the swiftest, and here the American dream is being won." This was solid American middle-class rhetoric. Yet the Caytons and other blacks experienced moments of discrimination, and when the editor turned from polite neutral comments to controversial political statements, advertisers cancelled orders. The fortunes of this proud family plummeted.

There was still some truth in that lecture to the famous Dr. Washington. Most blacks in Seattle and Tacoma enjoyed a pleasant Victorian life, relatively free, secure, and hopeful. They had responsible jobs and could hope for better times. Bush's son George went to the first state legislature in 1889, and Tacoma publisher John H. Ryan served there two decades later. Black workers, some of whom had arrived as strikebreakers, settled in mining towns such as Newcastle and Roslyn. Slowly, however, new elements, often less genteel than their predecessors, trickled into urban areas, threatening their fragile hold on the respect of the general community. In Washington's three largest cities, small black districts appeared near downtown. During the 1920s and 1930s, segregation was practiced in Seattle restaurants, theaters, and housing.

World War II labor shortages prompted calls for laborers from outside the Northwest. Blacks arrived from the South and the urban East in large numbers, gravitating to cities. In 1940 there were 7424 blacks in Washington; ten years later there were 30,691, a more than fourfold increase. Seattle's Central District became a solid minority area, spreading south along Twenty-third Avenue and east toward Lake Washington. Tacoma's blacks were concentrated in the Hilltop area and a smaller section near the city's southeast border. Spokane's new minorities settled south of the business district.

The impact was even greater in some smaller urban areas. The navy town of Bremerton had only twenty-eight blacks in 1939, but 2400 four years later. A hastily formed housing authority responded to the influx by constructing a segregated housing project eight miles outside of town. Bremerton blacks were regularly denied service by stores, shops, restaurants, and even professional people. Conditions were no better near the Hanford works. Several thousand blacks were brought into the area, but nothing was done to prepare for the arrival of unfamiliar and unwelcome minorities. Richland and Kennewick simply excluded blacks from residence, the latter becoming known as a "sundown town" that harassed minorities found on the street after dark. Pasco, a small town of blue-collar workers, at least allowed blacks to reside within its confines. Many settled east of town in tar-paper shacks and broken down trailers, scarcely better than what they had left. The DuPont Company built segregated housing and transported workers to its plant in segregated buses. Small concrete-block houses were eventually built in East Pasco, but the district lacked paved streets, water, sewage systems, and adequate shopping facilities, and residents suffered other forms of discrimination.

There were a few efforts to deal with racial problems during and just after the war. In 1944, Seattle established a multiracial Civic Union Committee that tried to resolve issues and increase public awareness. The State legislature enacted Governor Langlie's proposal for a State Board against Discrimination, the first in the nation, which endeavored with little success to outlaw discrimination in the work place.

World War II radically altered the racial demographics of Washington as urban populations mushroomed and new black neighborhoods and communities were created. If most blacks found living conditions better than they had left behind, there were still disappointments and frustrations. Many housing areas were closed to blacks. Salaries lagged behind the white standard, and some kinds of jobs were never available to blacks. Various subtle forms of discrimination occurred in housing, stores, schools, and social and political activities. This was the status quo for blacks in Washington until the state was swept up in the national civil-rights movement during the 1960s.

The growth of the Chicano* population of Washington, another direct result of World War II, was even more spectacular. In 1980 there were 120,000 Spanish-surnamed residents, mostly from Mexico, comprising the largest minority group in the state. The war had required maximum agricultural production, but as farm workers went into military service and urban defense, there was a desperate need for field workers, especially at planting and harvest time. Yakima Valley farmers tried hiring local schoolchildren, college students, vagrants, Camp Fire Girls, and even off-duty postal employees. But stopgap measures were insufficient; new approaches were needed.

In 1942 the United States and Mexican governments concluded an informal "bracero" agreement, allowing Mexican laborers to cross the border annually on a temporary wartime basis. The U.S. government provided transportation and housing and workers were bound by written contracts. The first braceros were brought into the Yakima Valley in April 1943 to work near Toppenish in sugar-beet fields owned by the Utah and Idaho Sugar Company. This initial effort was so successful that the practice spread to other areas of the valley and Western Washington. The Washington State University extension service reported that, "It would have been impossible to handle crops in Snohomish, Whatcom, Walla Walla and Skagit counties without imported workers."

The next spring, with a new Yakima County agency created to handle the program, almost a thousand Mexican laborers arrived, creating an oversupply. Housing was found in local labor camps, the Grandview ball park, and a vacated German POW camp. There were administrative problems, and sickness among the workers. Some valley residents discriminated against the bracero workers, but others welcomed them and joined them in observing national holidays and family celebrations. Notwithstanding its general success, the bracero program declined after 1948.

* Of the many terms which have been used to denote this population group, we consider *Chicano* to be the most appropriate for the people and the time period under discussion.

Irrigation and other factors encouraged expansion of agricultural production in Eastern Washington, where many crops depended on physical labor. But war's end in 1945 did not bring the anticipated return of the prewar agricultural work force, so Yakima Valley farmers began recruiting Chicanos from other parts of the United States. Spanish-language radio spots and posters advertising jobs in the Yakima Valley were spread throughout California, Texas, and other states. Migrants from the Southwest proved to be a more stable labor force than the braceros, and did not have to be recruited annually.

Eastern Washington became a regular seasonal stop on the migrant workers' cross-country swing. For most, the journey required four days of steady driving, usually with an extended family riding in a covered flat-bed truck. Local agencies, often using Spanish-speaking middlemen, helped newcomers adjust to the valley and meet personal needs. Many regular migrants developed attachments to particular communities and farms. Social activities revolved around the family, ethnic foods, and holiday celebrations. The annual influx of several hundred people allowed growers to maintain low wage scales.

By the 1950s many migrants were familiar seasonal members of valley communities east of the Cascades. Some abandoned the migratory life and stayed year around, introducing an enduring Mexican flavor to the culture of the area. There were Spanish-language radio broadcasts, theaters showing Mexican films, and a tortilla factory. A Spanish-speaking priest arrived to celebrate confirmations, communions, and regular masses. Yet, even as they maintained aspects of their own culture, the Chicanos became assimilated to the surrounding one.

The Yakima Valley experience was duplicated on a lesser scale in other agricultural areas of eastern and western Washington. Concurrently came a general movement into larger cities, until there were more Chicanos in urban than in rural areas.

The racial and ethnic tapestry of Washington was fundamentally and permanently altered by World War II. Along with Japanese Americans, blacks, and Chicanos, other minority ethnic groups in Washington were affected by World War II and its aftermath. Many Indians, for instance, left reservations for military service or war industry work, permanently affecting their traditional culture. Asians and Pacific Islanders underwent similar transformation. Then, in the early 1960s, the state underwent another transformation, and became more mature culturally, economically, and politically.

~ 10 ~

A New Washington Society

Like people, cities and regions experience rites of passage, certain moments and actions that signify a coming of age. Such turning points or watersheds help a community to mature. A world's fair may be one such civic rite of passage, drawing attention to an area and sometimes leaving a legacy for the future. The fair announces to an unsuspecting world, "Here we are; we have arrived."

The Pacific Northwest, including British Columbia, has hosted five world's fairs, each focusing upon some aspect of past, present, or future. The Lewis and Clark Exposition in Portland in 1905 commemorated the centennial of the great transcontinental expedition. Seattle's Alaska-Yukon-Pacific Exposition of 1909 promoted the region's relationship to those distant places. The Century 21 World's Fair held in Seattle in 1962 looked to the future and left the city an enduring cultural and recreational complex. Spokane's Expo '74 had an environmental theme and transformed a blighted downtown fringe into an inviting civic center and park. And Expo '86 in Vancouver, Canada, highlighted transportation and opened a broad waterfront to multiple uses.

Century 21 was a particular turning point for the Pacific Northwest. It was born in the mid-1950s during a luncheon between Don Follett of the Seattle Chamber of Commerce, newspaperman Ross Cunningham, and City Councilman Al Rochester. Originally intended to commemorate the fiftieth anniversary of the A-Y-P, the plan evolved into a regional event, and then a world's fair sanctioned by the Bureau of International Expositions. The local business community and city, state, and federal governments contributed support.

Seattle promoters latched on to the fair as a way to revitalize a static downtown core beset by competition from suburbs. The seventy-four acre site included a cluster of existing public buildings in need of rehabilitation and was nicely situated between Queen Anne Hill, the waterfront, and downtown.

As plans became concrete, the character and symbolism of the fair evolved with an eye to the future use of facilities. A space-age theme suggested a futuristic outlook consistent with the region's aerospace industry. The Space Needle, inspired by a German television tower, progressed from sketch pad to construction and became the universal symbol of fair and city. A monorail, extravagantly touted as the transportation method of the future, sped passengers between fairgrounds and downtown. An elegant science center, designed by Seattle-born architect Minoru Yamasaki, housed the core exhibit on a space-age theme, and remained a popular local attraction. The Washington Pavilion, its maze of exhibits displayed on several thousand aluminum cubes, continued in use as the Coliseum, a site for sports events, trade fairs, and conventions. The old Civic Auditorium was restyled into a plush opera house, with a more intimate theater located across a courtyard entry. The municipal ice arena was converted to a modern sports facility, a stadium was built where the old Civic Field had been, and a one-time National Guard armory became the Food Circus, featuring small eateries and shops. Elsewhere on the grounds exhibits of many nations and organizations surrounded a huge circular fountain.

A *Time* magazine cover story called Century 21 a "jewel of a fair." For many Seattleites it was a six-month party with an aura of color and excitement. The larger impact, though, remained after the fair closed. Century 21 signaled the maturation of the host city, state, and region. Twenty years later, one organizer recalled it as "a community benchmark, a point in destiny to separate the times before from the times afterward." Before Century 21, Seattle and Washington were tied to the wartime era, and seemed to think small and regionally. The fair ushered in an era of thinking big in national and world terms, of confidently looking forward to new objectives.

The early 1960s also represented a political watershed. Local concerns were becoming more closely entwined with national and world issues and with policies destined to have lasting effect. The election of Governor Daniel J. Evans in 1964 highlighted the arrival of a new active generation of political leaders. Republicans lost their long-time majority in the state's congressional delegation to younger Democrats. The new crop of representatives included future Senator Brock Adams and House Majority Leader Tom Foley. A newspaper headlined the results: "Election Marks End of Era; Oldsters Lose Out to Youth." Two holdovers from the earlier era, Senators Warren G. Magnuson and Henry M. Jackson, grew in national influence.

Arthur B. Langlie, son of Norwegian immigrants, was governor during World War II. At the University of Washington, he had been a well-known athlete with an unspectacular academic record. He might have remained a competent Seattle lawyer but for the Order of Cincinnatus. Disillusioned with the local political scene of the 1930s, the young founders of Cincinnatus pledged to improve the quality of civic leadership. Langlie became closely associated with the order, which encouraged and supported his campaigns for city councilman and mayor. As mayor, he handled city affairs well, gaining support even from some political opponents in his joust with the rising Teamsters leader, Dave Beck. Previously officially nonpartisan, Mayor Langlie became the Republican candidate for governor in 1940 and was elected amid a division among Democrats.

Never flashy, the moralistic Langlie played down partisanship in Olympia, seeking cooperation from diverse elements while inspiring confidence in his leadership. As wartime governor, he oversaw growing industrial development in the state and emerged as a leading spokesman for moderate Republicans. He, and most observers, viewed his reelection in 1944 as a foregone conclusion. Surprisingly, though, Langlie lost to U.S. Senator Mon Wallgren, from Everett.

Wallgren was more congenial and affable than his predecessor. He was also a close friend of President Harry S Truman and, according to detractors, a big spender who lived the high life at public expense. Even fellow Democrats conceded he was neither an effective political leader nor a strong governor. In 1948 voters turned again to Langlie. Honest and efficient, Langlie in his second term balanced a liberal social viewpoint with fiscal conservatism. Abhorring federal interference, he preferred decision making at local levels of government, but he was rarely an innovator. As his third term began in 1953, Langlie was growing increasingly partisan and often dogmatic, quarreling with legislators and other state officials. Nationally prominent within his party, he worked to nominate Dwight D. Eisenhower at the 1952 G.O.P. convention over conservative Robert A. Taft. Subsequently, Langlie often advised the new President on western matters. Urged on by Eisenhower, Langlie unsuccessfully challenged Senator Warren G. Magnuson in 1956 before retiring from public life.

Langlie's Democratic successor as governor was Albert D. Rosellini. From a prominent Italian American family, Rosellini challenged the old political belief that only candidates of Scandinavian or other North European descent could attain statewide office in Washington. The new governor had graduated from the University of Washington and joined a Seattle law firm before winning election to the state senate in 1939. He reveled in political give-and-take and became a leader of liberal Democrats and a frequent antagonist of Governor Langlie. Outgoing and practiced in politics, Rosellini brought color and vigor to the governorship. An effective administrator, he took pride in improving the quality of state institutions—an accomplishment that had eluded Langlie.

The election of Dan Evans in 1964, while not a complete break with the past, suggested the beginning of a new era. For twenty-four years, only three men had served as governor and they represented the New Deal–wartime generation. Evans and his associates were of the postwar political generation. His background as a civil engineer was reflected in the campaign slogan, "A Blueprint for Progress." Young, energetic, and articulate, "Straight Arrow Dan" had led Republican legislative opposition during the latter Rosellini years. Like his predecessors, Governor Evans was plagued by fiscal problems, quarrels over educational issues, and inadequate welfare programs. But the Evans years brought increasing involvement in broader concerns involving the environment, energy sources, civil rights, and the Vietnam War. More partisan than the early Langlie, Evans nevertheless garnered support from many Democrats and became highly popular and greatly respected. After three consecutive terms, a state record, he became president of The Evergreen State College. In the fall of 1983 Evans succeeded the late Henry M. Jackson in the U.S. Senate, then declined to make a reelection bid in 1988.

The election of Governor Dixy Lee Ray in 1976 marked several firsts. The first woman to hold the office in Washington, she was also the first governor to hold a Ph.D. degree, and the first to have held a high federal position. A Tacoma native, Ray was a marine biologist and at various times a University of Washington professor, a television lecturer, and director of Seattle's Pacific Science Center. In 1972, President Richard Nixon appointed her to the Atomic Energy Commission; as chairperson, she was the highest-ranking woman in the federal government. Later, Ray served as assistant secretary of state for scientific matters. Returning to Washington State in 1976, she announced her Democratic affiliation, won the party's gubernatorial nomination, and easily defeated Republican John Spellman for the state's highest office.

Outspoken and an outsider among established state Democrats, she depended upon her own group of personal loyalists. Her faith in technology and growth led to controversial pronouncements on such rising issues as oil pipelines, atomic energy and nuclear waste storage, and fishing disputes. She worked to diversify business and to increase trade with Asia, particularly the People's Republic of China. Intense opposition within her party prompted her defeat in the 1980 Democratic primary by long-time state senator Jim McDermott. In the general election, John Spellman succeeded in his second attempt to become governor.

Seattle University graduate Spellman had been King County executive and was best known for building the Kingdome. Likeable and mild-mannered, he was soon embroiled in serious economic problems resulting from inflation, a recession in basic industries, and cutbacks in federal programs. Although Republicans controlled the legislature, difficulties with party leaders plagued the governor's efforts to resolve these matters. Spellman's reticent style made him appear ineffective in dealing with state problems, at least to persons who preferred strong action.

In 1984 the voters again turned to a newcomer to statewide politics. Booth Gardner, millionaire stepson of Weyerhaeuser magnate Norton Clapp, had been a timber executive and a law professor with brief legislative service before becoming Pierce County executive. With shy mannerisms that belied his administrative talents, Gardner entered office determined to improve state finances, bring new industry into the state, and remedy pollution on Puget Sound. Yet his efforts also were plagued by financial difficulties including an inadequate tax base and declines in basic industries. While he remained personally popular, some observers grew to question the political effectiveness of his quiet, noncombative style.

The issues that faced Gardner and his immediate predecessors were of a different nature than those facing Langlie a generation earlier. Langlie wrestled with internal administrative issues: welfare, education, finance, highways, ferries, and state institutions. These issues were still present when Gardner was governor, but they were compounded by such new issues as energy needs, radioactive waste disposal, minority rights, and a wide range of environmental concerns, including fisheries enhancement, air and water pollution, preservation of natural areas, and the need to balance economic development with ecology. Whereas the concerns of Langlie's time—the war excepted—were primarily intrastate in nature, later governors were drawn into regional and national problems. From the early 1960s onward, politics evolved into a different era.

Meanwhile, Washington's congressional delegation, led by Senators Warren Magnuson and Henry Jackson, grew increasingly potent. Their careers had parallels. Both graduated from the University of Washington and were aggressive young prosecuting attorneys before being elected to the U.S. House of Representatives. Magnuson moved to the Senate in 1945 and Jackson in 1952. As their seniority increased, they became powerful figures who paid close attention to constituents' needs and seemed unbeatable in state elections. Both were members and chairs of powerful committees.

The consummate political pro, Magnuson took a particular interest in trade and health matters and was an early advocate of consumer protection. He had a well-deserved reputation for getting things through the congressional maze and seemed invulnerable until he was upset by Slade Gorton in the 1980 election. Magnuson was then 75, and his age and health were significant, if whispered, factors in his defeat. "Scoop" Jackson chaired the Energy Committee and was a knowledgeable proponent of a strong military defense—the "Senator from Boeing" to opponents and admirers alike. Presidents from both parties considered him for Secretary of Defense and he was a serious contender for the 1976 Democratic presidential nomination. Jackson remained a force in the Senate and the state right up to his sudden death in September 1983.

Washington had seven seats in the U.S. House of Representatives between 1950 and 1980, gaining an eighth after the 1980 census. Most postwar representatives were Democrats but all developed a camaraderie and cooperated on issues affecting the state. For several years two were women, Julia Butler Hansen of Cathlamet and Catherine May of Yakima.

The late 1970s were the glory days for Washington's congressional delegation, reputedly the most powerful in Congress, thanks in part to the seniority of the two senators. Tom Foley of Spokane headed the House Agriculture Committee and was moving up in party leadership. Before Brock Adams resigned in 1977 to become Secretary of Transportation, he chaired the important Budget Committee. Several Washington representatives were former Magnuson or Jackson staff members, while other alumni such as Sterling Munro, head of the Bonneville Power Administration, and Federal Trade Commission Chairman Michael Pertschuk, held positions in the executive branch. A telephone call from one of the senators to a federal official might well be received by a former employee. That is influence.

Washingtonians boast that they vote for the candidate rather than the party, an assertion supported by the postwar record. Popular candidates like Dan Evans and Henry Jackson piled up equally huge majorities even though they belonged to opposing parties. Frequently, voters have elected a governor of one party by a large majority, while in the same election giving the state's presidential vote to the other party. Governors frequently face legislatures controlled by the opposition.

Politicians have lamented that factors other than voter independence weakened party discipline. Voters do not register as Democrats, Republicans, or Independents as in most states. State law enables voters in primary elections to vote for the candidates of different parties for different offices; Republicans "cross over" to help choose Democratic nominees and vice versa. Thus, on occasion, voters were suspected of helping nominate weak candidates from the opposing party to strengthen the prospects of their own. In addition, after Franklin D. Roosevelt's popularity ushered in many little-known Democratic candidates, Republicans smarting from those defeats pushed through a law eliminating the straight-party lever from state voting machines. Voter independence became a trademark of Washington politics.

Not all Washington office holders emerged from conventional political backgrounds. During the 1950s, well-known sports figures such as amateur golfer Jack Westland, football coaches John Cherberg and Howie Odell, and basketball All-American John O'Brien enjoyed success at the polls. By the seventies, voters displayed a preference for familiar media personalities. Lloyd Cooney, a television executive widely known for on-air editorials, won a primary to challenge Warren Magnuson. Dixy Lee Ray was best known for her televised science lectures. Congressmen Al Swift and Rod Chandler were former newscasters, and John Miller a television commentator. On the same election day in 1978 television reporters Charles Royer and Ron Bair were elected mayors of Seattle and Spokane respectively.

Old-timers complained that Washington politics lacked the zest of earlier generations, when radicals and eccentrics gained notoriety and office. Even Magnuson was once celebrated for escapades with Hollywood starlets. Prohibition-era dance-band leader Victor A. Meyers, who held two state offices spanning thirty years, began his political career as a mayoral candidate parading Seattle streets in Mahatma Ghandi garb and leading a goat. In later years color returned only upon rare occasions. The unknown Richard A. C. Greene won the Republican nomination for state land commissioner in 1968 even though he made no personal appearances and was living in Hawaii the whole time. And in 1976 the OWL ("Out With Logic: On With Lunacy") Party made the ballot. Born in a late-night tavern conversation, its candidates included tavern owner Red Kelly for governor, his mother-in-law "Fast Lucy" Griswold, cocktail waitress Ruthie "Boom Boom" McInnes, and bar regulars Jack "The Ripoff" Lemon and Archie "Whiplash" Breslin. The OWL Party promised to market dehydrated water and transparent fog, to erect a covered syndrome between Tonasket and Tenino, and to fight the heartbreak of psoriasis. If elected, they promised, heads would roll: porta-potties would be pushed over the cliff behind the Governor's Mansion. Led by Fast Lucy's 42,000 votes, all the OWL candidates finished third behind the conventional politicians.

The OWL party did not bring back zaniness to Washington politics, but it spoofed how bland issues and politicians had become. People like Dan Evans, Henry Jackson, and Warren Magnuson were dependable and effective, but rarely exciting. Excitement, for better or worse, was missing from postwar Washington politics.

But the two Washingtonians perhaps most prominent nationally after World War II were not elected officials. One was a labor leader, the other a United States Supreme Court justice. One emerged from a raucous urban environment and the latter from small-town Eastern Washington. Both vividly personified the American Dream, the faith that any individual could acquire wealth and power through hard work. Yet their routes to success differed vastly from the typical "rags-to-riches" hero, Dave Beck rising from organized labor and William O. Douglas through academia.

Beck was only four years old in 1898 when he came to Seattle to grow up in the rough-and-tumble atmosphere of a city suddenly rich from Klondike gold. But the family was poor and Dave quit high school to drive a laundry truck. Returning after service in World War I, he joined the local Teamsters union. Soon, truck driving held less interest than labor politics, and in 1925 he became a full-time organizer. From the beginning, Beck supplemented persuasive tactics with threats, beatings, car sideswipings or window smashings by goon squads. At the same time, he developed the precepts that would guide his career. He was no revolutionary seeking a workers' takeover—in fact, radicals became his bitter opponents. Beck defended capitalism with the conviction that both employers and workers had legitimate needs compelling them to cooperate for their mutual benefit. Labor unions must "organize the bosses" and make them see that better wages and working conditions guaranteed a stable, reliable work force.

His control over truck drivers who carried goods to and from businesses gave Beck enormous influence over specific industries and over much of Seattle's economy. He improved wages, hours, and working conditions while granting favors to business supporters and punishing the uncooperative. During the 1930s, Beck moved the Teamsters into related industries and waged a long and often violent battle against Harry Bridges and the longshoremen over control of the Elliott Bay waterfront. Taking advantage of the Newspaper Guild strike against the Seattle *Post-Intelligencer* and lesser labor disturbances of the mid-1930s, Beck enlarged Teamsters membership while increasing his personal power. Meanwhile, most laborers were able to buy homes and move into solidly middle-class life styles. In the process Seattle, once a radical hothouse, became a conservative labor town with Dave Beck its most potent leader.

Beck also entered the larger civic arena, assuming influence rarely held by labor leaders. He served on numerous city and state boards and was a regent of the University of Washington; he declined invitations from both Roosevelt and Truman to be secretary of labor. Real estate and other investments brought him personal wealth. Simultaneously, Beck rose within the international leadership of the Teamsters, extending his influence along the Pacific Coast. In 1952 he became international president. While he held that position recurring rumors of corruption led to federal investigations. Beck had indeed received generous loans and benefits from the union, including a spacious waterfront compound. Convicted for income tax evasion in 1959, Beck served thirty months at the McNeil Island federal penitentiary. His labor career over, he remained a colorful Seattle figure, proud of the community he had helped to shape.

While young Dave Beck learned city ways, William O. Douglas was growing up in Yakima and getting to know the vast expanses of Eastern Washington. Douglas was six when his minister father died, and his mother raised her children in severe poverty and with strict discipline. The Douglases worked at odd jobs around Yakima and in surrounding fields to raise money for necessities and schooling. Frail after a bout with polio, Bill Douglas was determined to strengthen legs and body. He hiked, climbed, fished, hunted, and camped alone for days at a time in the coulees, hills, and mountains near his home.

Graduating from Whitman College, Douglas briefly taught high school in Yakima. Then, consumed by a fascination with law, he literally rode the rails to New York City and Columbia University Law School. Trained by some of the nation's best legal minds, he built an outstanding academic record, joined a New York law firm, and then taught law at Columbia and Yale. In 1936 Franklin D. Roosevelt appointed him to the newly created Securities and Exchange Commission, where he served two years as chairman, helping to shape New Deal ideology.

In 1939 Roosevelt appointed Douglas to the U.S. Supreme Court, where he remained until a stroke forced retirement in 1975. His thirty-six years on the Court was the longest service of any justice in history. His opinions advocated civil and individual rights and reduction of government control over the people. His were frequently minority views and often controversial, firmly held and lucidly expressed. Douglas believed that persons of all races and inclinations must share the freedoms and privileges expressed in the Bill of Rights, that unpopular views needed hearing, and that the privacy of the individual must be protected.

Notwithstanding the custom that Supreme Court justices avoid involvement in political matters, Douglas frequently made his views known. Roosevelt in 1944 and Truman in 1948 sought him as a running mate. He strongly expressed liberal views on public issues including conservation, relations with China, and the Vietnam war. Douglas's outspokenness aroused controversy, as did his three divorces and four marriages.

Outside of the court, Douglas was a well-known outdoorsman and author. He wrote over twenty books about politics, nature, world travel, and finally his own life. Douglas could describe an elk or a quiet pond as eloquently as he could argue a legal technicality. Throughout his career he maintained a cabin home in the mountains above Yakima to which he regularly returned for hiking the Cascades. Several of his hikes, including a much publicized walk along the Washington coast, were public demonstrations to encourage the preservation of scenic areas and trails. No other Washingtonian so effectively shaped the ideas, attitudes, and conscience of twentieth-century Americans as did Bill Douglas during his four decades of public life.

⁓

In the early days of the civil-rights movement, most white Washingtonians watched on their televisions screens the events in such places as Montgomery, and Little Rock, and Selma. With shocked but detached interest, they viewed these as problems of a less enlightened region; their own state, as far as they knew, was a haven of harmony where living conditions and opportunities for minorities were good. Few whites had enough contacts with minorities to make such judgments. During and since World War II the influx of blacks into the state had raised that group from 7,424 persons or 1.7 percent of the population in 1940 to 132,000 or 3 percent in 1986. Most lived in Seattle, Tacoma, Spokane, Yakima, and Pasco, where older neighborhoods evolved into black ghettos. Although most Washington blacks doubtless enjoyed better living conditions than their contemporaries in the South or in eastern ghettos, subtle inequalities existed in housing, employment opportunities, wages, and social matters. It was a truism that blacks, and particularly black women, were last hired and first fired. Only a prominent few rose above racial barriers.

In the immediate postwar years, local, state, and federal officials made piecemeal efforts to alleviate inequalities, with little public awareness. Events of the larger civil-rights movement began to highlight local concerns, and a young generation of militants sought to correct conditions their parents had tolerated. The newly formed Black Panthers and the Black Student Union challenged the moderate tactics of such traditional groups as the National Association for the Advancement of Colored People and the Urban League.

A few demonstrations took place in Washington cities, though the region was spared the major riots that afflicted many American cities during several summers in the late 1960s. Seattle's most telling episode occurred in the weeks following the assassination of Dr. Martin Luther King, Jr., in 1968. Minor disturbances in Seattle's Central District foreshadowed a full-blown riot that followed the arrest of two Black Panther militants and a search of their office. For several nights during the annual Seafair festivities, Seattle experienced rioting and rock-throwing. Other cities, particularly Tacoma and Pasco, had disturbances during the era. Yet, these were both less violent than the distant events viewed on the television news and more clearly outside the mainstream of Washington's civil-rights movement.

Moderates, both black and white, were anxious to find fair and lasting solutions to problems even as the rhetoric flowed. Arthur Fletcher developed highly respected self-help programs among Pasco blacks and became a political figure of note. A few blacks were elected to the legislature, and such leaders as the Reverend Samuel McKinney in Seattle and that city's Urban League director Edwin Pratt aroused consciousness and worked to improve relations. Much positive action centered around education. The larger school districts made efforts to desegregate, often voluntarily, culminating in Seattle's district-wide busing program in the late 1970s. Demonstrations erupted on college campuses, particularly at the University of Washington where black students demonstrated against athletic favoritism, admission policies, and the lack of minority studies and services for minority students. Change began, slowly, to take place. Nationwide, the black experience influenced other minority groups, such as Chicanos and Indians, to press for civil rights. Although centering on agricultural work and fishing rights, these movements also focused on improved education and the establishment of urban community centers.

The movement for women's rights was separate but parallel. Since acquiring the vote in 1910, Washington women had made only minor political strides, highlighted by the election of Bertha Landes as Seattle mayor in 1926. A few women served in high office or succeeded in business, but most stayed in traditional women's occupations and roles. Yet, Washington was early to ratify the Equal Rights Amendment to the U.S. Constitution in 1973 and to similarly amend the state constitution. Washington was one of the first states to ensure equal treatment of women seeking credit or insurance and it pioneered the concept of "comparable worth" to even out salary scales.

Meanwhile, the civil-rights movement had become entangled with the reaction to the war in Southeast Asia in the 1960s and 1970s. That war, in which American involvement became paramount after the Tonkin Gulf incidents of 1964, brought renewed economic benefits to Puget Sound industries as production and shipping increased. Supporters of the war included Senator Henry M. Jackson, who believed that American military actions were necessary to fulfill U.S. obligations to South Vietnam and to stop the spread of communism in Asia. Others viewed the conflict as a foreign civil war, not vital to American interests, and considered U.S. involvement morally wrong. Divergent views drove wedges between Americans as debate on the war grew. By 1968 the anti-war movement was becoming aligned with other causes and protests against what became known as "The Establishment."

Washington's anti-war protestors organized, spoke out, published bulletins, held mass demonstrations, and threatened violence. One small group of radicals who became known as the Seattle Seven served prison terms for vandalizing the federal courthouse in downtown Seattle. The University of Washington campus was the scene of emotional confrontations. Anti-war groups denounced the University for releasing student records to military and industrial recruiters and for making contracts with firms involved in war production. Following the invasion of Cambodia in May 1970 and the National Guard killings of four young people at Kent State University, a week of demonstrations disrupted the University of Washington. On May 5, an estimated ten thousand marchers took to the Interstate Five bridge heading for downtown Seattle and blocked traffic for several hours. The University was forced to close for a day. At Pullman, Washington State University ended the semester a week early and sent students home, to avoid possible violence and bloodshed.

In time, many Americans of different persuasions were questioning the purpose of the war and the apparent inability of U.S. troops to win decisively. American combat troops were withdrawn from Southeast Asia in 1973, and Vietnam was soon united under communist rule. As in earlier wars, returning troops passed through Puget Sound ports and airports. Soon, refugees from Southeast Asia were also arriving, bringing yet another population element to Washington state. As the civil-rights movement adopted less confrontational tac-

This "quiet city" was in fact part of a wartime industrial plant, under camouflage (Boeing Company Archives).

A Japanese American family from Washington, interned during World War II (photo by Clifford, Special Collections Division, University of Washington Libraries, neg. no. 1673)

Mexican American migrant agricultural workers in Yakima Valley during World War II (Yakima Valley Regional Library)

The Washington Public Power Supply System plant (courtesy of WPPSS, Richland, no. 850463-30)

Facing page: clockwise from top left, *Dave Beck (photo by Grady, Special Collections Division, University of Washington Libraries, neg. no. UW 2653); Senator Henry M. "Scoop" Jackson (courtesy of Helen Jackson); Justice William O. Douglas (Yakima Valley Regional Library); Senator Warren G. Magnuson (courtesy of Warren and Jermaine Magnuson)*

Washington had its share of unrest during the Vietnam War era. In May 1970 this rally was held at the University of Washington, to protest the war and mourn the deaths of students at Kent State University (Information Services, University of Washington).

Seventeen years later, on May 25, 1987, legislators and citizens dedicate a memorial to Washington citizens killed in Vietnam (photo by Dick Baldwin, courtesy of the Secretary of the Washington State Senate).

Olympia and the state capitol buildings, a far different prospect from the same scene a century ago (Washington State Department of Commerce and Economic Development)

tics and the Vietnam War ended, Washington and the nation turned toward other concerns.

∾ ✺ ∾

WPPSS, pronounced *whoops*.

The initials of the Washington Public Power Supply System proved the most suggestive acronym since Richard Nixon's Committee to Reelect the President became known as CREEP. WPPSS began innocently and sincerely, with the urgent desire of small power-producing units to satisfy future regional electricity needs. It ended as a $24 billion debacle and the greatest municipal bond default of all time.

WPPSS was formed in 1957 when seventeen public and private utilities united to build larger plants and thus produce more power than they could separately. The board of directors consisted of representatives from member organizations, "ordinary" citizens assuming a civic responsibility. "People have got to do something for the public, that's the way I feel," recalled a high-school principal turned farmer who was a Franklin County Public Utility District commissioner. "Some people work in churches, some people work in schools, some people work in PUDs." This was American volunteerism and civic duty at its most wholesome level. For its first undertaking, WPPSS built a small hydroelectric plant at Packwood Lake, south of Mount Rainier. With federal help and a successful bond sale, construction was completed seven months ahead of schedule in 1964. Such success augured more success, and WPPSS was already starting work on a nuclear steam plant at Hanford.

The federal government recognized that steam generated by the existing Hanford installations was going to waste and could be used to produce electricity. But the Eisenhower administration was reluctant to commit federal funds to a project in competition with private enterprise. WPPSS was willing to accept the challenge. Enabling legislation pushed through Congress by Senator Henry M. Jackson was signed by a willing President John F. Kennedy. Private utilities agreed to participate, receiving promises of cheap Bonneville Power Administration electricity in return. Completed ahead of schedule and under cost, the Hanford steam plant was generating power by 1966. Within two years, it was producing three times the energy of any other nuclear plant in the United States.

The heady and auspicious beginning of WPPSS suggested that small public and private agencies cooperating together could produce gigantic results. New utilities joined until the total membership reached eighty-eight. Even in the unsettling social climate of the late 1960s, problems were viewed optimistically as challenges to meet and overcome. Amid predictions of a national power shortage, eyes turned to the Pacific Northwest, for decades a reservoir of cheap hydroelectric energy. The Atomic Energy Commission, viewing nuclear energy as a largely untapped power source, and the Bonneville Power Administration, responsible for coordinating power resources throughout the region, encouraged such further plant construction by WPPSS. Prohibited from organizing its own engineering team, WPPSS hired outside consultants to devise construction plans.

Thus, a variety of outside forces coalesced to encourage expansion. Numerous experts predicted that the abundance of inexpensive power would decline while population growth and demand were accelerating. In 1976, BPA administrator Donald Hodel warned customers that if present trends continued, his agency could not guarantee adequate power supplies after July 1983. The Arab oil embargo of 1973–74 and the resulting lines at gas stations were fresh public memories. Many people concluded that dependence on petroleum and hydroelectricity could not continue; the nation needed alternative power sources. Utilities across the nation viewed nuclear power as the solution. Production would be inexpensive after the initial construction, and nuclear energy was generally regarded as safe.

Washington State had three decades of experience with nuclear power, and lots of enthusiasm. True, WPPSS board members were amateurs, farmers and small-town businessmen, lacking scientific expertise and strangers in the world of high finance. But they had a proven track record, professional consultants, abundant expert guidance from federal and state agencies, and a public willing to follow their lead. In the early 1970s, the board voted to construct five nuclear reactors, three in familiar surroundings at Hanford and two outside the Grays Harbor town of Elma on the Satsop River.

It was a disastrous decision. Environmental and ecological issues acquired an almost faddish interest, especially with respect to the means of generating energy. Predictions of the coming energy shortage proved erroneous in the extreme. The aluminum industry, for instance, a prolific user of electricity, had exaggerated future needs. WPPSS board members reported little to their agencies and less to the public. Don Shakow, a shrewd young economist, challenged the high forecasts of future power consumption predicted by Seattle City Light and persuaded the city council to avoid involvement in plants four and five. But there were few other individuals prepared to sort out the questions that needed asking.

The years following the decision to build the five plants were a nightmare of disputed contracts, delayed construction, inflation, cost overruns, and legal disputes. State laws, mandating different designs and contractors for the plants, added to the confusion. Poorly drafted contracts undermined efficiency and workers complained of waiting around with little to do. Supplies failed to arrive on time; paper work fell behind schedule; inspections were faulty. Completed work had to be torn out and redone, sometimes more than once.

During much of this time, WPPSS received little direction from government agencies. By 1980, however, rumors of trouble prompted investigations by the state senate and the federal General Accounting Office. The most visible result was the replacement of WPPSS manager Neil Strand with the highly respected Robert Ferguson. Ferguson consolidated operations, revised contracts, secured a no-strike pledge from labor, and made on-site managers accountable for work performed. His efforts, though, came too late. Ironically, observed environmental journalist Daniel Jack Chasan, "During most of the time WPPSS has been a synonym for bungling, it has been relatively well-run. Things really did get turned around after Ferguson was hired in 1980. By then, of course, it was too late to save WPPSS from itself."

In the end, it was the inability to sell bonds that finally brought WPPSS down. In May 1981, Ferguson stunned his board with new cost estimates for finishing the plants. The total, originally estimated at $4.1 billion, was now $23.8 billion. A new, huge bond sale would be necessary, but Ferguson warned that bonds were hard to sell and power demands were far below projections. In the early months of the Reagan Administration, financial markets were slumping generally and once-attractive municipal bonds had lost much appeal. In a hard decision reached after sleepless nights, Ferguson recommended a moratorium on completion of plants four and five. It was best to pull back.

This proposal represented a work slowdown rather than a complete halt. That step came a few months later, following the recommendation of a blue-ribbon committee appointed by the three Northwest governors. From this point on, WPPSS skidded out of control.

Protests mounted as grass-roots groups of "Irate Ratepayers" denounced WPPSS and urged local utilities to drop participation. In November 1981, voters overwhelmingly approved Initiative 394, which required major utilities to take a popular vote before incurring major indebtedness. Although later declared unconstitutional, the initiative was a clear statement of public dissatisfaction with WPPSS. Meanwhile, the Clark County PUD led other agencies out of WPPSS, and elsewhere protest candidates were elected to local utility district boards. Financial rating houses downgraded WPPSS, making it even more difficult to raise funds. Finally, the board conceded the inevitable, terminating plants four and five and moth-balling two others. One Hanford plant was all that would be completed. A year later, WPPSS defaulted on its debt—the greatest such default in American history. Now investors were as irate as ratepayers.

Even then it was not over. At Hoquiam, Shelton, Everett, and other communities across the state, "Irate Ratepayers" continued to denounce officials and resist paying off investors. Power customers in Washington and Oregon vowed that they would not allow their taxes and rates to be raised to meet obligations to Wall Street. Nevertheless, stripped of its mystique and a continuing object of ridicule, WPPSS endured. The single nuclear plant at Hanford was completed and began producing electricity in 1984. But few thought of WPPSS in terms of its achievements. More clearly etched in the public mind were the two unfinished cooling towers near Elma. Outlined against the Willapa Hills, they remained hulking monuments to the fiasco pronounced *whoops*.

Pushing seventy, George Boldt was a white-haired, balding jurist of scholarly decorum. In two decades on the federal bench he had dealt harshly with hoodlums, racketeers, and war protestors. Recently, he had spent time away from the court spearheading the Nixon Administration's fight against inflation. Yet, until he strode into his courtroom in Tacoma on February 12, 1974, his name was unknown, unlikely to appear on bumperstickers or in jokes like a household word. His anonymity ended with his decision in *U.S. v. Washington*, which declared that Washington Indians would be protected in their right to fish in accustomed places and in their accustomed manner to the extent of harvesting half the total catch. Thereafter referred to as the Boldt Decision (though it is rare for a case to be popularly called by the name of the presiding judge), this judgment rocked Indian-white relations more severely than any single event of the century past. It culminated a series of industrial changes, racial tensions, and personal frustrations reaching back over a hundred years.

Fish, particularly the five varieties of Pacific Northwest salmon, historically were basic to the diet and culture of Indians along the Columbia River and on Puget Sound. In almost identical language, each of the treaties negotiated by Isaac Stevens in the 1850s had stated: "The right of taking fish at usual and accustomed grounds and stations is further secured to said Indians in common with all citizens of the United States and of erecting temporary houses for the purpose of curing, together with the privilege of hunting and gathering roots and berries on open and unclaimed lands." Shellfish from "beds staked or cultivated by citizens" were the exception. "This paper," Stevens told the Indians, "secures your fish."

For half a century, the promise mattered little. Incoming multitudes of whites were less interested in commercial fishing than in logging, farming, and town building. Indian willingness to market salmon benefited all, and the establishment of the Columbia River's first fish cannery in 1866 was little noticed. But seventeen years later the river and its tributaries had fifty-five canneries in operation. By 1900, more fish were canned on Puget Sound than on the Columbia. Canning transformed the nature of fishing in the Northwest. Several inventions, including the sanitary can and the "Iron Chink" which cleaned salmon, aided the development of a large-scale commercial industry. Immigrants from Scandinavia and southeastern Europe took up fishing as their principal occupation, using traps, gill nets, and purse seines to bring in large harvests. These methods made possible the taking of fish before they returned to Indian fishing places or spawning areas. Wrote anthropologist Fay G. Cohen, "a salmon bound for its native stream was much more likely to end up packed in a can before it could reach either the nets of the Indians or its birthplace."

There were occasional Indian protests and court cases. As early as 1887, a Tumwater homesteader was ordered to remove a fence barring Indians from fishing at their customary spot. Subsequent court decisions tended to affirm treaty rights while also extending the authority of Washington State to regulate the industry. Some Indians fished illegally, eluding arrest. And so it went until the civil-rights era of the 1960s. A new generation of Indian leaders, many veterans of

World War II and Korea, experiencing discrimination in a country they had served, learned to use the courts and the media in an effort to assert rights long neglected.

In 1954, two young Puyallup activists, Bob Satiacum and James Young, adapted to their own purposes the "sit-in" technique being used by blacks in the American South. Below Interstate Five where it curves through Tacoma, they held a "fish-in" for steelhead, using hooks and nets deemed illegal by the state. Their highly publicized arrest—later disallowed by the state supreme court—encouraged similar demonstrations in the following years. Enforcement against violators was sporadic, with occasional arrests and jail terms. Demonstrations near metropolitan centers ensured press coverage and so did the participation of such celebrities as Marlon Brando and Dick Gregory. Meanwhile, the number of fish available for harvest continued to decline. Over-fishing by all groups, dam construction, and other factors shared the responsibility, but white fishermen became convinced that Indians using nets at off-limit places were the main culprits. Indian demonstrations drew counterdemonstrations, and the Puyallup and nearby Nisqually rivers became scenes of repeated agitation and violence. Indians complained that they were being shot at by snipers and that untended nets were cut. In the summer of 1970, a Puyallup encampment was raided and gassed by state and local police. Similar incidents, usually less violent, occurred along the Columbia.

Several court decisions gave limited support to the cause of the Indians, but fundamental issues remained unresolved when the Puyallup demonstrations caused federal officials to intervene. That fall, the Department of Justice joined the Indians suing the State of Washington on behalf of treaty tribes. In *U.S.* v. *Washington,* Judge Boldt was called upon to explore and clarify many aspects of the fishing question. During the three years the case was in preparation, tension mounted. One prominent Indian leader, Hank Adams, of the Quinault Reservation, was shot and seriously wounded while guarding nets.

The Boldt Decision affirmed the right of Indians to "half the catch" (an ambiguous phrase which gave rise to much legal debate), allowed Indians to fish off their reservations, and limited state regulation of such fishing, but it did not end the controversy. On January 26, 1976, the U.S. Supreme Court refused to hear an appeal from the state, thus upholding the Boldt Decision. Still, many whites refused to accept the outcome peaceably. New violence occurred when the state stepped in to limit non-Indian fishing. The shooting off the Kitsap Peninsula of a white fisherman by a state fisheries agent trying to ticket him was the most dramatic of several tense incidents. It prompted Governor Dan Evans to affirm Washington's acceptance of the Boldt Decision as the law of the land.

Such incidents also prompted Judge Boldt to assume personal responsibility for enforcing his ruling. He appointed Dr. Richard Whitney, a fisheries expert from the University of Washington long experienced in dealing with Indian and state fishing controversies, to chair an advisory board that would also include an Indian representative and a non-Indian fisherman. The board was charged with resolving disputes before they reached court. Meanwhile, the federal government established a task force to set guidelines for management and enhancement of fisheries in the Northwest. Also, some opponents tried to dilute the effects of the Boldt Decision by legal means, with proposals to cut back federal funding for Indian programs and to abrogate the Stevens treaties. The state also sought reconsideration in the Supreme Court and this time the justices agreed to hear arguments. On July 2, 1979, the Court ruled six to three to uphold most aspects of the Boldt Decision.

Finally the case had been concluded—or so it seemed. State officials, Indians, and whites settled down to the logistics of implementing the Boldt Decision, and worked to enhance overall fishing resources. Over the years, the Indian share of the catch has approached their alloted 50 percent and over-fishing has been reduced. Many non-Indians have suffered economically as a result. Recent disputes involving Indian rights have most often been handled in the courts, with little violence or publicity, and the government has affirmed that the law, however unpopular, would be upheld. By the time George Boldt died in March 1984, a new era of cooperation seemed to have set in, along with a new realistic view of Indian-white relations.

A short article in the January 1975 *Harper's* magazine described a survey on the quality of life in America's fifty largest cities. Measureable characteristics such as median income, the ratio of rich to poor, the level of education, and the number of library books had been collected from reliable sources. Several "best" and "worst" cities were listed in each of some twenty categories. The conclusion was a ranked listing of all fifty according to their "liveability." At the top of the list was the "most liveable" city in America: Seattle.

The survey was little more than an academic parlor game; similar surveys reach strikingly different conclusions. "Quality of life" is an intangible. Still, a reputable publication with no apparent bias had selected Seattle as the nation's most desirable large city in which to live. What was true of its largest city, residents of Washington rejoiced, must be true of the state as well. If the 1962 world's fair was a turning point in the region's advance to wider renown, the *Harper's* study provided confirmation.

One important factor in the desirability of the state may be its diversity. Geographically and climatically, Washington is two states in one, divided by a mountain range. One can drive from sea level to the snow-covered base of Mount Rainier in little more than an hour. Waters range from ocean to an inland sound to lakes and rivers large and small. Washington's hills are round or rugged, dry or moist, golden brown or green, barren or thick with timber. The great plateau of eastern Washington is marked by channeled scablands left from glacial scrapings and cut through by coulees of ancient vanished rivers. Winding through the state, the Columbia River, even though altered by dams and reservoirs, flows past canyon walls, rolling hillsides, and a mountain-breaking gorge to its mist-shrouded mouth, where it meets ocean breakers.

Washingtonians think that their myriad outdoor attractions, as varied as the region itself, make the state a special place. Puget Sound residents like to boast that it is the boating capital of the world. Not uncommonly, persons of moderate means own a vacation home or a small craft to sail or cruise on the Sound or on lakes and rivers. Winter provides opportunities for skiing and snow sports in the Cascades or other mountain areas. Hiking, backpacking, and camping are enjoyed by large and increasing numbers of people. Thousands have climbed to the 14,410-foot summit of that regional symbol, Mount Rainier; lesser peaks are as compelling and sometimes more demanding. Fishing varies from deep-sea ventures to idle castings in remote streams. Big and small game and fowl attract hunters to all corners of the state. Many outdoor activities are doubly attractive because of their accessibility to urban areas. More than a few urbanites could, if they so desired, fish in the early morning before work, sail to and from work, and go skiing in the evening. Weekend excursions are a tradition for many.

The state has also added scenic, recreational, and historic areas to its growing park system. Since World War II, the federal government has expanded Olympic National Park and opened North Cascades National Park. Following the 1980 eruptions of Mount St. Helens, the federal government, in cooperation with Burlington Northern Railroad, created a national monument in the devastated area. The Washington Wilderness Act of 1984 placed over a million acres of mountain wilderness under federal protection, and scenic areas of the Columbia River gorge were set aside by Congress in 1986. Washington's parks reflect an outdoor, recreational mode geared to the active, informal life style of its citizenry.

Recent years have seen an increase in urban amenities, diverse and increasingly sophisticated. World's fairs left Seattle and Spokane with parks, opera houses, sports arenas, and convention facilities. Tacoma's appropriately wooden Tacoma Dome is convertible for varied functions. In big and small cities alike, classic movie theaters have been renovated to house stage productions and concerts. Seattle supports more professional theater companies than most cities of comparable size, enabling actors to maintain a living; a symphony, a ballet company, an opera company, art galleries, and touring productions further brighten its cultural offerings. Even medium-sized towns are likely to have musical groups and theatrical productions as well as facilities for touring artists and lectures.

Urban areas also emphasize the out-of-doors. Near the turn of the century, Tacoma transformed an unused military reserve into Point Defiance Park, preserving virgin timber and other natural features in combination with picnic and play areas, formal gardens, and a replica of Fort Nisqually. After the 1974 world's fair, Spokane developed river islands and its famed mid-city falls into an urban park alongside the business district. Seattle, with established parks gracing hillsides and shorelines, created new ones in such unlikely settings as a freeway lid and an abandoned gas plant.

Since the professional SuperSonics basketball team arrived in Seattle in 1967, it has been joined by the Seahawks in football and the Mariners in baseball. Much of the state has adopted these as their own, but smaller cities also have professional, semiprofessional, or amateur sports teams with a wide local following. The invigoration of Northwestern cities is reflected in—and promoted by—the rising quality of restaurants, bars, hotels, and entertainment complexes. Along with this has grown an appreciation for older homes, buildings, and areas. Several cities have renovated their original business districts and landmark structures, while small communities such as Leavenworth and Winthrop have developed town themes that attract tourists.

There are, nonetheless, cracks in the quality of Washington life, many resulting from problems with an economy that has not always supported efforts to achieve the good life. Many parts of the state depend upon a single industry or product. Periodically, fluctuations and setbacks in lumber, wheat, or aircraft production interrupt the state's prosperity. In the late 1960s, the loss of the long-awaited government contract to build a supersonic transport plane devastated Boeing, forcing a reduction in employment from one hundred thousand to less than forty thousand. The entire metropolitan Seattle area reeled from the effect. Many of those laid off were engineers with seniority who had never contemplated unemployment. The silver lining was that many remained in the area, using their expertise to start new industries, and Boeing itself began to diversify.

By the mid-1970s, the forest products industry, traditional mainstay of the region, was in trouble. Slowdowns in housing construction were exacerbated by strong competition from southern softwood forests and neighboring British Columbia; areas like Grays Harbor and the Willapa Hills, which relied heavily on lumbering, were hit hard. Wheat growers and other food producers in Eastern Washington faced economic difficulties similar to farmers elsewhere in the United States. High costs of production and the need for expensive mechanized equipment lowered profitability in agricultural parts of the state. Attempts to bring in new, "clean" industries were partially successful, but certain features of state tax laws tended to lessen Washington's attractiveness for small business enterprise.

A gnawing realization developed that some of the state's blessings were overrated. Declining salmon runs, overused clam beds, and disappearing game limited some forms of outdoor recreation. The many boats on Puget Sound and larger lakes produced pollution and overcrowding. Skiing was close to metropolitan areas, but there were no first-class winter resorts. Meanwhile, some environmental victories, such as protection of the Columbia River gorge hindered economic development of depressed areas. Rural residents complained that their livelihoods were sacrificed to give city folk a place to play. Water and air pollution often defied cleanup efforts.

Astute observers suspected that Washingtonians were congratulating themselves too soon on their recent cultural achievements. Critics of Seattle's rising skyline of glass and steel saw in it nothing more than unimaginative replicas of buildings in other cities. A newcomer's comment that Seattleites thought their symphony "was better than it actually was," applied to other attributes of modern life as well. Downtown areas struggled to maintain an identity against the onslaught of suburban malls which tended to be carbon copies of one another. A drive through downtown Tacoma, Everett, Aberdeen, Walla Walla, and other cities made obvious their struggle to survive against outlying attractions.

Social problems also increased. A modern myth attributed to the Pacific Northwest a high suicide rate, supposedly the result of gray skies producing gray moods, and the concept of the coast as a dead end from which the disaffected could move no farther. In truth, Washington's suicide rate was lower than most other western states. It ranked thirteenth in divorce rates and about average in alcohol consumption. Incidents of disease and mental illness and other indicators of psychological and emotional disturbances remained high in Washington. Crime rates, especially those involving property crimes, remained higher than in other parts of the nation. Several spectacular crimes attained national notice: the murders attributed to Ted Bundy, the Wai Mei killings in a Seattle gambling club, Spokane's "South Hill" rapes, and the still unsolved string of Green River murders. Life in Washington was less wholesome, it would seem, than boosters might insist.

Culturally, Washington had few genuine claims to prominence. In the world of art, a "Northwest School" heralded by *Life* magazine in 1953 had centered around Mark Tobey, Morris Graves, Kenneth Callahan, and Guy Anderson. These artists and later others utilized colors, themes, and motion in a manner reflective of an Asian as well as a Pacific Northwest Indian influence. By the 1980s, Washington's most prominent painter was Jacob Lawrence, his black heritage illustrated in colorful and dramatic canvases.

Washington made some significant literary contributions, although few of its leading writers truly reflected the state. Early in the twentieth century, J. Allen Smith and Vernon L. Parrington of the University of Washington produced influential works in political science and American cultural studies. Both helped mold opinions in their fields, but their work could have been done anywhere. Recently novelists Don Berry and Ivan Doig have received acclaim for books reflecting a distinct northwestern spirit; both live in Seattle but they write primarily about Oregon and Montana. Ernest K. Gann of the San Juan Islands and Anacortes devises adventure plots against an international background, and Frank Herbert of Port Townsend reached even farther to create the planet Dune. Nationally acclaimed poets such as Theodore Roethke, David Waggoner, and Carolyn Kizer have used Northwest themes and climate in their works. The best-known piece of writing to emerge from Washington was neither great literature nor did it boost the state's self-image. Betty MacDonald wrote humorously of her experiences on an Olympic Peninsula chicken ranch in *The Egg and I*. Nationally popular, it spawned a series of movies and helped create a perception of Washington as a land of eccentric, backwoods folk.

In the field of popular culture, Washington has bequeathed to the world such diverse entertainers as Bing Crosby, Quincy Jones, Ray Charles, Jimi Hendrix, and several rock groups of the 1970s, none of whom particularly reflected the regional culture in their achievements. More representative were the Depression-era folk songs of Woody Guthrie, an "outsider" briefly brought in by the Bonneville Power Administration to portray the people affected by dam construction.

Writing at the Battelle Institute "think tank," Raymond Gastil compared the Pacific Northwest with other regions of the United States. The Northwestern resident, he suggested, "is probably somewhat more likely to have what passes for a general education, less likely to attend church, more likely to spend his time in outside, participant sports or camping, less likely to be a spectator." Washington offers its citizenry opportunities for a life mixing active and "laid-back" styles, less influenced by class distinctions than in many parts of America. As they reach their centennial year, Washingtonians might ponder from whence they came and whether the "good life" is enough to sustain them in their future.

Afterword

Anniversaries always inspire reflection on the past and speculation about the future. The hundredth anniversary of a state raises serious questions, as well as nostalgia. Out of ten decades of experiences, which have proven to be most significant? Which have affected the life of the state most profoundly—the heroes and headlines, or perhaps events and persons who went unnoticed in the hurly-burly of their times? Can lessons learned from a century of statehood be applied to the next hundred years? And what does a general historical overview reveal about the connections between yesterday, today, and tomorrow?

Like many of the United States, Washington was created artificially, its borders determined by distant and ill-informed politicians and bureaucrats. Considering the geography of the region, two administrative entities—one east and one west of the Cascades—might have functioned more smoothly. Instead, the history of Washington since territorial days has been a ceaseless and often futile effort to impose politics upon geography. Politics tends to dominate the news, from the four-page Olympia *Columbian* to the high-tech coverage of modern television. But politics has often been remote from central historical events. Of the four key developments directing Washington to 1989, only one involved public policy, and that was a matter of foreign affairs.

On May 12, 1792—near the end of George Washington's first presidential term—Yankee trader Robert Gray guided his vessel into "a large river of fresh water." After spending a week near the mouth of this stream, which he named Columbia after his ship, Gray sailed away, never to return. Five months later, British officers under George

Vancouver carried out the first exploration of the lower river. Gray's discovery, however, had laid the foundation for subsequent American claims to the Northwest coast. Were it not for that New England merchant captain, the Union Jack or the Maple Leaf might today fly over the land that became Washington. Cricket might be the main sports attraction and high tea the daily social event in fine hostelries. (One might also speculate on the consequences if Spain had not kept secret its 1775 discovery of the Columbia.) Here, in the enormous latter-day complications of a simple act by a modestly distinguished seaman, is a prime instance of the capricious nature of history.

Fifty-six years later, in the midwinter of 1848, a mechanic named James Marshall discovered gold in California. At first, this epochal event nearly depopulated the Pacific Northwest, as people rushed south—months before the larger national hysteria of 1849. But the gold rush soon led to the building of a lumber commonwealth on Puget Sound. Unable to supply San Francisco and other boom towns from more convenient sources, timber merchants erected a complex of steam-powered sawmills along the western shore of Puget Sound and the Hood Canal. Created to serve the distant golden bayside city, these manufactories commenced a century-long dominance of Washington industry by loggers and lumbermen.

Four decades passed before the Northern Pacific Railroad opened its tunnel through the Cascades in 1888, completing the direct transcontinental link between Puget Sound and the eastern United States. Washington's geographic isolation was ended. Passengers and freight could move across country with speed and relative comfort. A huge influx of people during the 1880s made the territory eligible for statehood. And wealthy men from the Great Lakes, Frederick Weyerhaeuser the most notable, arrived to invigorate the lumber industry and drive it to top ranking among all states.

The span of a human life separated the coming of the railroad from the attack on Pearl Harbor in December 1941. This fourth key event set in motion developments affecting Washington at least to its centennial. Using power made possible by the recent fortuitous completion of Grand Coulee and Bonneville dams, the state's aluminum industry was founded and Boeing underwent a mammoth expansion of production. The Hanford plutonium works made Washington a birthing place of the atomic age. New population groups arrived, altering the accustomed social fabric. In a few hurried years, the modern industrial economy of Washington, its environmental and social consequences more grave than any posed by lumbering, arrived full-scale.

Fur trade exploration, personified by Robert Gray, produced the American Pacific Northwest. The California gold rush founded Washington's lumber industry and established its dependence upon export trade. Transcontinental railroads brought in people and money, opened wheat fields, and made statehood possible. Between Pearl Harbor and V-J Day, new modern industries established an enduring link between Washington's economic health and the business of war, be it hot or cold.

Over the decades, popular and scholarly commentators alike have attempted to define the distinct quality of Pacific Northwest existence. There supposedly is, and always has been, a special life style west of the Rockies and north of California. Inhabitants of the region, for reasons difficult to pin down, supposedly are more civilized than those in less blessed areas. Some observers point to rainfall or to the forest as key factors, but their theories do not include the land east of the Cascades. Analyses inspired by that dry section, meanwhile, stress the value of agriculture or the peculiarities of irrigation, but they too become mired in complication while traversing the mountain pathways to contradiction.

The truth, one fears, is that the supposed uniqueness of Washington depended upon the state's former isolation. Between 1848 and 1941, from California gold to Hawaiian disaster, the historical course of America passed the Pacific Northwest by, leaving it a backwater. World War II, however, brought new people as well as new industry. Hundreds of thousands of migrants, their rate of arrival accelerating in the postwar era, seemed determined to remake Washington in the image of the outside world, especially of fast-paced California. Television, jet planes, and the computer, those semi-beneficial milestones of modern technology, broke barriers of time and space and made Washington part of a truly united American nation.

If the self-reliant and independent Washingtonian, something of a transplanted New Englander, ever really existed, he or she was increasingly rare after 1945. Residents of the state now watch television programs along with a national audience and rely for news and opinion upon broadcasts from New York. Their transportation system focuses on an interstate highway network, upon which they operate foreign-made automobiles in a manner learned from the free-ways of Southern California. And, given their economic dependence on federal largesse—defense contracts, dams, irrigation projects, military and naval bases—they rely upon the "other Washington" to sustain them in prosperity.

Sources and Suggested Reading

Introduction: The Statehood Year

The best starting point for the study of Washington State history must be *The Works of Hubert Howe Bancroft,* especially the volumes *The History of the Northwest Coast, The History of Oregon,* and *The History of Washington, Idaho, and Montana* (San Francisco: A. L. Bancroft & Company, 1884–1890). Over the years most general histories of the state have been textbooks covering the entire Pacific Northwest. Perhaps the most generally used has been Charles M. Gates and Dorothy O. Johansen, *Empire of the Columbia: A History of the Pacific Northwest* (New York: Harper & Brothers, 1957). The most recently published text for the college level is Gordon B. Dodds, *The American Northwest: A History of Oregon and Washington* (Arlington Heights, Ill.: The Forum Press, 1986) and, for the secondary school level, Charles P. LeWarne, *Washington State* (Seattle: University of Washington Press, 1986). Other texts include Oscar Osburn Winther, *The Great Northwest: A History* (second edition, New York: Alfred A. Knopf, 1952); Mary W. Avery, *History and Government of the State of Washington* (Seattle: University of Washington Press, 1961); and Cecil Dryden, *Dryden's History of Washington* (Portland: Binfords & Mort, 1968).

Published in conjunction with the national bicentennial in 1976 as part of "The States and the Nation" series and intended for the general public were Norman H. Clark, *Washington: A Bicentennial History,* and Gordon B. Dodds, *Oregon: A Bicentennial History* (New York: W. W. Norton & Company; Nashville: American Association for State and Local History, 1976).

A valuable new anthology containing twenty-three essays and useful introductory sections is G. Thomas Edwards and Carlos A. Schwantes, editors, *Experiences in a Promised Land: Essays in Pacific Northwest History* (Seattle: University of Washington Press, 1986). See also William G. Robbins, Robert J. Frank, and Richard E. Ross, editors, *Regionalism and the Pacific*

Northwest (Corvallis: Oregon State University Press, 1983). Earlier useful anthologies include Stewart H. Holbrook, editor, *Promised Land: A Collection of Northwest Writing* (New York: McGraw-Hill Book Company, 1945); Ellis Lucia, editor, *This Land Around Us: A Treasury of Pacific Northwest Writing* (New York: Doubleday, 1969); and W. Storrs Lee, editor, *Washington State: A Literary Chronicle* (New York: Funk & Wagnalls, 1969).

Other books dealing with particular topics that readers might find of interest are Sally B. Woodbridge and Roger Montgomery, *A Guide to Architecture in Washington State: An Environmental Perspective* (Seattle: University of Washington Press, 1980); James W. Phillips, *Washington State Place Names* (Seattle: University of Washington Press, 1971); Robert Hitchman, *Place Names of Washington* (Tacoma: Washington State Historical Society, 1985); Norbert MacDonald, *Distant Neighbors* (Lincoln: University of Nebraska, 1988), a comparative history of Seattle and Vancouver, B.C.; and John W. Reps, *Panoramas of Promise: Pacific Northwest Cities and Towns on Nineteenth-Century Lithographs* (Pullman: Washington State University Press, 1984).

Information for this chapter was drawn from a number of sources, including several state and local histories. One which deals with the centennial decade is David Buerge, *Seattle in the 1880s* (Seattle: Historical Society of Seattle and King County, 1986). The statements by John Muir are quoted from Lee, *Washington State*, pp. 367–69. A helpful bibliography is David L. Nicandri, "Washington State: A Bibliography," *Pacific Northwest Quarterly* 74:114–15 (July 1983).

1: The Land Is Opened

A standard, scholarly account of Washington's geological background is Bates McKee, *Cascadia: The Geologic Evolution of the Pacific Northwest* (New York: McGraw-Hill Book Co., 1972), while persons with a casual interest will benefit from the travel-guide approach in David D. Alt and Donald W. Hyndman, *Roadside Geology of Washington* (Missoula, Mont.: Mountain Press, 1984). Stephen L. Harris, *Fire and Ice: The Cascade Volcanoes* (Seattle: Mountaineers, 1976) is a highly readable account of a dramatic geological force; the Pacific Search Press joined in publishing a revised edition in 1980 after the eruptions of Mount St. Helens. The relationship of humans to the land is the topic of Richard White, *Land Use, Environment, and Social Change: The Shaping of Island County, Washington* (Seattle: University of Washington Press, 1980), which has a broader application than its subtitle implies. Numerous scholarly articles have been printed on archeaological research in the Northwest and are summarized in an illustrated volume for the general reader, Ruth Kirk and Richard D. Daugherty, *Exploring Washington Archaeology* (Seattle: University of Washington Press, 1978.)

Philip Drucker, *Indians of the Northwest Coast* (Garden City, N.Y.: Natural History Press, American Museum Science Books, 1963), is a standard account of the topic, while Tom McFeat, editor, *Indians of the North Pacific Coast* (Seattle: University of Washington Press, 1966), is a compilation of useful articles. Robert H. Ruby and John A. Brown have published books on several specific Indian tribes, with their *Indians of the Pacific Northwest* (Norman: University of Oklahoma Press, 1981) an overall look at the groups. James G. Swan was an early close observer of Northwest Indians who gathered much information about them. His classic work, *The Northwest Coast; Or, Three Years' Residence in Washington Territory*, originally published in 1857, is available in paperback, with an introduction by Norman Clark (Seattle: University of Washington Press, 1972). For a record of the arts and material culture of the Indians of the Northwest Coast in the early reservation period, see *The Indians of Puget Sound: The Notebooks of Myron Eels* (Seattle: University of Washington Press, 1986). This monograph by the missionary is edited by George Pierre Castile, whose introduction places Eels, Indian policy and administration, and the Indians' reaction to change in historical context. There is also much information in Hermann Haeberlin and Erna Gunther, *The Indians of Puget Sound* (Seattle: University of Washington Press, 1930), and Erna Gunther, *Ethnobotany of Western Washington: The Knowledge and Use of Indigenous Plants by Native Americans* (revised edition, Seattle: University of Washington Press, 1973).

Exploration is traditionally a popular subject with historians and with the public. Journals and logs of the major explorers, Vancouver, Gray, Lewis and Clark, and Wilkes among them, are available in published form as are many diaries and journals of persons who accompanied them. Pertinent sections of George Vancouver's journal were originally printed early in this century and later reprinted with appropriate explanations in Edmond S. Meany, *Vancouver's Discovery of Puget Sound: Portraits and Biographies of Men Honored in the Naming of Geographic Features of Northwestern America* (Portland: Binfords & Mort, 1957). The standard biography is Bern Anderson, *Surveyor of the Sea: The Life and Voyages of Captain George Vancouver* (Seattle: University of Washington Press, 1960), which was reprinted in 1966 under the title *The Life and Voyages of Captain George Vancouver: Surveyor of the Sea*. David Lavender, *Land of Giants: The Drive to the Pacific Northwest, 1750–1950* (New York: Doubleday, 1958), includes a highly readable account of explorers on both sea and land. Spain's role is best described in Warren L. Cook, *Flood Tide of Empire: Spain and the Pacific Northwest, 1543–1819* (New Haven: Yale University Press, 1973). Two books by Derek Pethick, *First Approaches to the Northwest Coast* (Vancouver: J. J. Douglas, Ltd., 1976) and *The Nootka Connection: Europe and the Northwest Coast, 1790–1795* (Vancouver: Douglas & McIntyre, 1980), concentrate on the British Columbia coast but have applications for the area to the south. John Frazier Henry's *Early Maritime Artists of the Pacific Northwest Coast, 1741–1841* (Seattle: University of Washington Press, 1984) is a beautiful collection of paintings that offers much of value to persons interested in maritime exploration. Early chapters in Murray Morgan, *Puget's Sound: A Narrative of Early Tacoma and the Southern Sound* (Seattle: University of Washington Press, 1979), concern explorations in the Sound, especially its southern portion.

Much has been written about various aspects of the Lewis and Clark expedition, but the standard account remains John Bakeless, *Lewis and Clark: Partners in Discovery* (New York: William Morrow, 1947); James P. Ronda, *Lewis and Clark among the Indians* (Lincoln: University of Nebraska Press, 1984), includes more recent research. A concise abridgement of their journals is Bernard DeVoto, editor, *The Journals of Lewis and Clark* (Boston: Houghton Mifflin, 1953). The complete *Journals of the Lewis and Clark Expedition,* edited by Gary Moulton, are being published in eleven volumes by the University of Nebraska Press, with the fifth volume due in 1988.

Bernard DeVoto, *Across the Wide Missouri* (Boston: Houghton Mifflin, 1947; pbk. reprint, 1964), is a near-classic account of the fur trade for the serious general reader. A good popular description of Fort Vancouver, by a National Parks historian, is "Fort Vancouver: Fur Trade Capital of the Pacific Northwest," *The American West* 15:12–19, 68–71 (Sept.-Oct. 1977). Clifford Merrill Drury remains the essential biographer of the Whitman group of missionaries, with *Marcus Whitman, M.D.: Pioneer and Martyr* (Caldwell, Idaho: Caxton Printers, 1937), *Elkanah and Mary Walker: Pioneers among the Spokanes* (Caldwell, Idaho: Caxton Printers, 1940), and *Marcus and Narcissa Whitman and the Opening of Old Oregon* (Glendale, Calif.: The Arthur H. Clarke Company, 1973).

2: The Land Is Settled

The movement of Americans west in the 1840s and 1850s has been a fundamental component of American myth and legend, dramatized in novels, movies, and television. Among the better novels of this genre is A. B. Guthrie, *The Way West* (New York: Sloan, 1949). An excellent historic account is in David Lavender, *Land of Giants: The Drive to the Pacific Northwest, 1750–1950* (New York: Doubleday, 1958), and the indispensable study, drawn from exhaustive research in diaries and other source materials, is John D. Unruh, Jr., *The Plains Across: The Overland Emigrants and the Trans-Mississippi West, 1840–1860* (Champaign: University of Illinois Press, 1979). A useful view of overland expeditions as "Nomadic Communities of the Trail" is given in Chapter 4 of Robert V. Hine, *Community on the American Frontier: Separate but Not Alone* (Norman: University of Oklahoma Press, 1980), while Dorothy Johansen argues for a study of the "pull factors" that attracted certain kinds of people to the Northwest in "A Working Hypothesis for the Study of Migrations," *Pacific Historical Review* 20:1–12, (Feb. 1967), reprinted in G. Thomas Edwards and Carlos A. Schwantes, editors, *Experiences in a Promised Land: Essays in Pacific Northwest History* (Seattle University of Washington Press, 1986), pp. 40–50. Among recent accounts of women on the trail is Lillian Schlissel, *Women's Diaries of the Westward Journey* (New York: Schocken Books, 1982). Reminiscences by pioneers include Phoebe Goodell Judson, *A Pioneer's Search for an Ideal Home* (Lincoln: University of Nebraska Press, 1984 reprint of 1925 edition), and Ezra Meeker, *Pioneer Reminiscences of Puget Sound: The Tragedy of Leschi . . .* (Seattle: Lowman & Hanford, 1905; rpt. Seattle: Historical Society of Seattle and King County, 1980).

Many historical accounts of towns and cities have appeared recently, of uneven quality. Olympia and its environs is the subject of Gordon Newell, *Rogues, Buffoons, and Statesmen* (Seattle: Superior Publishing Company, 1975), while another early settlement is described in Marjorie Powell Mottishaw, "Quiet, Peaceful, Old Steilacoom," *Pacific Northwest Quarterly* 46: 1–4 (Jan. 1955). Excellent studies of the two largest cities are Roger Sale, *Seattle Past to Present* (Seattle: University of Washington Press, 1976), and two histories by Murray Morgan, *Skid Road: An Informal Portrait of Seattle* (revised edition, Seattle: University of Washington Press, 1982) and *Puget's Sound: A Narrative of Early Tacoma and the Southern Sound* (Seattle: University of Washington Press, 1979). Port Townsend is the topic of an old volume, James C. McCurdy, *By Juan de Fuca's Strait: Pioneering Along the Northwestern Edge of the Continent* (Portland: Binfords & Mort, 1937), and a new compilation of facts, narratives, and anecdotes, Peter Simpson, *City of Dreams: A Guide to Port Townsend* (Port Townsend, Wash.: Bay Press, 1986).

Washington Territory's first governor and Indian treaty maker is the topic of a definitive biography by Kent Richards, *Isaac Stevens: Young Man in a Hurry* (Provo, Utah: Brigham Young University Press, 1979), and his treaties form the backdrop of *Uncommon Controversy: Fishing Rights of the Muckleshoot, Puyallup, and Nisqually Indians* (Seattle: University of Washington Press, 1970). Settlement patterns and Indian-white relations east of the Cascades are well examined in D. W. Meinig, *The Great Columbia Plain: A Historical Geography, 1805–1910* (Seattle: University of Washington Press, 1968). The epic struggle of the Northwest's most famous Indian chief is related in Merrill D. Beal, *"I Will Fight No More Forever": Chief Joseph and the Nez Perce War* (paperback edition, Seattle: University of Washington Press, 1966).

3: The Timber Commonwealth

There is an enormous body of literature on the history of Washington forest exploitation. Robert E. Ficken, *The Forested Land: A History of Lumbering in Western Washington* (Seattle: University of Washington Press, 1987), covers the subject in comprehensive fashion. Thomas R. Cox, *Mills and Markets: A History of the Pacific Coast Lumber Industry to 1900* (Seattle: University of Washington Press, 1974), places it in regional perspective. Thomas R. Cox et al., *This Well-Wooded Land: Americans and Their Forests from Colonial Times to the Present* (Lincoln: University of Nebraska Press, 1985), provides the national context. The theme of forest usage is dealt with from an environmentalist perspective in Richard White, *Land Use, Environment, and Social Change: The Shaping of Island County, Washington* (Seattle: University of Washington Press, 1980).

Several lumber companies have received careful study. Edwin T. Coman, Jr., and Helen M. Gibbs, *Time, Tide, and Timber: A Century of Pope & Talbot* (Stanford, Calif.: Stanford University Press, 1949), and Ralph W. Hidy, Frank Ernest Hill, and Allan Nevins, *Timber and Men: The Weyerhaeuser Story* (New York: Macmillan, 1963), are authorized treatments based upon research in company records. Charles E. Twining, *Phil Weyerhaeuser: Lumberman* (Seattle: University of Washington Press, 1985), focuses on the company's leadership from 1933 to 1956, including the development of sustained-yield management. Another important concern is covered in Richard C. Berner, "The Port Blakely Mill Company, 1876–89," *Pacific Northwest Quarterly* 57:158–71 (Oct. 1966), and in Robert E. Ficken, "The Port Blakely Mill Company, 1888–1903," *Journal of Forest History* 21:202–17 (Oct. 1977). Iva L. Buchanan, "Lumbering and Logging in the Puget Sound Region in Territorial Days," *Pacific Northwest Quarterly* 27:34–53 (Jan. 1936), deals with several of the early firms. Seattle's famous Yesler mill is examined in John R. Finger, "Seattle's First Sawmill, 1853–1869: A Study of Frontier Enterprise," *Journal of Forest History* 15:24–31 (Jan. 1972). Thomas R. Cox, "Lumber and Ships: The Business Empire of Asa Mead Simpson," *Journal of Forest History* 14:16–26 (July 1970), details the career of the owner of the North Western Lumber Company. The story of one of the major Great Lakes firms is told in Murray Morgan, *The Mill on the Boot: The Story of the St. Paul & Tacoma Lumber Company* (Seattle: University of Washington Press, 1982).

Timber theft is handled by Frederick Yonce in "Lumbering and the Public Timberland in Washington: The Era of Disposal," *Journal of Forest History* 22:4–17 (Jan. 1978). Ivan C. Doig, "John J. McGilvra and Timber Trespassing: Seeking a Puget Sound Timber Policy, 1861–1865," *Journal of Forest History* 13:6–17 (Jan. 1970), examines one effort to combat thievery.

On the changing industrial front at the turn of the century, see Robert E. Ficken, "Weyerhaeuser and the Pacific Northwest Timber Industry, 1899–1903," *Pacific Northwest Quarterly* 70:146–54 (Oct. 1979). John H. Cox, "Trade Associations in the Lumber Industry of the Pacific Northwest, 1899–1914," *Pacific Northwest Quarterly* 41:285–311 (Oct. 1950), handles the origin of association activities.

Understanding of the forestry movement begins with Samuel P. Hays, *Conservation and the Gospel of Efficiency: The Progressive Conservation Movement, 1890–1920* (Cambridge, Mass.: Harvard University Press, 1959). Harold T. Pinkett, *Gifford Pinchot, Private and Public Forester* (Champaign: University of Illinois Press, 1970) is the best biography of the chief forester. Harold K. Steen, *The U.S. Forest Service: A History* (Seattle: University of Washington Press, 1976) places Pinchot in the context of agency history.

The subject of forest fires is treated in definitive fashion in Stephen J. Pyne, *Fire in America: A Cultural History of Wildland and Rural Fire* (Princeton, N.J.: Princeton University Press, 1982). Stewart H. Holbrook, *Burning an*

Empire: The Story of American Forest Fires (New York: Macmillan, 1944) is an older treatment containing an account of the Yacolt Burn. The development of regional forestry is treated in George T. Morgan, Jr., "Conflagration as Catalyst: Western Lumbermen and American Forest Policy," *Pacific Historical Review* 47:167–87 (May 1978); in Robert E. Ficken, "Gifford Pinchot Men: Pacific Northwest Lumbermen and the Conservation Movement, 1902–1910," *Western Historical Quarterly* 13:165–78 (April 1982); and in Lawrence Rakestraw, "Before McNary: The Northwestern Conservationist, 1889–1913," *Pacific Northwest Quarterly* 51:49–56 (April 1960).

4: The Wheat Commonwealth

The classic work of Eastern Washington history is D. W. Meinig, *The Great Columbia Plain: A Historical Geography, 1805–1910* (Seattle University of Washington Press, 1968). A synthesis of regional historiography is John Fahey, *The Inland Empire: Unfolding Years, 1879–1929* (Seattle: University of Washington Press, 1986).

Two outstanding works deal with the region's Indian background: Alvin M. Josephy, Jr., *The Nez Perce Indians and the Opening of the Northwest* (New Haven: Yale University Press, 1965), and Robert Ignatius Burns, S.J., *The Jesuits and the Indian Wars of the Northwest* (New Haven: Yale University Press, 1966). Robert H. Ruby and John A. Brown, *A Guide to the Indian Tribes of the Pacific Northwest* (Norman: University of Oklahoma Press, 1986) is a handy source of basic facts. The same authors have written on specific Eastern Washington Indians in *Half-Sun on the Columbia: A Biography of Chief Moses* (Norman: University of Oklahoma Press, 1965) and in *The Spokane Indians: Children of the Sun* (Norman: University of Oklahoma Press, 1970). The essential work on government policy is Francis Paul Prucha, *The Great Father: The United States Government and the American Indians* (Lincoln: University of Nebraska Press, 2 vols., 1984).

On economic matters, Randall V. Mills, *Stern-Wheelers up Columbia: A Century of Steamboating in the Oregon Country* (Palo Alto, Calif.: Pacific Books, 1947), is the standard account of river navigation. Dorothy O. Johansen, "The Oregon Steam Navigation Company: An Example of Capitalism on the Frontier," *Pacific Historical Review* 10:179–88 (June 1941), examines the famous transportation monopoly. The definitive study of cattlemen is J. Orin Oliphant, *On the Cattle Ranges of the Oregon Country* (Seattle: University of Washington Press, 1968). Alexander Campbell McGregor, *Counting Sheep: From Open Range to Agribusiness on the Columbia Plateau* (Seattle: University of Washington Press, 1982), does the same for sheep ranching and related activities. The role of the railroads in settlement is dealt with in Ross R. Cotroneo, "Western Land Marketing by the Northern Pacific Railway," *Pacific Historical Review* 57:299–320 (Aug. 1968).

General agricultural trends are examined by Robert C. Nesbit and Charles M. Gates in "Agriculture in Eastern Washington, 1890–1910," *Pacific*

Northwest Quarterly 37:279–302 (Oct. 1946). James F. Shepherd deals with wheat in "The Development of Wheat Production in the Pacific Northwest," *Agricultural History* 49:258–71 (Jan. 1975) and in "The Development of New Wheat Varieties in the Pacific Northwest," *Agricultural History* 54:52–63 (Jan. 1980). The rise of irrigation is covered in Rose Boening, "History of Irrigation in the State of Washington," *Washington Historical Quarterly* 9:259–76, 10:21–45 (Oct. 1918, Jan. 1919), and in Calvin B. Coulter, "The Victory of National Irrigation in the Yakima Valley, 1902–1906," *Pacific Northwest Quarterly* 42:99–122 (April 1951).

The development of Spokane is treated in four works by John Fahey: *Inland Empire: D. C. Corbin and Spokane* (Seattle: University of Washington Press, 1965); *The Ballyhoo Bonanza: Charles Sweeney and the Idaho Mines* (University of Washington Press, 1971); "The Million-Dollar Corner: The Development of Downtown Spokane, 1890–1920," *Pacific Northwest Quarterly* 62:77–85 (April 1971), and *Inland Empire: Unfolding Years* (cited above). Regional lumbering is studied in W. Hudson Kensel, "The Early Spokane Lumber Industry," *Idaho Yesterdays* 12:25–31 (Spring 1968).

Several contemporary accounts of the Columbia River scene are worth examination. Isaac Stevens's commentaries appear as volume 12 in *Reports of Explorations and Surveys . . . for a Railroad from the Mississippi River to the Pacific Ocean* (36th Cong., 1st sess., House Ex. Doc. 56. Washington, D.C.: Thomas H. Ford, 1860). The influential "Report of an Examination of the Upper Columbia River" by Thomas W. Symons was published as Ex. Doc. No. 186, 47th Cong., 1st session. A number of travel books and articles are helpful, including: Frances Fuller Victor, *All Over Oregon and Washington* (San Francisco: John H. Carmany & Co., 1872); G. H. Atkinson, "A Winter Trip to the Upper Columbia Basin," *West Shore* 7:286 (Dec. 1881); Samuel Rodman, Jr., "Explorations in the Upper Columbia Country," *Overland Monthly* 7:255 (March 1886); and Wallace J. Miller, *A Trip Along the Columbia River* (Pacific Publishing Company, 1890).

5: The Era of Reform

Various articles by Carlos A. Schwantes and his book, *Radical Heritage: Labor, Socialism, and Reform in Washington and British Columbia, 1885–1917* (Seattle: University of Washington Press, 1979), examine the Knights of Labor and other roots of reform and radicalism in Washington. The anti-Chinese movement is recounted in Robert E. Wynne, *Reaction to the Chinese in the Northwest and British Columbia, 1850 to 1910* (New York: Arno Press, 1978), while Murray Morgan presents an extensive discussion of its Tacoma phase in *Puget's Sound: A Narrative of Early Tacoma and the Southern Sound* (Seattle: University of Washington Press, 1979); see also Jules Alexander Karlin, "The Anti-Chinese Outbreak in Tacoma, 1885," *Pacific Northwest Quarterly* 39:2 (April 1948). Roger Sale, *Seattle, Past to Present* (Seattle: University of Washington Press, 1976), and Murray Morgan, *Skid Road: An Informal Portrait of Seattle* (revised edition, Seattle: University of Washington Press, 1982), contain discussions of the same period, and Roger Daniels, *Asian America: Chinese and Japanese in the United States since 1850* (Seattle: University of Washington Press, 1988), examines both the reasons for Asian emigration and the experience of first-generation immigrants. On an important territorial governor, see Alan Hynding, *The Public Life of Eugene Semple: Promoter and Politician of the Pacific Northwest* (Seattle: University of Washington Press, 1973).

Little has been published on populism in Washington. There is Thomas Wayne Riddle's unpublished Ph.D. dissertation, "The Old Radicalism in America: John R. Rogers and the Populist Movement in Washington" (Washington State University, 1976), and David B. Griffiths, "Far-western Populist Thought: A Comparative Study of John R. Rogers and Davis H. Waite," *Pacific Northwest Quarterly* 60:183–92 (October 1969). On utopian endeavors, see Charles P. LeWarne, *Utopias on Puget Sound, 1885–1915* (Seattle: University of Washington Press, 1975), and " 'And Be Ye Separate': The Lopez Island Colony of Thomas Gourley," in James W. Scott, editor, *Pacific Northwest Themes: Historical Essays in Honor of Keith A. Murray* (Bellingham: Western Washington University, Center for Pacific Northwest Studies, 1978), pp. 83–97.

Like populism, the progressive movement in Washington appears in little published material, although Robert D. Saltvig, "The Progressive Movement in Washington" (Ph.D. dissertation, University of Washington, 1966), is a strong study. See also Mansel Blackford, "Reform Politics in Seattle During the Progressive Area, 1902–1916," *Pacific Northwest Quarterly* 59:177–85 (October 1968). Daniel M. Ogden, Jr., and Hugh A. Bone, *Washington Politics* (New York: New York University Press, 1960), is short but helpful. Seattle's prominent minister is the subject of Dale E. Soden, "Mark Allison Matthews: Seattle's Minister Rediscovered," *Pacific Northwest Quarterly* 74:50–58 (April 1983), and "In Quest of a 'City on the Hill': Seattle Minister Mark Matthews and the Moral Leadership of the Middle Class," in Carl Guarneri and David Alvarez, editors, *Religion and Society in the American West: Historical Essays* (Lanham, Md.: University Press of America, 1987), pp. 355–73. Senator Miles Poindexter is the subject of Howard W. Allen, *Poindexter of Washington: A Study in Progressive Politics* (Carbondale: Southern Illinois University Press, 1981). *Women in the Pacific Northwest: An Anthology,* edited by Karen J. Blair (Seattle: University of Washington Press, 1988), includes "Of Women's Rights and Freedom: Abigail Scott Duniway," by Ruth Barnes Moynihan, "May Arkwright Hutton: Suffragist and Politician," by Patricia Voeller Horner, and "The Fight for Woman Suffrage and the Oregon Press," by Lauren Kessler. T. A. Larson, "The Woman Suffrage Movement in Washington," *Pacific Northwest Quarterly* 67:49–62 (April 1976), is an excellent account of the topic.

On Washington socialism, see Schwantes, *Radical Heritage,* and LeWarne, *Utopias on Puget Sound.* Much of the history may be found in master's theses such as Paul B. Bushue, "Dr. Hermon F. Titus and Socialism in Washington State" (University of Washington, 1967), and Barbara Winslow, "The

Decline of Socialism in Washington, 1910–1925" (University of Washington, 1969).

Colorful and often associated with violence, the Industrial Workers of the World has attracted more attention from both the public and historians than movements that are doubtless more significant. The essential history of IWW nationally, Melvin Dubofsky, *We Shall Be All: A History of the Industrial Workers of the World* (Chicago: Quadrangle Books, 1969), includes much about the Northwest, as does Joyce L. Kornbluh, editor, *Rebel Voices: An IWW Anthology* (Ann Arbor: University of Michigan Press, 1968). Robert L. Tyler, *Rebels of the Woods: The I.W.W. in the Pacific Northwest* (Eugene: University of Oregon Press, 1967), has some excellent features but is not thorough. Norman H. Clark, *Mill Town: A Social History of Everett, Washington, from Its Earliest Beginnings on the Shores of Puget Sound to the Tragic and Infamous Event Known as the Everett Massacre* (Seattle: University of Washington Press, 1970), and Robert L. Friedheim, *The Seattle General Strike* (Seattle: University of Washington Press, 1964), contain background and depth far greater than their titles imply. John McClelland, Jr., presents a thorough account of the Centralia events and their aftermath in *Wobbly War: The Centralia Story* (Tacoma: Washington State Historical Society, 1987). For the flavor of the times from the viewpoint of a radical, see Harvey O'Connor, *Revolution in Seattle: A Memoir* (New York: Monthly Review Press, 1964); from the opposite perspective, read the account by Seattle's mayor of the General Strike and how he broke it in Ole Hanson's *Americanism vs. Bolshevism* (New York: Doubleday, Page, 1920). The dramatic story of Louise Olivereau is told in Sarah E. Sharbach, "A Woman Acting Alone: Louise Olivereau and the First World War," *Pacific Northwest Quarterly* 78:32–40 (Jan.-April 1987).

6: From Great War to Great Depression

The overall homefront context for the Great War is covered in David M. Kennedy, *Over Here: The First World War and American Society* (New York: Oxford University Press, 1981). Norman Clark, *Mill Town* (Seattle: University of Washington Press, 1970), details the Everett Massacre, including its precursors and consequences. Robert L. Friedheim chronicles the events of 1919 in Seattle in *The Seattle General Strike* (Seattle: University of Washington Press, 1964). Wartime military construction is the subject of Bernard L. Boylan, "Camp Lewis: Promotion and Construction," *Pacific Northwest Quarterly* 58:188–95 (Oct. 1967). Matters related to the forest products industry throughout the war and the 1920s are treated in Robert E. Ficken, *The Forested Land: A History of Lumbering in Western Washington* (Seattle: University of Washington, 1987). Similar coverage of agriculture is found in John Fahey, *Inland Empire: Unfolding Years, 1879–1929* (Seattle: University of Washington Press, 1986).

For the great lumber strike of 1917–1918, see Robert E. Ficken, "The

Wobbly Horrors: Pacific Northwest Lumbermen and the Industrial Workers of the World, 1917–1918," *Labor History* 24:325–41 (Summer 1983). Harold M. Hyman, *Soldiers and Spruce: Origins of the Loyal Legion of Loggers and Lumbermen* (Los Angeles: University of California Institute of Industrial Relations, 1963), is the standard work on its subject. Two of Robert L. Tyler's publications are also of value: *Rebels of the Woods: The I.W.W. in the Pacific Northwest* (Eugene: University of Oregon Press, 1967) and "The United States Government as Union Organizer: The Loyal Legion of Loggers and Lumbermen," *Mississippi Valley Historical Review* 47:434–51 (Dec. 1960).

Completion of the present state capitol buildings spanned three decades and was interrupted by the war; Norman J. Johnston, *Washington's Audacious State Capitol and Its Builders* (Seattle: University of Washington Press, 1988), traces not only the design and construction but also the state politics that hindered and helped the process, and includes a vivid portrait of Governor Roland Hartley. State politics in the 1920s are covered in Robert E. Ficken, *Lumber and Politics: The Career of Mark E. Reed* (Seattle: University of Washington Press, 1979). Norman Clark, *The Dry Years: Prohibition and Social Change in Washington* (Seattle: University of Washington Press, 1965; pbk. reprint 1988), is a model study of the "noble experiment."

Reclamation schemes for the Columbia Basin are covered in Bruce C. Harding, "Water from Pend Oreille: The Gravity Plan for Irrigating the Columbia Basin," *Pacific Northwest Quarterly* 45:52–60 (April 1954), and in Bruce Mitchell, "Rufus Woods and Columbia River Development," *Pacific Northwest Quarterly* 52:139–41 (Oct. 1961). A popular treatment of power development is offered in Steward H. Holbrook, *The Columbia* (Rinehart and Co., 1956). The 308 Report was published as "Columbia River and Minor Tributaries," House Document No. 103, 73d Cong., 1st session.

7: Washington's New Deal

The best general history of the New Deal's impact on western America is Richard Lowitt, *The New Deal and the West* (Bloomington: Indiana University Press, 1984). On the social and political impact of the Great Depression, see William H. Mullins, "Self-Help in Seattle, 1931–32: Herbert Hoover's Concept of Cooperative Individualism and the Unemployed Citizens' League," *Pacific Northwest Quarterly* 72 (Jan. 1981), and Murray Morgan, *Skid Road: An Informal Portrait of Seattle* (pbk. reprint, Seattle: University of Washington Press, 1982). Western expenditures of the Roosevelt Administration are analyzed in Leonard Arrington, "The New Deal in the West: A Preliminary Statistical Inquiry," *Pacific Historical Review* 38 (Aug. 1969), and in Donald Worster, *Rivers of Empire: Water, Aridity, and the Growth of the American West* (New York: Pantheon Books, 1985).

Industry's Depression experience is covered in Robert E. Ficken, *The For-*

ested Land: A History of Lumbering in Western Washington (Seattle: University of Washington Press, 1987). The lumber code fiasco is treated in William G. Robbins, "The Great Experiment in Industrial Self-Government: The Lumber Industry and the National Recovery Administration," Journal of Forest History 25:128–32 (July 1981).

On labor, the starting point is Irving Bernstein, Turbulent Years: A History of the American Worker, 1933–1941 (Boston: Houghton Mifflin, 1970). The best sources on Dave Beck are Donald Garnel, The Rise of Teamster Power in the West (Berkeley: University of California Press, 1972), and Jonathan Dembo, "Dave Beck and the Transportation Revolution in the Pacific Northwest, 1917–41," in G. Thomas Edwards and Carlos A. Schwantes, editors, Experiences in a Promised Land: Essays on Pacific Northwest History (Seattle: University of Washington Press, 1986). There is also a chapter on Beck in Murray Morgan's Skid Road (cited above). For unionization in the lumber industry, see Vernon H. Jensen, Lumber and Labor (New York: Farrar & Rinehart, 1945).

Construction of Grand Coulee Dam is detailed in George Sundborg, Hail Columbia: The Thirty-Year Struggle for Grand Coulee Dam (New York: Macmillan, 1954), and Murray Morgan, The Dam (New York: Viking Press, 1954). The general subject of Columbia River dam building is handled in Charles McKinley, Uncle Sam in the Pacific Northwest: Federal Management of Natural Resources in the Columbia River Valley (Berkeley: University of California Press, 1952). On the BPA, two important articles are Philip J. Funigiello, "The Bonneville Power Administration and the New Deal," Prologue 5 (Summer 1973), and Herman C. Voeltz, "Genesis and Development of a Regional Power Agency in the Pacific Northwest, 1933–43," Pacific Northwest Quarterly 53:65–69 (April 1962). The impact of dam building on salmon is examined in Anthony Netboy, Salmon of the Pacific Northwest: Fish vs. Dams (Portland: Binfords & Mort, 1958). Richard Neuberger's New Deal journalism is assembled in Our Promised Land (New York: Macmillan, 1939).

Essential context for the Olympic National Park conflict is offered in Alfred Runte, National Parks: The American Experience (Lincoln: University of Nebraska Press, 1979). Elmo R. Richardson, "Olympic National Park: Twenty Years of Controversy," Forest History 12:6–15 (April 1968), examines the park's creation in detail.

8: Homefront Washington

The best history of the regional homefront is Gerald D. Nash, The Americana West Transformed: The Impact of the Second World War (Bloomington: Indiana University Press, 1985). Two studies from the national perspective are also of use: John Morton Blum, V Was for Victory: Politics and American Culture During World War II (New York: Harcourt Brace Jovanovich, 1976), and Richard Polenberg, War and Society: The United States,

1941–1945 (Philadelphia: J. B. Lippincott, 1972). A good introduction to the concept and American experience of the "good war" is Studs Terkel, *"The Good War": An Oral History of World War II* (New York: Pantheon, 1984).

There is an enormous historical literature on the Japanese relocation. The best treatments are Roger Daniels, *Concentration Camps U.S.A.: Japanese Americans and World War II* (New York: Holt, Rinehart & Winston, 1972) and Peter Irons, *Justice at War: The Story of the Japanese American Internment Camps* (New York: Oxford University Press, 1983). Roger Daniels, *Asian America: Chinese and Japanese in the United States since 1850* (Seattle: University of Washington Press, 1988), addresses the impact of World War II and the succeeding Cold War era on Japanese Americans. Personal accounts of the relocation may be found in Monica Sone, *Nisei Daughter* (pbk. reprint, Seattle: University of Washington Press, 1979), and John Okoda, *No-No Boy* (pbk. reprint, Seattle: University of Washington Press, 1980). The mutuality of racist sentiments in the Pacific conflict is stressed in John W. Dower, *War Without Mercy: Race and Power in the Pacific War* (New York: Pantheon, 1986).

Considerable information on wartime Seattle is found in Karen Anderson, *Wartime Women: Sex Roles, Family Relations and the Status of Women during World War II* (Westport, Conn.: Greenwood Press, 1981); see also Karen Beck Skold, "The Job He Left Behind: Women in the Shipyards During World War II," in Karen J. Blair, editor, *Women in the Pacific Northwest: An Anthology* (Seattle: University of Washington Press, 1988). The impact on blacks is covered in Howard Droker, "Seattle Race Relations During the Second World War," *Pacific Northwest Quarterly* 67 (Oct. 1976).

Hanford construction is treated in three detailed histories: Richard Rhodes, *The Making of the Atomic Bomb* (New York: Simon and Schuster, 1986); Vincent C. Jones, *Manhattan: The Army and the Atomic Bomb* (Washington, D.C.: Center of Military History, 1985); and Richard G. Hewlett and Oscar E. Anderson, Jr., *The New World, 1939–1946* (University Park: Pennsylvania State University Press, 1962). Popular reaction to the atomic bomb is examined in Paul Boyer, *By the Bomb's Early Light: American Thought and Culture at the Dawn of the Atomic Age* (New York: Pantheon, 1985).

9: Postwar Washington

Published accounts of the postwar years remain scant and information must often be derived from newspapers and periodicals. Two magazines, the issues-oriented *Seattle* (published between 1964 and 1970), and *Pacific Search* (renamed *Pacific Northwest*), published from 1966 to the present, are particularly useful. Calvin F. Schmid and Stanton E. Schmid, *Growth of Cities and Towns, State of Washington* (Olympia: Washington State Planning and Community Affairs Agency, 1969), is essential for population and demographics, as are *Population Trends for Washington State,* published annually by the Washington State Office of Financial Management, and official reports of the Bureau of the Census, U.S. Department of Commerce.

Gerald D. Nash, *The American West Transformed: The Impact of the Second World War* (Bloomington: Indiana University Press, 1985), is weighted heavily toward California but contains much on Washington. Effects of the war are discussed in a popular history, Nard Jones, *Evergreen Land: A Portrait of the State of Washington* (New York: Dodd, Mead & Company, 1947), Roger Sale, *Seattle, Past to Present* (Seattle University of Washington Press, 1976), Gerald B. Nelson, *Seattle: The Life and Times of An American City* (New York: Knopf, 1977), and Harold Mansfield, *Vision: The Story of Boeing. A Saga of the Sky and the New Horizons of Space* (New York: Duell, Sloan & Pearce, 1966).

On Richland, see Paul Loeb, *Nuclear Culture: Living and Working in the World's Largest Atomic Complex* (New York: Coward, McCann & Geoghagan, 1982), and "Richland: The Town the Atom Built," a mimeographed pamphlet published by the Atomic Energy Museum in Richland (n.d.).

On Bellevue, see Lucile McDonald, *Bellevue: Its First 100 Years* (Fairfield, Wash.: Ye Galleon Press, 1984). The development of METRO is discussed in Sale, *Seattle, Past to Present,* and James Ellis's several contributions are the subject of John Fischer, "The Easy Chair: Seattle's Modern-Day Vigilantes," *Harper's* 238:14–26 (May 1969).

Washington's wartime and later governor is the subject of George William Scott, "Arthur B. Langlie: Republican Governor in a Democratic Age" (Ph.D. dissertation, University of Washington, 1971). Local events of the McCarthy era are recounted in Vern Countryman, *Un-American Activities in the State of Washington* (Ithaca, N.Y.: Cornell University Press, 1951.) A critical phase of the local investigation is interpreted in Jane Sanders, *Cold War on the Campus: Academic Freedom at the University of Washington, 1946–64* (Seattle: University of Washington Press, 1979), while Melvin Rader describes his successful account to clear his name in *False Witness* (paperback edition, Seattle: University of Washington Press, 1979).

For information about the contemporary experience and enduring traditions of ethnic groups, see Roger Daniels, *Asian America: Chinese and Japanese in the United States since 1850* (Seattle: University of Washington Press, 1988); Carlos Bulosan's memoir of Filipino life, *America is in the Heart* (reprinted with a new introduction by Carey McWilliams, Seattle: University of Washington Press, 1973); Vi Hilbert, *Haboo: Native American Stories from Puget Sound* (Seattle: University of Washington Press, 1985); and Pamela Amoss, *Coast Salish Spirit Dancing: The Survival of an Ancestral Religion* (Seattle: University of Washington Press, 1978). A valuable new anthology, containing twelve essays and a bibliographical guide, is *Women in the Pacific Northwest: An Anthology,* edited by Karen J. Blair (Seattle: University of Washington Press, 1988). This collection documents and interprets a broad range of experiences of the region's women. A section on "Race and Ethnicity" includes "Black Women of the Pacific Northwest: A Survey and Research Prospectus," by Susan H. Armitage and Deborah Gallacci Wilbert, as well as essays on women's roles on the Colville Indian Reservation and in Scandinavian communities.

Fundamental to understanding the black experience in Washington are Esther Hall Mumford, *Seattle's Black Victorians 1852–1901* (Seattle: Ananse Press, 1980), and Horace R. Cayton, *Long Old Road: An Autobiography* (paperback edition, Seattle: University of Washington Press, 1970). Wartime changes are discussed in Howard A. Droker, "Seattle Race Relations During the Second World War," *Pacific Northwest Quarterly* 67:163–74 (October 1976), reprinted in G. Thomas Edwards and Carlos A. Schwantes, editors, *Experiences in a Promised Land: Essays in Pacific Northwest History* (Seattle: University of Washington Press, 1986), pp. 353–68. A contemporary study by the state is *Race and Violence in Washington State: Report of the Commission on the Causes and Prevention of Civil Disorder* (Olympia: Commission on the Causes and Prevention of Civil Disorder, 1969). An incident distant from Puget Sound population centers is recounted in Gordon Bowker, "A Town Divided: Pasco, Wash. is full of tumbleweeds and trouble," *Seattle* 75:32–39 (June 1970).

Erasmo Gamboa has written on Spanish-speaking Americans in "Mexican Migration into Washington State," *Pacific Northwest Quarterly* 72:121–31 (July 1981), and "Mexican Labor in the Pacific Northwest, 1943–1947: A Photographic Essay," *Pacific Northwest Quarterly* 73:175–81 (October 1982). See also Richard W. Slatta and Maxine P. Atkinson, "The 'Spanish Origin' Population of Oregon and Washington: A Demographic Profile, 1980," *Pacific Northwest Quarterly* 75:108–16 (July 1984).

10: A New Washington Society

As with the previous chapter, much valuable information is gleaned from contemporary newspapers and periodicals, especially *Seattle* and *Pacific Search/Pacific Northwest* magazines. A useful article by a native son turned national editor is Thomas Griffith, "The Pacific Northwest," *The Atlantic* 237:46–93 (April 1976). Seattle's 1962 world's fair is the subject of Murray Morgan, *Century 21: The Story of the Seattle World's Fair* (Acme Press, 1963), and a reminiscence by Cyrus Noe, "Innocence Revisited: 20 Years After the Fair, a Flack Remembers," *Pacific Northwest* 16:23–32, with an accompanying feature, "Days of the Future Passed," by Heather Lockman.

On political developments, see Hugh A. Bone, "The 1964 Election in Washington," *Western Political Quarterly* 8:514–22 (June 1965). Major political figures are the subjects of George William Scott, "Arthur B. Langlie: Republican Governor in a Democratic Age" (Ph.D. dissertation, University of Washington, 1971); William W. Prochnau and Richard W. Larson, *A Certain Democrat: Senator Henry M. Jackson; A Political Biography* (Englewood Cliffs, N.J.: Prentice-Hall, 1972); and "Dixy Rocks the Northwest: An unspoiled state and a contentious Governor face crucial choices," *Time* 110:26–35 (December 12, 1977). Gordon Newell provides some background of politics in the state capital in *Rogues, Buffoons and Statesmen*

(Seattle: Superior Publishing Company, 1975), and the "founder" recalls the OWL party in Red Kelly, with Bart Potter, "Let's Have a Party. . . ," *The Weekly* (Seattle) 11:30 (July 23–29, 1986), pp. 28–30.

Although much has been written about Dave Beck, a full biography remains to be done. John D. McCallum's *Dave Beck* (Seattle: The Writing Works and Gordon Soules Book Publishers, 1978) is largely McCallum's own self-serving account of the era of Beck's rise. A valuable interpretation is Jonathan Dembo, "Dave Beck and the Transportation Revolution in the Pacific Northwest, 1917–41," in G. Thomas Edwards and Carlos A. Schwantes, editors, *Experiences in a Promised Land: Essays in Pacific Northwest History* (Seattle: University of Washington Press, 1986). William O. Douglas describes his early life in Eastern Washington in *Go East, Young Man, The Early Years: The Autobiography of William O. Douglas* (New York: Random House, 1974).

A full study of the problems surrounding the Washington Public Power Supply System remains to be untangled, but Daniel Jack Chasan has made an admirable start with *The Fall of the House of WPPSS: The $2.25-Billion Horror Story That Haunts the Nuclear Industry, the Bond Market, and the Northwest* (Seattle: Sasquatch Publishing, 1985). James Leigland and Robert Lamb analyze the WPPSS crisis as a failure in management in *WPP$$: Who is to Blame for the WPPSS Disaster?* (Cambridge, Mass.: Ballinger Publishing Company, 1988). See also David Myhra, *Whoops/WPPSS: Washington Public Power Supply System Nuclear Plants* (Jefferson, N.C.: McFarland & Co., 1982).

The Indian fishing disputes and the Boldt Decision are the topic of a report prepared for the American Friends Service Committee, *Uncommon Controversy: Fishing Rights of the Mucleshoot, Puyallup, and Nisqually Indians* (Seattle: University of Washington Press, 1970), which argues for a peaceable solution, and an update by Fay Cohen, *Treaties on Trial: The Continuing Controversy over Northwest Indian Fishing Rights* (Seattle: University of Washington Press, 1986). The case leading to the Boldt Decision is *United States v. Washington*.

Roger Sale, *Seattle, Past to Present* (Seattle: University of Washington Press, 1975), and Norman H. Clark, *Washington: A Bicentennial History* (Norton, and American Association for State and Local History, 1976), have useful sections concerning the civil-rights movement, but one must also turn to running issues of *Seattle* magazine. Also essential is *Race and Violence in Washington State: Report of the Commission on the Causes and Prevention of Civil Disorder* (Olympia: Commission on the Causes and Prevention of Civil Disorder, 1969).

Two articles praising Seattle as a liveable city are Arthur M. Lewis, "The Worst American City: A scientific study to confirm or deny your prejudices," *Harper's* 250:67–71 (January 1975), and Sarah Pileggi, "Seattle: City Life at its Best," *Sports Illustrated* 57:54–68 (July 19, 1982). Roger Sale, *Seattle, Past to Present* deals perceptively with the quality of life in that city and its environs. Selected statistics and state rankings are available in FYI Information Services, *The New Book of American Ratings* (New York: Facts on File

Publications, 1984). Cultural characteristics of the region are discussed in Edwin R. Bingham and Glen A. Love, editors, *Northwest Perspectives: Essays on the Culture of the Pacific Northwest* (Seattle: University of Washington Press, 1979). The short chapter on "The Pacific Northwest" in Raymond D. Gastil, *Cultural Regions of the United States* (Seattle: University of Washington Press, 1975), is useful in comparing this with other sections of the country.

Index